THE BEST OF OZ

THE BEST OF OZ

Ordo Templi Orientis

THE GRAND LODGE OF AUSTRALIA

MARCH EQUINOX - ANNO VVI - 2020 E.V.

Copyright © 2020 OTO Grand Lodge of Australia

All rights reserved. This book or any portion thereof may not be reproduced or used in any manner whatsoever without the express written permission of the publisher except for the use of brief quotations in a book review.

First Printing, 2020
ISBN 978-0-646-81577-0
Ordo Templi Orientis
GPO Box 1193
Canberra, ACT 2601
AUSTRALIA

www.otoaustralia.org.au

Cover Design: Ben Hay (honeyrogue.com)
Editor: Brendan Walls
Layout: Padraig Maclain

Contents

Foreword	1
By Krzysztof Azarewicz	
Introduction	5
By Brendan Walls	
Origins of the Modern O.T.O in Australia	9
By Adam Pellen	
Aurora Australis: Topological Reflections on the Modern M∴M∴M∴ in Australia	13
By Grand Master Shiva X°	
'New Commentary' Theology: Notes Towards Reorganising the EGC Part 1	63
By Grand Master Shiva X°	
'New Commentary' Theology: Notes Towards Reorganising the EGC Part 2	79
By Grand Master Shiva X°	
'From the GM' (AUGL in Japan)	87
By Grand Master Shiva X°	
Toiling in the (Local) Fields of Our Lord	113
By Grand Master Shiva X°	
Remembering Parsi Krumm-Heller (1925-2008 e.v.) Obituary	119
By Grand Master Shiva X°	
Introduction to J. Daniel Gunther's 'Initiation in the Aeon of the Child'	127
By Grand Master Shiva X°	

VENI COOPER-MATHIESON   133
    By Frater Hermellyon
WOMAN GIRT WITH A SWORD KEYNOTE ADDRESS   141
    By Grand Master Shiva X°
OUR CHURCH - THE CLARITY OF VOCATION   153
    By Tau Amrit
EGC RETREAT KEYNOTE ADDRESS   157
    By Grand Master Shiva X°
SHADOW OF THE THELEMITES: THE ABBOT, THE ABBEY   165
AND THE NIGHTMARE
    By Grand Master Shiva X°
IN THE FLESH - MANIFESTING LIBER 194   185
    Interview with Frater O.I.P. , E.C. President
FREEDOM REQUIRES DISCIPLINE   199
    By Phillip Tripp
ALAS! FOR THE KINGDOM WHEREIN ALL THESE ARE   203
AT WAR
    Interview with Brother Phil Pope
APOKALYPSIS 418   215
    By Stephen J. King
TEMPLE MOUNT: THE ORIENTAL TEMPLAR CRUSADE   257
FOR VERITÀ
    By Stephen J. King
LIVING IN THE SUNLIGHT   295
    By Grand Master Shiva X°

Foreword

Krzysztof Azarewicz

Do what thou wilt shall be the whole of the Law.

Charing Cross train station was busy as usual at that time of the day. I rushed through the crowds and walked fast towards Bloomsbury. I have always found the little streets of that area of London very charming, but then I wasn't paying attention to them as I wanted to get to the famous Atlantis Bookshop before closing time. A friend of mine had recommended a new issue of the Australian OTO magazine called 'Waratah' and apparently only a few copies were left. A quick glimpse through the pages confirmed it was something unique. It was beautifully produced and both content and artwork were very impressive. I obviously purchased a copy.

Later that year, the Atlantis organised a party to celebrate a launch of P.R. Stephensens' *The Legend of Aleister Crowley*. The book was published by individuals involved in the production of Waratah and it confirmed high editorial standards and production values. The launch gave me an opportunity to meet the book editor, Stephen J. King, who soon after kindly added me to the list of subscribers receiving 'OZ', the official newsletter of the Australian Grand Lodge of Ordo Templi Orientis.

From issue 15 (March, 2010 e.v.) OZ was distributed in electronic format only. However, it didn't matter. I enjoyed it a lot, as every instalment was packed with incredibly interesting material and appeared on a regular basis. Every Solstice and Equinox I could expect in my inbox an email containing an attachment with the new issue.

Usually, after reading an introductory piece from the Grand Secretary who presented a summary of the activities taking place across the country in the last quarter, I focused on the local bodies reports. For me, as the then Lodge Master, this was an invaluable source of inspiration and a plethora of new ideas. The Grand Master Frater Shiva X° was well aware of the impact the newsletter had worldwide. In issue 16 (June, 2010 e.v.) he wrote:

> OZ makes it to Croatia, Serbia, Italy, Japan, China, Hong Kong, Norway, South Africa, Canada and New Zealand. I hold high hope and promise for many of these national sections, believing they will be instrumental in shaping the 21st century OTO. And for me it is heartening and encouraging to know that in some way we as a Grand Lodge have inspired and encouraged, guided and reassured, their Great Work. That is a great achievement, and an even greater responsibility. So, with measure and good cheer, don't underestimate the value of your work for the Order, or the work of your local body.

Likewise, stay open and respectful of the work of others. Keep the reports coming in.

OZ was a proof of consolidation and continuing growth of the Australian Grand Lodge, but it offered something more than reports. Essays. Visionary, profound, challenging, thought-provoking, sophisticated essays. They caused me to reflect on my practice and approach as a Thelemite, an initiator and Frater Superior's Representative in Poland. In fact, my strategy of the development of our national OTO section was largely inspired by ideas presented in OZ. I'm pleased to say they were successfully integrated into our transactional *modus operandi* and transformative *magnum opus*. I must confess I even made my own edition of 'The Best of OZ'. I copied all inspirational articles and excerpts of a section called 'From the Grand Master' (sometimes known as 'King's Rave') into a special file. Quite often I still refer to them and use some of the ideas presented there as a compass which helps me navigate across meanders of socio-magical challenges and ordeals.

In some sense the magical work is not fully accomplished if its results don't manifest on the material plane, in the world of the final He of Tetragammaton. Transformation has to take place on all planes; the Word has to be made flesh to dwell among us. The alchemical *opus* requires a process of fixation by which a previously volatile substance is changed into a solid form, the Spirit is turned into a Body. I'm very pleased that the best essays published in OZ are manifested in the book, and I do hope that they will be as inspirational to the reader as they were and still are for me.

Love is the law, love under will.

KRZYSZTOF AZAREWICZ
Gdansk, February 2019 e.v.

Introduction

Hear thou the voice of fire

'...around thee darts the Lightning Flame and all things appear amid thunders.'

- *The Chaldæan Oracles of Zoroaster*

'Do you come from a land down under?
Where women glow and men plunder?
Can't you hear, can't you hear the thunder?
You better run, you better take cover...'

- *Men At Work*

OTO members in Australia have been lucky to receive OZ magazine four times a year for 13 years now, but all good things come to an end and after 50 issues, we're devising new ways of communicating to our people, and the World. Some of these methods will work, some won't; more on that in a minute.

It was after reading the submissions for the final edition (*Ascona* and *Living In The Sunlight* mostly) that I thought it would be a terrible shame to leave these pieces languishing half-read in people's inboxes; also, to simply preach to the choir and not let them out into the World for the edification of a wider audience. This is the first time most of these pieces will be available to non-OTO and International OTO members.

OZ turned pretty quickly from a 'national newsletter' into a chronicle of contemporary Thelemic thought. Even now, the most tentative articles here seem quite audacious.

OZ was first published in 2006, not long after the Australian Grand Lodge formed, and in a way, this volume forms something of a biography of AUGL.

In Australia we try stuff out. 'Give it a bash' we say. From the beginning (65,000 or so years ago), our very survival in this largely inhospitable place has been a matter of trial and error. OTO here has been no different. A rigid approach to establishing the Order here would have led to miserable failure. Our survival has been forged through flexibility and resourcefulness: adaptability.

'Resilience' is a mantra here, and really, it has been the defining trait of Australian OTO from the beginning. One need only read *Progradior and The Beast* and see what kind of difficulties Frank Bennett had to endure to know what resilience means.

I'm writing this in Hobart, as my family has been forced to evacuate our home in the South which is currently surrounded by bushfires. I don't know if I'll have a home to return to tomorrow, and yesterday, I got as much Oasis equipment into the car as I could fit. I had to decide which items were non-essential enough to leave behind. This kind of thinking is fairly typical of the OTO here. Which things should be left to the flames, and which should make it into the car called 'Millions-of-Years'.

Some of the ideas teased out in OZ were consigned to the flames, but perhaps someone, somewhere will take them and kindle a great light.

Many thanks to Troy Mackellar for copy editing; and Padraig Maclain for proofing and layout.

'Hear thou the voice of fire...'

The Chaldæan Oracles of Zoroaster.

BRENDAN WALLS

Grand Secretary General

Grand Lodge of Australia, Ordo Templi Orientis

ANNO VIV - 27 JANUARY, 2019 E.V.

Origins of the Modern O.T.O in Australia

Brother Adam Pellen

There is a process in one's life wherein what was once contemporary slides into the distance and becomes history. When I was approached to write a piece delineating my small part in the genesis of the Order in this country I had to cast my mind back over a distance far greater than I realised I had traversed.

The mid-late seventies saw me as a teenager studying graphic design, listening to punk and progressive rock, and with a burgeoning curiosity in what may be loosely termed 'the Occult'. My introduction to Crowley had come via Symonds's *The Great Beast*. The tattered paperback still sits on a bookshelf at home. Despite its now obvious shortcomings, it told of a man with whom, I flatter myself, I had much in common. 'Do what thou wilt shall be the whole of the Law' bypassed intellectual considerations and registered deep within me. From this time I have considered myself a Thelemite, and sought to fan the flames of this passion.

Travelling the 17 miles by train as often as I could, I explored the city's book stores. On one excursion I purchased the Thoth deck. Included was the address of the OTO in America.

Beside me is a copy of the letter I wrote in my finest cursive to the Order in July 1977. My first question expressed a hope that they may help in obtaining Crowley's books. I also asked if the Order was operative in this country. A month later I received a reply from a Brother Bill Heidrick. He offered some suggestions regarding acquiring the books I was after but advised that there was no organised Order work happening in Australia. He went on to say that the Order had received a number of enquiries from Australia and that the formation of an associate chapter was possible.

Our correspondence[1] continued and in a letter dated 11th September 1977 Brother Bill asked if I would act as a representative of the Order in Australia. This would involve acting as a central point of contact for all enquiries from this country and New Zealand. I completed the Associate Membership form and sent a postal order for ten American dollars to Berkeley, California. Brother Bill gave me a list of names and addresses of recent Australian correspondents

---

[1] My thanks go to Brother Joel for providing copies of my correspondence with the OTO in America and to Brother Chris for asking and encouraging me to write this. Thanks also to our King who, in honour of my humble role, has dubbed me 'Great Uncle Adam', which is highly preferable to 'the Missing Link' as someone else suggested. As mentioned above, I still retain most, if not all the early correspondence along with some early OTO periodicals (i.e. the 'Magickal Link'). It made me realise how much the world had changed, reading the old letters. Apart from my first hand-written letter, the remainder were typed on my red Olivetti type-writer and when Brother Bill offered to send me tapes (reel to reel) I asked if he could send cassettes and I possessed such modern machinery to play them. - Adam

with a synopsis of each. One he'd annotated 'a bit of a nutcase - says he's surrounded by devil worshippers' which firmed my resolve to employ a post office box. It seemed appropriate when I was randomly allocated PO Box 333!

Over the next year or so I received around twenty letters and provided what information I could, associate membership forms, and the hope that we could begin an offshoot of the Order here. I did meet with some correspondents who happened to pass through Adelaide. I was disappointed that I had no contact with anyone from my own state; most letters arriving from the eastern side of our country and from New Zealand. This, along with other circumstances (not least my having no funds to travel), saw little progress at my end. I stayed in touch with all my contacts and still have some very interesting letters in a box in the cellar. Brother Bill continued to assist me in my personal studies and we kept one another up to date with our Australian contacts.

Brother Bill wrote to me on 17th July 1980 and told me that Heather Jennings (whom he describes as 'beautiful and charming - AND does the dishes!') had arrived and was staying with him. Heather and I had been in touch for some time and although we hadn't met I felt quite close. This marks a bitter-sweet moment for me. Heather went on to found the Order in this country which is something we must all be grateful for. I was, of course, saddened that I was unable to be a part. That is, until now. A lot has happened in my life since then, but this is where my role in the birth of the Order in this country ends.

OZ 24. Anno IVxx - 21 June 2012 e.v.

AURORA AUSTRALIS

Topological reflections on the modern M∴M∴M∴ in Australia

GRAND MASTER SHIVA X°

'I also want to express how good it feels to have heard from the new OTO of OZ...I remember... [Crowley's] phrase about the 'Thelemic light' having gone out down under with...[Frank Bennett's] death... Good to know the lamp is lit again.'

Tobias Churton[1]

A Policeman let loose on Society

Do what thou wilt shall be the whole of the Law.

Political Scientists describe *anarchy* quite differently to how I first experienced it as a teenage punk rocker. For a structural realist like the University of Chicago's John Mearsheimer for example, anarchy is far removed from the chaos and disorder of the rebel anthems of my youth. 'Anarchy is an ordering principle' he says, 'it simply means that there is no centralized authority or ultimate arbiter that stands above

---

[1] Churton, T. 2012. Personal correspondence with author, 24 January.

states.'² Its opposite according to this paradigm is *hierarchy*. Hierarchy is identified with centralized authority, and importantly, as 'the ordering principle of *domestic* politics'.³ Nation-states are hierarchical, while international relations are anarchic. By this analysis there is no central authority above the nation states and their pursuit of power, hegemony and security.

Aleister Crowley had his own ideas about anarchy and hierarchy. You could say that he personified both. In *The Book of Lies* Frater Perdurabo declared 'I am not an Anarchist in your sense of the word: fancy a Policeman let loose on Society!'⁴ His accompanying Commentary stated 'The only solution of the Social Problem is the creation of a class with the true patriarchal feeling, and the manners and obligations of chivalry.'⁵ He would apply his 'solution' to the British section of the OTO, the M∴M∴M∴ : "It must be possible", reads Liber CLXI, 'to train men to independence, to tolerance, to nobility of character, and to good manners, and this is done in the OTO by certain very efficacious methods...'⁶ It could even be argued that the OTO *became*

---

² Mearsheimer, J. 2006. 'Structural Realism', pg. 73, viewed 18 April 2012

http://www.oup.com/uk/orc/bin/9780199298334/dunne_chap04.pdf
³ My italics. Ibid. pg. 73
⁴ Crowley, A. 1988 ed. The Book of Lies, Wesier, York Beach ME, ch. 81 'Louis Lingg' p. 172.
⁵ Ibid. pg. 173.
⁶ Liber CLXI 'Concerning the Law of Thelema'.

Crowley's solution. The Order's organisational structure would factor in most aspects of the anarchy-hierarchy spectrum in a complex array of checks and balances: 'It combines monarchy with democracy; it includes aristocracy, and conceals even the seeds of revolution.'[7] The OTO Constitution relies upon a central authority standing above the kingdom-states, vested in the Outer Head of the Order (OHO) and the international headquarters or Central Office. And it was envisaged that this new world Order would implement a universal plan for human emancipation, publicly released as Liber OZ, whilst establishing and celebrating Thelema as a universal religion.[8]

Although history has so far relegated the OTO mission and presence to the counter-cultural fringe, the 'social problem' it was there to address has gone viral, and the inconvenient truth about anarchic international relations is that it *is* an inconvenient truth - irrespective of what the values-based rhetoric of western liberal democracy might have to say about it. Critics to this assessment may perhaps point to the United Nations as some type of 'ultimate arbiter', though a cynic could easily dismiss the UN as a playground for the dominant states, and a body in constant constitutional crisis with a historical achievement riddled with ineffectiveness. Still others might point to globalisation or market forces,

---

[7] Liber CXCIV 'An Intimation with Reference to the Constitution of the Order'.

[8] I take up these themes elsewhere, See Shiva X°. 2011. 'Aspiring to the Holy Order', OTO, Sydney & Tokyo.

however mainstream economics relies heavily upon reductionist and individualistic accounts of human behaviour and knowledge acquisition.[9] By metaphor of scale, these drivers morph into the positions and interests of the nation-state.[10] While it may not be fashionable within the current OTO counterculture to propose that the Order has a nascent social, spiritual and political relevance on a global scale, it might well be its emergence that informs our growth and development over the next 100 years - as much a hope as it is a challenge.

A danger inherent to the anarchy-hierarchy dichotomy is that in the quest for hegemony states opt for what Mark Elvin of the Australian National University calls the 'logic of short term advantage.' He coined the term in relation to the tragic Qing Dynasty famine in China, arguing that systemic corruption of the civil service meritocracy and rampant environmental degradation were its causes.[11] You could apply the 'logic of short term advantage' to other events in humanity's historical and contemporary record. Elvin has his critics, in particular those who disregard environmental

---

[9] See Duguid, P. 2005. ' "The Art of Knowing": Social and Tacit Dimensions of Knowledge and the Limits of the Community of Practice', The Information Society: An Information Journal 21:2, viewed 10 April 2012, http://dx.doi.org/10.1080/01972240590925311
[10] For metaphor of scale, see Latour, B. nd. 'On actor-network theory: a few clarifications plus more than a few complications', viewed 24 April 2012, http://www.cours.fse.ulaval.ca/edc-65804/latour-clarifications.pdf
[11] Elvin, M. 2004. The Retreat of the Elephants; an Environmental History of China, Yale University Press, London.

considerations and assert that the pursuit of knowledge, capital and economic and political power, are the real drivers of civilization's growth.[12] From a sustainability perspective however, the problem with this view as the University of Sydney's Dr. Michael Paton has suggested, is that it situates 'humanity above or outside its physical and environmental constraints.'[13] I have called this disjunctive way of thinking 'pentecostal,'[14] in that it seems to derive, ultimately, from the dogma that God is above and outside man. It follows by that reasoning and the hierarchy of being it asserts, that man is then above and outside nature.

Contrary to pentecostal logic, the OTO has declared that 'there is no god *but* man'[15] and it follows from this that we assert an entirely new *participation mystique* with nature. This was eloquently expressed by Hymenaeus Beta when he said 'I believe Our Lady is bringing us to a new relationship to her Sister the Earth, and that this new ecological awareness is vital to our survival on Earth... We are not in for a return to the earth-mother-goddess paganism of the

---

[12] Ma, D. 2004. 'Growth, Institutions and Knowledge: A Review and Reflection on the Historiography of 18th–20th Century China', Australian Economic History Review, 44, 3, pp. 259-277.

[13] Paton, M. nd. 'The Environmental History of China and the Sustainable Management of Governments', viewed 21 April 2012, http://sydney.edu.au/business/__data/assets/pdf_file/0003/56622/The_Environmental_History_of_China.pdf
I'm grateful to Dr. Paton for giving me access to his currently unpublished papers on sustainability and southern culture.

[14] See Acts 2:1-4.

[15] See for example Liber LXXVII OZ.

past, but something much more interesting.'[16] The spark of Godhead is within us, the core of every star.[17] We now celebrate the creative force of nature, within and without - 'Thou that art One, Our Lord in the Universe the Sun, our Lord in ourselves whose name is Mystery of Mystery'[18] - enabling us to strip away the veils that shroud this inmost light, the True and Living God Most High.[19]

Curiously and perhaps paradoxically, we get opportunity to identify and organise these integral components of Self through selfless service to our Order,[20] while in so doing further identifying and organising the integral components of the OTO itself: 'For, in True Things, all are but images one of another; man is but a map of the universe, and Society is but the same on a larger scale.'[21] The Key rests in the Order's first philosophical instruction - *adaptation to environment*. By necessity this is the purview and work of the OTO national sections. It cannot be unthinkingly imported in the name of short term advantage from one to another or prescribed by a Central Office. The centricity of the OTO

---

[16] Hymenaeus Beta XI°. 1997. 'Women's Conference Address', The Magical Link, Fall, p.10.
[17] See AL:II:6.
[18] Liber XV 'Ecclesia Gnostica Catholica Canon Missa', Section IV, 'Of the Ceremony of the Opening of the Veil'.
[19] See also Gunther, J.D. 2009. Initiation in the Aeon of the Child: the inward journey, Ibis, Lake Worth, pp.52-58.
[20] I take up this theme elsewhere, See Shiva X°. 2011. 'Under the Shadow of the Wings', OTO, Sydney & Tokyo.
[21] Liber CXCIV, op cit..

rests within ourselves and our engagement with our own unique environments, not in or from any one OTO country or Kingdom.

The most godless country on earth

To live above or outside the natural world is alien to the *mythopoetic* 'Spirit of Place' of my home, Australia. This archetypal dimension to life here - what our indigenous brethren refer to as the Dreaming - cannot be accessed or encountered with the pentecostal mindset. This has led a number of religious commentators on Australia, including Pope Benedict XVI, the Rev. James Denney the 19th century Scottish Presbyterian theologian,[22] and Professor Tom Frame, director of St Mark's National Theological Centre in Canberra,[23] to all totally miss the point and echo - or even quote directly - the words of the Rev. Samuel Marsden, one of the first Anglican clergy in Australia. In the late 1700s Marsden declared Australia 'the most godless country on earth.'[24] From his own disjunctive perspective,

---

[22] Collins, P. 2005. 'Australians are not godless, they're hungry', Sydney Morning Herald, 23 August, viewed 23 April 2012, http://www.smh.com.au/news/opinion/australians-are-not-godless-theyre-hungry/2005/08/22/1124562800483.html

[23] Buttrose, L. 2009. 'Sport, grog and godliness', The Australian, 5 September, viewed 23 April 2012, http://www.theaustralian.com.au/news/opinion/sport-grog-and-godliness/story-e6frg6zo-1225769660554

[24] Richardson, P. 1995. 'Letter from Australia: An Australian perspective on disestablishment', New Directions, November, viewed 23 April 2012, http://trushare.com/06NOV95/NO95AUST.htm

Marsden was probably right. About 200 years later in his iconic 1964 book, *The Lucky Country*, author Donald Horne went so far as to suggest that Christianity was simply out of step with secular Australian values.[25] Yet, it is a secularism steeped in an unconscious mythopoetic.

The mythopoetic worldview was advocated by the analytical psychologist Carl Jung, departing from Freud on the subject, who would have reduced the same to infantile projections. Jung insisted upon a *participation mystique* with the environment beneath the surface of superficial consciousness, writing in 1943 'I am deeply convinced of the - unfortunately - still very mysterious relation between man and landscape.'[26] Jung's ideas were significantly developed by James Hillman in his *anima mundi* discourse,[27] and within a specifically Australian context, more recently by David Tacey of La Trobe University. Tacey suggests that Western European cosmology is reversed in Australia, giving rise to a completely different spiritual phenomenology. "We don't 'have' spiritual experiences in Australia," he writes, "rather, they 'have us', and hold us in their grip."[28] He notes that "in Australia, the country of reversals, the upside down land, the

---

[25] Ibid.
[26] Adler, G (ed.). 1989. C.G. Jung: Letters, vol. 1, Princeton UP, New Jersey, p. 338.
[27] Hillman, J. 1982. 'Anima Mundi': The Return of the Soul to the World', Spring, pp. 71-93.
[28] Tacey, D. nd. 'Spirit of Place', Earthsong 1, viewed 22 April 2012, http://earthsong.org.au/publications/journal/issue-1/issue-1-feature-article/

Antipodes whose symbol is the tilted Southern Cross, the celestial realm appears to be 'below' us, in the earth itself, in the soil, rocks, and plants of this ancient land. Here, the spirit has not departed the earth and retreated to its heavenly abode. The spirit is in the earth, under our feet, and below our normal level of vision and understanding."[29] Our natural spiritual orientation is, if you like, averse. Again, such an orientation is not 'a return to the earth-mother-goddess paganism of the past',[30] but simply a southern reception and perception of the 'Greeting of Earth and Heaven!'[31] And something much more interesting.

Spirit of Place

Some of my most intense encounters with our Spirit of Place occurred over 2004 whilst conducting an Opus not generally known for triggering numinous experiences - drafting up Grand Lodge Bylaws! Joseph Campbell once wrote that 'The deity of one's worship is a function of one's own state of mind. But it is also a product of one's culture. Catholic nuns do not have visions of Buddha, nor do Buddhist nuns have visions of Christ.'[32]

Nor do OTO leaders have visions of Aboriginal spirits.

---

[29] Ibid. See also Tacey, D. 1995. Edge of the Sacred: Transformation in Australia, HarperCollins Publishers, Balckburn.
[30] Women's Conference Address, op cit.
[31] Liber XV, op cit., Section III, 'Of the Ceremony of the Introit.'
[32] Campbell, J. 1986. The Inner Reaches of Outer Space: Metaphor as Myth and as Religion, Harper & Row, New York, p.67.

Campbell's point was to recognize your visions as transparent to transcendence. Mine were for the most part a series of simple geometrical forms that came upon me unprepared and uninvoking, universal or archetypal symbols perhaps, but most easily located in the western tradition. Yet, they spoke to me of *this* land and its people, and in particular, about how to organise the then soon to be established OTO Kingdom. The most vivid and cosmic encounter was an entirely different class of symbol that mashed together inner and outer space - it is the most public of the series as with the help of Australian artist Barry Hale it became my X° seal, yet it is also my most private in that it relates to the IX° of OTO and my work as a X°. On that one I have to be silent, but it was the last received, quite literally sealing the Opus.

I would however like to briefly mention some of the others and show how once processed, they were applied to the social scientific experiment of the OTO organisation.

The first was of a regular *dodecahedron*, one of the Platonic solids (12 pentagonal faces, 3 meeting at each vertex). In Plato's *Timaeus* the dodecahedron is attributed to the zodiac, and there's also a number of other mystical interpretations of its form and significance throughout the western esoteric tradition. What I was not aware of until recently was that at about the time of this vision the French astrophysicist Jean-Pierre Luminet had just put forward his theory that the shape of the Universe was Poincare's (dodecahedral) sphere -

a theory yet to be proven although elements of it were later confirmed in 2008.[33]

The zodiac symbolism of 12 has endless associations, but importantly, has its place in OTO's ritual and fraternal traditions.[34] After encountering the dodecahedron I was drawn to the view that it was also in our Governing structure as well. In this regards, the Greek Amphictyony came to mind - the association of 12 city-states responsible for sacred sites. The Great Amphictyonic League looked after the Oracle at Delphi and the temples of Apollo and Demeter. It was said to have been founded by Amphictyon, in one tradition held to have been *born of the sacred soil*. The late new age writer, John Michel, did an interesting if often imaginative study of amphictyonic government systems in his *Twelve-Tribe Nations and the Science of Enchanting the Landscape* (1991).[35]

In the times following this vision, the dodecahedron's 12 faces with 3 meeting at each vertex made me rethink an aspect of Baphomet's M∴M∴M∴ Constitution. Article Seven states:

---

[33] Luminet, J.P., Weeks, J., Riazuelo, A., Lehoucq, R., Uzan, J.P. 2003. 'Dodecahedral space topology as an explanation for weak wide-angle temperature correlations in the cosmic microwave background,. Nature 425 (6958), pp. 593-5.

[34] For the latter see Liber CI 'An Open Letter to Those Who May Wish to Join the Order Enumerating the Duties and Privileges.'

[35] For a recent and revised edition, Michel, J. and Rhone, C. 2008. Twelve-Tribe Nations: Sacred Number and the Golden Age, Inner Traditions, Rochester.

'There shall be a Supreme Council of Nine members appointed from the Sovereign Grand Inspectors General. The National Grand Master General shall be the President of the Council (*ex officio*) and all other members of the Executive shall be *ex officio* members of the Supreme Council which shall act as an advisory Committee.'[36]

Given the Executive has 3 members (The National Grand Master General, Grand Secretary General and Grand Treasurer General), adding these *ex officio* ('by virtue of office') members to the 9 *appointed* SGIGs gave me a total of 12 for the Supreme (Grand) Council.[37] This differed from my presumption that the Council had to be 9 *inclusive* of the 3 *ex officio*. The 9 + 3 has its place in our ritual symbolism, whilst side by side they give us our beloved '93'. At the Hermetic Brotherhood of Light level in Australia we are exploring this arrangement in different ways, including by qabalah, astrological psychology, harmonic vibration and the OTO practices taught at this level, although these experiments and their informing ideas are in their infancy. We've also actively organised the OTO according to this

---

[36] 'Ancient Order of Oriental Templars, Mysteria Mystica Maxima, Constitution of British Section.' This was first published in modern times in The Magical Link, Fall 1997.

[37] The modern OTO calls the national 'Supreme Council' the 'Supreme Grand Council.' The Supreme Council is left to designate the International Headquarters Council of OHO, Secretary General and Treasurer General. See the OTO International Bylaws.

framework. Importantly, I do not claim that this is Baphomet's intended constituent number for the Supreme (Grand) Council, only that it is a workable possibility, and that if we look at the equivalent *advisory* body in the International Constitution, this "Advisory Council" consists of 12 members inclusive of the OHO.[38] In modelling off 12 (or whilst developing, up to 12) rather than 9 (or up to 9) I think Australia might differ from the arrangement of our sister Grand Lodges.

The next vision took the first even further. Here, the dodecahedron changed into a *hendecagon* (an eleven-sided polygon), though of the more psychedelic, *petrie polygon* type variety. In turn this changed into the more familiar 11 pointed star. This particular star features in ritual OTO tradition, and the number 11 features in OTO organisation: the 'Electoral College consists of Eleven Persons in each country,' 'the appointment is for Eleven Years', and 'Volunteers must renounce for that period all further progress in the Order'[39]; further, 'The Electoral College possesses one most singular power. Every eleven years, or in the case of a vacancy occurring, they choose two persons from the Ninth Degree, who are charged with the duty of Revolution.'[40] And in the introductory lines of Liber CXCIV a province of the OTO is considered established

---

[38] Constitution of the Ancient Order of Oriental Templars, Article VI.
[39] Liber CXCIV, op cit.
[40] Ibid.

'when it possesses eleven or more Profess-Houses.'[41] The impression from the star seemed to be that visionary meaning was now shifting from form (in the first vision) to function, and in particular that the entire series of images related to Lovers Triad Governance (in this case now, at the Senate level). It was fairly easy from there to identify the star transformation as related to the X° being unapproachable below the VI° - a shift from the 12 of the SGC to the 11 *from* the SGC active and approachable in the M∴M∴M∴. This was followed by a period of recurring dreams and active imaginings involving chivalrous, rosicrucian and alchemical symbolism although always in distinct and contemporary Australian settings. Through study moreso than intuition I was able to identify these secondary visions as related to the alchemical process of the *Sublimatio*.

In brief, the sublimatio is part of the purification process whereby the volatile spirit is extracted from matter or body, which in its largest psychological sense relates to the redemption of the Self from its unconscious state.[42] On an everyday level, it's about taking the high ground to see the 'bigger picture', a precursor to being 'well grounded' and 'down to earth.' In a way, this was exactly what I was trying to do with Grand Lodge planning at the time. Sublimatio is

---

[41] Ibid.
[42] See Edinger, E. 1994. Anatomy of the Psyche: Alchemical Symbolism in Psychotherapy, Open Court, Chicago and La Salle, pp. 117 - 145.

the elevating process of vaporization, while its descent or condensation is known as the distillation.[43] Applied to OTO, this distillation was to be represented by the descent or devolution of the 'SGC', from 'Sovereign Grand Commander' (a title of the X°) to the 'Supreme Grand Council' (of the VII°) through to the 'Sublime Grand Commander' (the title of the VII° in the Senate of Knight Hermetic Philosophers) - so, from Sovereign to Supreme to Sublime - a concurrent process to the Sublime Grand Commander 'elevating' the Senate's discourse and membership through equilibrated facilitation. In the Senate degree Crowley said the 'intellectual and moral attitude is further defined'[44] and the Sublime Grand Commander would work to bring this out, or elevate it, within the Senate's membership by applying the principle of equilibrium (as taught in the VII°) to all possible moral and intellectual ideas raised in their work.[45]

From the sublimatio download the *modus operandi* of our Senate emerged. Firstly, it should be noted that we operate the Senate according to the descriptor given in Liber CXCIV, considering this grade 'the first of the governing bodies, properly speaking' and '*within* this body is the

---

[43] The Sublimatio should not be confused with Freud's theory of sublimation, see C.G. Jung: Letters, vol. 1, op cit. p. 171.
[44] Excerpt from Confessions published as Baphomet XI°. 1989. 'What is Freemasonry? An Excerpt on the Reconstituted OTO', in Equinox III:10 (1990 ed.), 93 Publishing, New York, p.204.
[45] Ibid. See description of the VII°.

Electoral College of the OTO'[46] i.e. we do not treat the Electoral College as *the* Governing Body, but as a component part of it. The Sublime Grand Commanders (the 11, or up to 11) of the Senate of Knight Hermetic Philosophers would be assigned a regional Senate body, each area having a local representative from the Electoral College (EC). Issues of regional Governance would be discussed there, and when relevant or required, sent to the national Electoral College who would serve as the *central* sanctioning body of the Senate. So for example, the check and balance is that regional Senate preferences might be overturned at the national level, the EC possibly 'displeasing the majority' in the name of 'progress and illumination.'[47] And of course, EC decisions can be appealed to the Supreme Grand Council.

This federalist structure continues to be experimental - an unsatisfactory and vague term when it comes to organisational governance and management, but meant in the spirit of Franklin Roosevelt's 'bold and persistent experimentation'. It can perhaps best be qualified by saying that on one level the Senate's design accords with Strategic Niche Management (SNM) theory, defined as an approach 'to facilitate the introduction of radically new sustainable technologies through societal experiments. Its ultimate aim is to contribute to a broad shift to more sustainable development, through an integral combination of

---

[46] My italics. Liber CXCIV, op cit.
[47] Ibid.

technological progress and system-wide social-institutional transformation.'[48] On another level, as the Australian Foreign Minister and elder political statesmen, the bookish and intellectual Bob Carr said, 'There may lie the way forward. Improvisation - smart leaders collecting the best that is around and making it up as they go along... Forget theory and improvise.'[49]

Overwhelmingly, the evidence suggests that the federalist Senate structure within our constitutional monarchy works, and although it has taken a number of years to see that, there's now evidence it empowers members and their constituent OTO bodies, promotes a greater understanding and management of the OTO, develops governing skills and sharpens philosophical acumen. Again, I do not claim that this is Baphomet's intended Senate model, or his vision for an OTO Kingdom (which in this model essentially sees a maximum of 11 regions within the Kingdom develop), only that it is a workable possibility uniquely adapted to our environment. Ironically, the current and former Australian Governments have advocated similar approaches, but way after us, under the title 'Cooperative Federalism'[50] - with

---

[48] Caniels, M and Romijin, H. 2008. 'Actor network in Strategic Niche Management: Insights from social network theory', Futures, 40, pp. 613-629.

[49] Carr, B. 2012. 'Social Democracy Crisis', Australian Financial Review, 'Review", 2 March pp. 10–11.

[50] See for example, Crean, S. 2011. 'Call for new 'bottom-up' cooperative federalism to boost regions', Media Release, Minister for Regional Development, viewed 24 April 2012,

substantially less success than the OTO I might add. From the Senate model we've developed a regional plan known internally as the OTO pentagrammaton (recalling the pentagonal faces of the dodecahedron) - in every OTO region that emerges we want to have (at least) a Lodge, a Chapter, a Church, a Senate (inclusive of an Elector), with much of the discourse at Senate level exploring regional solutions for the long term scalability and sustainability of this model. And perhaps one day we'll have those 11 or more profess houses as well.

As an aside, due to the way we work our Senate rites, it may be interesting to note that similar visionary experiences to the ones I've related here have independently occurred in some members of the VII°, leading to new symbolic meanings with related research and insight developing.

The OTO Experience

With these evolving structural topologies as a backdrop, other features of the OTO have also taken their own shape. Our Man of Earth bodies, while on one level the same as they are the world over, have a few slight distinctions. Our Camps are chartered to III° members, the Master chartered

---

http://www.minister.regional.gov.au/sc/releases/2011/october/sc131_2011.aspx
See also Wanna, J., Phillimore, J., Fenna, A., Harwood, J. 2009. 'Common cause: Strengthening Australia's Cooperative Federalism. Final Report to the Council for the Australian Federation', Council for the Australian Federation, viewed 26 April 2012,
http://www.caf.gov.au/documents/FP3%20-%20final.pdf

to *only* initiate the Minerval Degree - an application of Baphomet's 'Camp of Minerval' idea, with Oases Masters chartered to work 0°–III°. Grand Lodge has also embraced the Frater Superior's relatively recent position, authorising Lodge Masters to be chartered to initiate 0°–PI. In the case of IV° and PI in Australia, Grand Lodge requires these are worked with some VII° assistance. The main point however, is that the Lodge Master can be the initiator, rather than the VII°, as used to be the case in the past. We have found this to not only provide a coherent allocation of initiatic authority throughout the Man of Earth local bodies, but also excellent training for our Lodge Masters, and something that inspires them and broadens their experience of our System. A standing item for the Senate is Man of Earth succession planning, as we want the Lodge Chair to pass as often as is practicable to ensure variety and capacity building within our middle ranks. Only foundation body charters are being issued, followed by authorising letters of appointment from the Electoral College. I should add that my most recent experiment has been to shorten the term of appointment of the EC President within their overall 11 year term as an Elector, rotating the Presidency much like the Chairs of Lodges, to keep things fresh, better draw upon the unique skills of all electors, and develop the EC's leadership and governing abilities both as a group and as individuals.

At the Lovers level we are preparing for Chapters of Rose-Croix to be chartered to members of the Knight Hermetic Philosopher (Senate) degree, in line with another of the

Frater Superior's more recent positions. This is something we not only embrace, but something that will sit extremely well with our Senate model, its operational plan and the future growth of the RC. It is a significant departure from the former requirement that our Most Wise Sovereigns (MWS) and High Priestesses (HP) needed to be VI° - a requirement that, especially as a X°, troubled me as it seemed to invite a conflict of interest between the military function of the VI° and the social welfare work of the RC. We've also implemented and continue to develop the Frater Superior's distinction between the Knight of the Red Eagle (KRE) and Knight Hermetic Philosopher (KHP) rites of the Senate. Again, this is a shift away from how many of the older generation, myself included, went through the Senate in a combined degree, yet sits much better not only with our teachings and symbolism at the Senate level, but with the current assignment of KRE to Lodge Master and KHP to MWS/HP.

Our invitation to V° process is simple and straightforward and does away with the pointless mystery, fuss and bureaucracy which in my view has plagued this process (in Australia) in the past, to the detriment of the real business of advancing our members to 'the natural stopping-place of the majority of men and women.'[51] Treating the KEW as 'but a bridge between the first and second series,'[52] at the

---

[51] Liber CXCIV, op cit.
[52] Ibid.

conclusion of that Ceremony we give the new KEW a certain V° form initiates of the Rose Croix would be familiar with. Upon satisfaction of its criteria and signing (whenever or if ever that might be) and its required attestation by others as prescribed, it gets sent to the Electoral College for a determination on sanction. We treat this form as the 'new pledge-form'[53] Baphomet refers to in his description of the KEW in Liber CXCIV, and leave it right from the start in the hands of the new Knight, rather than in the hands of a Chapter. The decision to complete the form rests with the Knight, rather than with a Chapter to decide when to dispense it. Non-essential paperwork, which was beginning to creep in under former processes, is eradicated. We have found this juxtapositioning extremely motivating, encouraging and inspiring for our KEWs, and for the astute Knight, gives further hints about the Path in Eternity at this stage in our System, and the true Obligation of a 'new Knight vowed to devote his life to the Establishment of the Law of Thelema.'[54]

A theology of joy and beauty

The Ecclesia Gnostica Catholica (EGC) or Gnostic Catholic Church is deserving of a paper in its own right given its complexity, the controversy it occasionally invites, and its place within a western religious context. However, some reflections are worth noting here.

---

[53] Ibid.
[54] Ibid.

Firstly, as a Primate I respectfully disagree with some of the recent representations put forward about the EGC For example, in an unofficial episcopal publication, *To Perfect This Feast*, the authors state 'Aleister Crowley remains the only superior we recognize with the authority to guide us in the performance of the Gnostic Mass.'[55] This does not quite square off with the fact that we all derive our authority to perform the Mass from the *present* Frater Superior. My further concern with this comment is that it may be taken outside of what I think is the intended context - fidelity to the text of Liber XV - and used by others to justify *more* of what the authors have argued against, 'the variations we have witnessed... over the last three decades.'[56] I would qualify my comments by saying that some variation in performance is not only inevitable, but in my experience, healthy. The textual directions given in Liber XV are in more than one place ambiguous, and beyond Liber XV, Baphomet left next to no guidelines on performance. It seems only natural then that many interpretations and styles will emerge, and that these variations will have to be assessed through the interpretative grille of our Mystery by appointed (not self-appointed) Church authorities.

The boundaries or scope for variation in performance should in my opinion be the sole purview of the Patriarch or

---

[55] Wasserman J., Wasserman, N. 2010 2nd rev. ed. To Perfect This Feast: A Commentary on Liber XV The Gnostic Mass, Sekmet Books, West Palm Beach, p.13.
[56] Ibid.

Matriarch of the Church, and to a lesser extent his or her sole direct representatives the Primates. From there it lives through the episcopal relationships of our Bishops with our Priestesses and Priests. Performance guidelines cannot be isolated from the preparation and administration of our Sacrament, or treated independent of doctrine. Aleister Crowley seems to have appreciated this, as might be evidenced by his comments about the Anthem 'should other anthems be *authorized* by the Father of the Church.'[57] For this reason, in Australia we hold that the official or authoritative text of Liber XV is always the latest one edited by the OHO of the time, or a version *specifically* given his or her imprimatur.

I also disagree with the promotion of our Church as a separate organisation to the OTO[58] To the best of my knowledge there is no evidence that this was Baphomet's intent, and it seems clear to me that one function of the OTO is to train the Church's clergy in the preparation of our Sacrament through progressive initiation. The separatist viewpoint lends itself to potential schism, as the logical inference of such a recontextualisation is that you can then

---

[57] My italics. Liber XV, The Gnostic Mass, note to section VII.
[58] See To Perfect this Feast, op. cit. p. 7 "...this is not an official publication of either organisation", and Kaczynski, R. 2009. The Weiser Concise Guide to Aleister Crowley, Red Wheel/Weiser, San Francisco. Part I of this book, 'Mystical and Magical Societies' has 3 Chapters on (respectively) the A∴A∴, the OTO and the Ecclesia Gnostica Catholica. The inference is that EGC is a 'Mystical and Magical Society' in its own right.

have an EGC Clergy who are independent or a breakaway of the OTO. This is not to say that we cannot look to the EGC to have a much more public role, function and service in the wider community, and for the Church to establish and provide for the religious needs of congregations and communities of non-initiates. While it is early days for this type of EGC presence in Australia, it is something we are working towards as a key driver of our long term strategy.

To this end, my first act as Primate was to identify the sacramental 'celebrations' given in Liber XV[59] with Crowley's 'New Comment' interpretation of AL II:41.[60] There is some evidence suggesting this would have met with Therion's blessings in Liber DCCCXXXVII, where commenting on AL:II:34–44, he declares 'Here is the Calendar of our Church... All you have to do is to be yourself, to do your will, and to rejoice.'[61] The alignment of the ecclesiastical sacraments such as baptism and confirmation, as well as the ecclesiastical calendar, to the New Comment exposition may invite criticism or concern for its theological connotations. If so, I would call it a

---

[59] These are stated in the explanatory notes to Section VIII of Liber XV, op cit., 'Of the Mystic Marriage and Consummation of the Elements.'
[60] See Crowley, A. 1996 ed. L. Wilkinson and Hymenaeus Beta. The The Law is for All: The Authorized Popular Commentary to The Book of the Law, New Falcon, Tempe and Las Vegas, p. 124. While funerary rites are not referred to in the notes on celebrations, they may be inferred from the New Comment and from the Collects of Liber XV.
[61] Liber DCCCXXXVII 'The Law of Liberty, A Tract of To Mega Therion 666 That is a Magus 9 = 2 A∴A∴.

theology of joy and beauty in line with Therion's comments above, and I feel the alignment with AL by far the most sustainable and wholesome way forward for the sacraments of the Church taking us into the future. It does however change things to what may well be accepted Church practice overseas. For example, if you align baptism with the New Comment on a feast for life, you are a) making a theological statement about what the sacrament of baptism represents in the Church, and b) clearly not baptising adults. These are all practical and philosophical issues the Church in Australia will have to tease out in the future, the first step to which has been developing the episcopate required to do this.

Relevant to both the public space of the Gnostic Catholic Church and the private space of the Sovereign Sanctuary of the Gnosis is the doctrinal statement given in the EGC Manifesto that 'The priestess must now function as well as the priest.'[62] Were I forced to look to only one source of optimism and hope for our next 100 years, it would be this, and I am on record (with my people, at least) for predicting that the 21st century will be the century of the Priestess.[63] Once again, 'We are not in for a return to the earth-mother-goddess paganism of the past, but something much more

---

[62] 'Manifesto of the Gnostic Catholic Church', in Hymenaeus Beta, 1990. 'On the Gnostic Catholic Church', The Magical Link, Vol III No 4, p. 30.
[63] This theme is taken up in Shiva X°. 2007. 'New Commentary Theology III: the enchanted doxologies of Virgo Intacta'

interesting.'[64] This *functionality* will go beyond the unique skills, aptitude and capabilities our Sisters can bring to organisational and ceremonial roles, nor will it be framed in identities or projections one Sister described as 'overly fanatical tough tomboy feminists wearing trousers like blokes? Angry, provocative goddesses holding ourselves above men with revenge and retaliation burning in our eyes? Being almighty knowing oracles that expect to be put on a pedestal? And more? Probably some or all of the above at different times... Maybe that's the woman trying to be what she thinks a soldier is, rather than a woman that is a soldier.'[65]

I would say that 'something much more interesting' will develop, extending from an entirely new feminine contribution to and understanding of, our hermetic science and central secret, as well as new ways of engaging and learning with and from each other, and the means of expressing our Gnosis. It could perhaps be argued, though I'm sure I will have my critics, that our 'body of doctrine' to date is a male body, and that what we seek in our doctrinal understanding of our Mystery is a sexed, or perhaps better, two sexes in one, corporeality, in order to embrace and experience the Spirit inherent to us all. In such an endeavour, at least from the theological viewpoint, we move

---

[64] 'Women's Conference Address', op. cit.
[65] Sr. Aygul Servito VII°. 2012. 'Chicken Scratchings and an Egg for the Chicks', OZ, 23, March, p.8.

way beyond the corporeal theories of Freud, Lacan, Merleau-Ponty, Foucault, Deleuze, Derrida[66] and others (if not the western canon itself), and through a lived spiritual experience contribute, or potentially contribute, to a new and presently unknown philosophical, intellectual and spiritual space. I should also add biological, especially if you subscribe to the notion that biology is inherently social, and subject to social inscription, something I would suggest we do on both mystical and moral levels in the social experiment and social laboratory of the OTO.[67]

The Frater Superior once suggested that 'Someday, perhaps not soon, a woman adept in the OTO Sovereign Sanctuary will manifest the genius to compose a Mass in which the female takes the more active role, and the male the more passive (as with Siva and Sakti in Hinduism) - in which the Deacon, speaking for the Priestess, can claim communion with the women in history that have perceived the divinity of man.'[68] Perhaps sooner, women aspirants in Australia or elsewhere will manifest the genius to spiritualize and celebrate - for all of us - the corporeal experiences unique to women in a Church of the future that can provide the

---

[66] See Grosz, E. 1994. Volatile Bodies: Towards a Corporeal Feminism, Indiana UP, Bloomington.
[67] This statement should be considered in relation to Ch. XXVII 'Structure of Mind based on that of Body (Haeckel and Bertrand Russell)', in Crowley, A. 1954. Magick Without Tears, Thelema Publishing Company, Hampton, pp. 129–131.
[68] 'Women's Conference Address', op. cit., p.10.

spiritual framework and space for this? Time will tell, but we are in 'for something much more interesting' and it behoves us to be open to it *now*, and in this matter women not men should be leading the way.

Perhaps then the OTO *public* celebration and contribution will be to 'await, no longer a science of sexuality, its formalization and abstraction, but an art of sexuality, not its analysis but its celebration as diverse becoming, not knowing and thereby containing it, but elaborating it and extending it.'[69] Perhaps in a celebration of openness we will better understand 'the surprise of sexuality, its liability to unpredictability, to openness, formlessness, boundlessness'[70] and in a manner that I think the OTO is extremely well placed to initiate, bring about 'the generation of a new productivity between and of the two sexes'[71] that in turn affects how we conceive of and act in the world.

Social Scientific Illuminism

One of the more understated achievements of the modern OTO and our Frater Superior in particular, has been the organising of the vast corpus of historical OTO instructions into a coherent and comprehensive OTO Curriculum.[72] In

---

[69] Grosz, E. 2005. Time Travels: Feminism, Nature, Power, Duke UP, Durham and London, p.214.
[70] Ibid.
[71] Volatile Bodies, op cit. p. 210.
[72] 'OTO Curriculum' and 'Official Instructions of the OTO' in Crowley, A, Desti, M, Waddell, L. 1997 ed. Hymenaeus Beta. Magick, Liber ABA, Book Four Parts I-IV, Weiser, York Beach, pp. 476–485.

his later life Crowley admitted that OTO material was 'not as ordered and classified as one would wish'[73] and the Curriculum addresses this. How are we best placed to use the Curriculum systematically, or is it just a historical compilation that members can pick and choose from as need dictates?

Perhaps the best answer is that we can do both, and while our members do approach the Curriculum independently - as many of us have done for years - we decided here that from the *international* Curriculum we should construct a *national* Syllabus that would inform *local* group and *individual* study, thereby aligning Curriculum to the principle networks of OTO activity. We also recognized from the start that any attempt to systematically use the Curriculum would have its limitations Syllabus-wise: new research and publications for example are always being released and impossible to keep track of in their entirety.

We assigned to our degrees what we considered relevant and useful instructional papers from the Curriculum. It is now in its second year, and whilst an iterative and experimental endeavour in its earliest stages, it has been well received and currently covers Minerval through to V°. Many of my senior members have said privately to me that they wished it was around when they were growing up through the junior ranks of OTO. So do I. And as the learning culture has evolved, as

---

[73] Magick Without Tears, op. cit., Ch. 13 'System of the OTO', p. 70.

it has done even after only 1 year of implementation, the Syllabus too has expanded to include other works and original contributions from our members. The scope of group activity - by far the hardest part of the Syllabus to implement - will take some time to develop, but it is way too early to either assess or analyse this yet, either qualitatively or quantitatively. We are trying to encourage in a non-prescriptive manner grass roots, innovative and creative group approaches fitted to local environments which in turn will feed into Syllabus renewal and exchange in the future, but the experiments have only just begun.[74]

How we selected materials for the Syllabus was a mix of common sense and consensus of informed opinion, explicit ritual instruction (e.g. if you are told to study *this* or meditate upon *that* we looked for papers which addressed it) and what I will call 'OTO attributes'. By this I mean that we took the OTO moral qualities described in Liber LII[75] such as courage, honour, zeal etc as the ideal attributes we want our V° members to possess. We then deconstructed the degrees through to V° to identify where we saw a focus on some or all of these particular qualities in any one rite. We then looked for papers within the OTO Curriculum that mapped to those qualities and assigned them to that particular degree. At other times, we selected papers with

---

[74] See for example, Mayes, C. 2005. Jung and Education: elements of an archetypal pedagogy, Rowman & Littlefield Education, Lanham, Toronto & Oxford.
[75] Liber LII 'Manifesto of the OTO'

what you could call mystic license, knowing what our candidates may be exposed to in later degrees, or based upon our own insights and experiences working through the System.

In general, the methods we've employed are predicated on a simplistic model I use to explain the complexities of the OTO Constitution to our junior members when I get that opportunity - that from Minerval through to V° you could be considered a *student*, whereas above V° you could be considered *staff* who have devoted their lives in service to the Order. The emphasis here is on 'simplistic model' - we're always students of the System after all. The model rests on the traditional assignment of the OTO as an *Academia*.[76] All of our 'staff' will have their own practical or theoretical research interests, some will take on different types of teaching roles, and all will proceed to sit on one, some or all of the 'Academy's' bodies, such as the Senate, or Tribunal, or Council, or Executive Management, or have social welfare or ecclesiastical roles, etc. However, the fundamental principle of the Academy is that *all* share a primary duty of care towards our 'students'. I try and encourage the 'staff' to take an 'academic' approach - not in terms of rigid intellectualism and academic output, but rather in how they manage their OTO time. Some will focus on administration, or research, or teaching, or some or all of these briefs on top of their field duties. Most importantly, the OTO National

---

[76] ie. the traditional 'Academia Masonica', see Liber LII, ibid.

Executive tries to keep the OTO as flexible, lean and as bureaucracy free as possible so our senior members have the time for their research and/or teaching. In reality, we have a long way to go before we've perfected this approach to the Academy, with mentoring and supervising of research to come, as well as research communities opening up.

A key to understanding the Syllabus is an experimental constructivist idea (and perhaps one day a proven methodology) that I have termed *Social Scientific Illuminism*. Basically this is a group approach to and experience of Crowley's unique pedagogy, Scientific Illuminism, to facilitate the Order's specialized training of groups by way of progressive initiation.[77] In other words, social 'scientific illuminism would be characterized by meticulous and objective record keeping of laboratory experiments, a concern about possible 'sources of error', the broader research community's access to other scientists' research results, and the sanctioning of practices by an authorizing body'[78], all through a group lens. Observation and experiment.

The focus of this 'education revolution' as we call it locally, has been to articulate an OTO narrative and discourses within our community, to concentrate on *our* teachings and

---

[77] See the Editorial to Equinox III:1. 1919. Universal Publishing Company, Detroit, p.9.
[78] Morrison, M.S. 2007. Modern Alchemy: Occultism and the Emergence of Atomic Theory, Oxford UP, New York, p.47.

practices as an Order, and what it means to be OTO - to be culturally located in our curriculum and traditions, rites and customs, as a distinct System (despite the occasional overlap) from the much more widely known Curriculum of A∴A∴. It's a get back to basics approach, where in this day and age the basics can all too easily be overshadowed - especially in our younger or junior members - by the gossip and unreliable information of the occult ghetto denizens of cyberspace, and the egoic projections of the 'many who think themselves to be Masters who have not even begun to tread the Way of Service that leads thereto.'[79] It's about taking care of our young and training them properly in OTO, or perhaps better, exploring our sacred and sublime Mysteries together.

I know full well that on the face of it to write about Curriculum or to even espouse a remotely scientific approach to OTO activity might sound boring and disengaging, or at least unfamiliar, to many. The challenge is to turn that around and articulate our Mystery in accessible, creative, and challenging yet inclusive ways. For, I have no doubt that when Crowley called our Central Secret a 'scientific secret' with which there is 'nothing... the human imagination can conceive that could not be realized in practice'[80] he meant it. And when he said of OTO 'you only become a magician, and a priest of the Holy One - a very

---

[79] Liber LXI 'A∴A∴. The Preliminary Lection.'
[80] 'What is Freemasonry', op cit., p. 203.

fine and balanced 6° = 5, but no more,'⁸¹ far from devaluing the OTO he gave us a very real spiritual context, and surely, a moral and fraternal obligation and responsibility to help each other reach our potential, individual and collective, in this regards. And he obviously had something very definite in mind when he decided that the OTO, unlike the open Curriculum of A∴A∴, would have 'much secret knowledge... besides that openly published'⁸², even stating it was 'desirable' that Aspirants to the Major Adept grade of A∴A∴ 'should have attained the 9th degree of OTO.'⁸³

We have a tradition which has a depth and richness in its own right, with much to learn, research, preserve, develop, improvise, teach and celebrate.

I say, so mote it be!

The Elephant in the Temple

In December of 1916 Aleister Crowley wrote to Frank Bennett in Australia saying, 'Please distinguish carefully between A∴A∴ and OTO. The latter is a practical organisation devoted to the establishment of the work of the former.'⁸⁴ Exactly what that might mean warrants

---

[81] 'OTO Curriculum', op cit. p.476.
[82] 'A∴A∴ Curriculum, Course VIII' (Major Adept) in Book Four, op cit. p. 458.
[83] Ibid.
[84] Crowley, A. 1916. Letter to Frank Bennett, December, OTO Archives. See also 'Aspiring to the Holy Order', op. cit., for a discussion about devotion 'to the establishment of the work of the former.'

considerable reflection in terms of the function of the OTO and is one of the research perspectives and problematics we are investigating here. It is in this devotional sense to establishing the work of A∴A∴ that I have stated in the past that OTO is in *service* to the A∴A∴. Given the amount of unscholarly and emotive criticism this has evoked in the international community, I perhaps should have just stuck to 'devoted', a term which has both practical and magical connotations in my view, but possibly beyond the scholarly or historical grasp of current criticism.

In his later years, Crowley reiterated his position saying the OTO was '(a) convenient in various practical ways, (b) a machine for carrying out the orders of the Secret Chiefs of A∴A∴, (c) by virtue of the Secret a magical weapon of incalculable power.'[85] The latter is a direct reference to IX° of OTO. Something quite deep is being said there.

On a practical level, we have followed the precedent set by International Headquarters in their publications by listing the official address of A∴A∴ in relevant OTO papers such as our Syllabus, to 'distinguish carefully' between the Orders and their different modes of operating and curricula, while referring members drawn to the work of A∴A∴ to its official point of contact. All of the feedback I've been able to obtain from our members suggests this has been received positively,

---

[85] Magick Without Tears, op. cit., Chapter LXXI 'Morality (2)', pp. 323–324.

and has served to clarify much of the needless confusion on this matter. We have supplemented this by collaborative work with A∴A∴ such as hosting lectures from their instructors, or lecturing together. I hold the view that the traditional 'alliance'[86] between the Orders has been obfuscated in the years following Crowley's death, and moving forward into the future we need to analyse this if indeed we are to continue 'carrying out the orders of the Secret Chiefs' - a task that requires the trials and errors, but ultimate reward, of sustaining and maintaining the magical link. Our research to date suggests this alliance is evolutionary rather than static and capable of uncovering new (or at least, new for us) aspects and approaches to our System.[87]

Commenting on the challenges the alliance faces, within the OTO world community, I recently wrote this frank mail to a Sister of the Order overseas:

> 'The almost systemic problem we have with these types will never go away in OTO until and unless we have strong and enlightened national leadership with a strong educational reform agenda on what the OTO is and is not, delivered with acute tact and sensitivity to cultural and generational change. This

---

[86] Liber LII, op. cit.
[87] See for example, 'Aspiring to the Holy Order' and 'Under the Shadow of the Wings', op.cit. See also Lohengrin VII° 'First Instruction in Kundalini Yoga', Fifth Degree Syllabus, 2012 iteration, AUGL OTO.

also requires a frank, fair and honest assessment of our history that transcends sentimentality and defensiveness - of the great divides (and great delusions) that have happened post-Crowley. Maybe, in some areas anyway, it's too early for that - memories are still fresh or even still too painful etc... Who knows. Yet we possibly run risk of failing to have a convincing narrative in the interim, which will leave us ineffective and bland, rather than inspirational & doing our job.'[88]

If we are to remain divided on such issues, let it be 'for love's sake, for the chance of union.'[89]

Night thoughts of an OTO outsider

The Australian OTO is the only Grand Lodge to have retained a section in Grand Lodge Bylaws on the Guilds, which is to say that we can have Australian as distinct from international Guilds. I did this as I felt it better served Australian members and 'the prosecution of their own good' who may choose to organise or join Guilds. At the same time philosophically, I remain uncertain about the effectiveness and logic of the international model, or even if these Guilds are really all that international or predominantly US-centric. This is a good example of how we don't always agree at senior levels, and where I accept

---

[88] Shiva X°. 2012. Private correspondence [name withheld], 5 April.
[89] AL:I:29.

that my own views are not held by the majority of my esteemed senior brethren. This notwithstanding, I do however wonder about the 'independent Parliament of Guilds'[90] and how that might work. Although this is a chicken and the egg situation I suspect, perhaps we should have developed an idea of how that Parliament might be constituted and function, before we proceeded with the current Guilds model?

I have also wondered about the *ad hoc* Ordeal appointed by the Grand Tribunal referred to in Liber CI (in its original context related to defending brethren accused of offences against criminal law).[91] As a theoretical positioning, I have wondered whether just as so much of the traditional M∴M∴M∴ literature needs to be examined in its British context and its reform of British systems (such as the class system), can we locate in the *ad hoc* Ordeal appointed by Grand Inquisitor Commanders a reform to the legal system - in particular, outside of the obvious historical symbolism, a form of the *inquisitorial* system of law as distinct from the *adversarial* system? Are there applications of the inquisitorial system that can be applied to the Grand Tribunal today, as confronting as that might be for countries indoctrinated in the adversarial mindset and its fundamental reliance upon presumption of innocence? We should in this regards consider that outside of the United Kingdom, most

---

[90] Liber CXCIV, op. cit.
[91] Liber CI, op. cit.

Commonwealth countries and the United States, the inquisitorial system of law is more widely used than the adversarial.

I've wondered how you could equitably and representationally systematise a process for the Man of Earth to choose from among themselves the two men and two women to serve the King 'in order that the feelings of the general body may be represented.'[92] I suspect that this will organically arise in Australia from the Man of Earth at some point, and at such time the next challenge will be to work out the practical terms of service. In a few experiments to date though, I've found that Man of Earth representations can differ substantially from reports about the same I receive from Inspectors, and the feelings of the Third Triad can inform my decision making.

Finally, I believe the mandatory time between our introductory degrees is long overdue for a rethink. I doubt very much our present arrangement is what Baphomet ever intended, and that he envisaged progression through these grades similar to the procedures - practical and financial - of Craft Freemasonry. I have wondered whether this has contributed to our attrition rates in these grades, or misassumptions about OTO, or misguided activities or commentary done in the Order's name - members with too much time on their hands when what was intended was a far

---

[92] Liber CXCIV, op. cit.

more rapid and agile process. This in turn affects how our candidates engage with our allegory and symbolism, our tasks and obligations, and what overriding focus imprints and impressions of symbolic initiation are retained and initiated in the psychic life of the candidate.

These are but some of the many thoughts I can have about the OTO. But what of the future?

What I have tried to show in this paper is that the OTO of tomorrow is down to us today - our spirit, our inventiveness, our aspiration, our devotion, our practice, our patience and our ability to organise nationally. Perhaps the answers are in the rap song my eleven year old son is bellowing along to now as I type this: 'This is ten percent luck, twenty percent skill, fifteen percent concentrated power of will, five percent pleasure, fifty percent pain and a hundred percent reason to remember the name.'

That name is Ordo Templi Orientis.

I am not an Anarchist in your sense of the word: fancy the King of a Republic of Genius!

Love is the law, love under will.

OZ 24 ANNO IVxx - JUNE 2012 E.V.

REFERENCES FOR AURORA AUSTRALIS

AL

AL:I:29, AL:II:6, AL:II:34–44

Biblical

Acts 2:1-4

Books

Adler, G (ed.). 1989. *C.G. Jung: Letters, vol. 1*, Princeton UP, New Jersey.

Campbell, J. 1986. *The Inner Reaches of Outer Space: Metaphor as Myth and as Religion*, Harper & Row, New York.

Crowley, A, Desti, M, Waddell, L. 1997 ed. Hymenaeus Beta. *Magick, Liber ABA, Book Four Parts I-IV*, Weiser, York Beach.

Crowley, A. 1988 ed. *The Book of Lies*, Wesier, York Beach ME.

Crowley, A. 1996 ed. L. Wilkinson and Hymenaeus Beta. *The The Law is for All: The Authorized Popular Commentary to The Book of the Law*, New Falcon, Tempe and Las Vegas.

Crowley, A. 1954. *Magick Without Tears*, Thelema Publishing Company, Hampton.

Edinger, E. 1994. *Anatomy of the Psyche: Alchemical Symbolism in Psychotherapy*, Open Court, Chicago and La Salle.

Elvin, M. 2004. *The Retreat of the Elephants; an Environmental History of China*, Yale University Press, London.

Grosz, E. 2005. *Time Travels: Feminism, Nature, Power*, Duke UP, Durham and London.

Grosz, E. 1994. *Volatile Bodies: Towards a Corporeal Feminism*, Indiana UP, Bloomington.

Gunther, J.D. 2009. *Initiation in the Aeon of the Child: the inward journey*, Ibis, Lake Worth.

Kaczynski, R. 2009. *The Weiser Concise Guide to Aleister Crowley*, Red Wheel/Weiser, San Francisco.

Mayes, C. 2005. *Jung and Education: elements of an archetypal pedagogy*, Rowman & Littlefield Education, Lanham, Toronto & Oxford.

Michel, J. and Rhone, C. 2008. *Twelve-Tribe Nations: Sacred Number and the Golden Age*, Inner Traditions, Rochester.

Morrison, M.S. 2007. *Modern Alchemy: Occultism and the Emergence of Atomic Theory*, Oxford UP, New York.

Tacey, D. 1995. *Edge of the Sacred: Transformation in Australia*, HarperCollins Publishers, Balckburn.

Wasserman J & Wasserman, N. 2010 2nd rev. ed. *To Perfect This Feast: A Commentary on Liber XV The Gnostic Mass*, Sekmet Books, West Palm Beach

Equinox

Equinox III:10. 1990 ed. 93 Publishing, New York.

Equinox III:1. 1919. Universal Publishing Company, Detroit.

Journal & Newspaper Articles

Aygul Servito VII°. 2012. 'Chicken Scratchings and an Egg for the Chicks', OZ, 23.

Buttrose, L. 2009. 'Sport, grog and godliness', *The Australian*, 5 September, <http://www.theaustralian.com.au/news/opinion/sport-grog-and-godliness/story-e6frg6zo-1225769660554>

Caniels, M and Romijin, H. 2008. 'Actor network in Strategic Niche Management: Insights from social network theory', *Futures*, 40.

Carr, B. 2012. 'Social Democracy Crisis', *Australian Financial Review*, 'Review", 2 March.

Collins, P. 2005. 'Australians are not godless, they're hungry', *Sydney Morning Herald*, <http://www.smh.com.au/news/opinion/australians-are-not-godless-theyre-hungry/2005/08/22/1124562800483.html>

Crean, S. 2011. 'Call for new 'bottom-up' cooperative federalism to boost regions', Media Release,

Minister for Regional Development,

<http://www.minister.regional.gov.au/sc/releases/2011/october/sc131_2011.aspx>

Duguid, P. 2005. ' "The Art of Knowing": Social and Tacit Dimensions of Knowledge and the Limits of the

Community of Practice', *The Information Society: An Information Journal* 21:2, <http://dx.doi.org/10.1080/01972240590925311>

Hillman, J. 1982. 'Anima Mundi': The Return of the Soul to the World', *Spring*.

Hymenaeus Beta, 1990. 'On the Gnostic Catholic Church', *The Magical Link,* Vol III No 4.

Hymenaeus Beta XI°, 1997. 'Women's Conference Address', *The Magical Link*, Fall.

Latour, B. nd. 'On actor-network theory: a few clarifications plus more than a few complications' <http://www.cours.fse.ulaval.ca/edc-65804/latour-clarifications.pdf>

Lohengrin VII°. 2012. 'First Instruction in Kundalini Yoga', Fifth Degree Syllabus, 2012 iteration, AUGL OTO.

Luminet, J.P., Weeks, J., Riazuelo, A., Lehoucq, R., Uzan, J.P. 2003. 'Dodecahedral space topology as an explanation for weak wide-angle temperature correlations in the cosmic microwave background,. *Nature* 425 (6958).

Ma, D. 2004. 'Growth, Institutions and Knowledge: A Review and Reflection on the Historiography of 18th - 20th Century China', *Australian Economic History Review*, 44, 3.

Mearsheimer, J. 2006. 'Structural Realism', <http://www.oup.com/uk/orc/bin/9780199298334/dunne_chap04.pdf>

> Paton, M. nd. 'The Environmental History of China and the Sustainable Management of Governments', <http://sydney.edu.au/business/__data/assets/pdf_file/0003/56622/The_Environmental_History_of_China .pdf>

Richardson, P. 1995. 'Letter from Australia: An Australian perspective on disestablishment', New Directions, November, <http://trushare.com/06NOV95/NO95AUST.htm>

Shiva X°. 2007. 'New Commentary Theology III: the enchanted doxologies of Virgo Intacta', *OZ*, 5.

Tacey, D. nd. 'Spirit of Place', *Earthsong* 1, <http://earthsong.org.au/publications/journal/issue-1/issue-1-feature-article/>

Wanna, J., Phillimore, J., Fenna, A., Harwood, J. 2009. 'Common cause: Strengthening Australia's Cooperative Federalism. Final Report to the Council for the Australian Federation', Council for the

Australian Federation,

<http://www.caf.gov.au/documents/FP3%20-%20final.pdf>

Lectures

Shiva X°. 2011. 'Aspiring to the Holy Order', OTO, Sydney & Tokyo.

Shiva X°. 2011. 'Under the Shadow of the Wings', OTO, Sydney & Tokyo.

Libers and other papers

Ancient Order of Oriental Templars, Mysteria Mystica Maxima, Constitution of British Section.

Constitution of the Ancient Order of Oriental Templars.

Liber XV Ecclesia Gnostica Catholica Canon Missa.

Liber LII 'Manifesto of the OTO'.

Liber LXI 'A∴A∴. The Preliminary Lection.'

Liber LXXVII OZ.

Liber CI 'An Open Letter to Those Who May Wish to Join the Order Enumerating the Duties and Privileges.'

Liber CLXI 'Concerning the Law of Thelema'.

Liber CXCIV 'An Intimation with Reference to the Constitution of the Order'.

Liber DCCCXXXVII 'The Law of Liberty, A Tract of To Mega Therion 666 That is a Magus 9 = 2 A∴A∴.

OTO International Bylaws.

Correspondence:

Crowley, A. 1916. Letter to Frank Bennett, December, OTO Archives.

Churton, T. 2012. Personal correspondence with author, 24 January, OTO Archives.

Shiva X°. 2012. Private correspondence [name withheld], 5 April.

'NEW COMMENTARY' THEOLOGY - PART 1

Notes towards reorganizing the EGC

GRAND MASTER SHIVA X°
(PRIMATE, ECCLESIA GNOSTICA CATHOLICA)

Aleister Crowley once described the OTO Gnostic Mass as 'the central ceremony of its [the Order's] public and private celebration.' This often quoted comment (from Crowley's *Confessions*) alludes to the public and private nature of the OTO itself: on the one hand the Mass is a sacramental rite of public celebration and worship, while on the other hand the Mass celebrates in dramatic form the private worship and sacramental formulae of our Sanctuary of the Gnosis. That the Mass expresses these polarities ensures the rite truly celebrates *our* Mystery of Mystery. It gives us the opportunity, as clergy and congregation, to not only directly experience *gnosis*, but to experience such individually *and* collectively in the presence of our Saints. With this comes our obligation to continuity—the miracle of the Mass must be taught and preserved, in due course passing from generation to generation. For this to happen, the onus is on us to keep our Church real, vital and relevant.

There is also a more practical interpretation of 'public' and 'private': in the day to day operations of OTO groups celebrating Mass, a private Mass is an OTO only affair, whereas a public Mass has non initiates present. This is the gist of the definition of 'public' and 'private' used in the *International EGC Handbook*. In a sense, such a definition exposes some of the ambiguities if not contradictions in the script of *Liber XV*. For example, how can you have a public Mass when private OTO 'steps' and 'signs' are used, to which you've been sworn to secrecy? We have a modern day workaround for this (using OTO steps and signs in the Mass that are no longer in use by the Order in our initiations, see *Book Four*), but it does suggest that the Mass was originally conceived as an OTO only affair—in Baphomet's own words, the Mass was 'prepared for the use of the OTO' (*Confessions*). I think Baphomet embedded into the Canon of the Mass not only the rubric for its performance, but also a basic organizational blueprint for a Gnostic and Catholic Church of the future, hence these types of inconsistencies. Whether by design or circumstance, he left it up to us to develop this, to sort out the ambiguities and contradictions, and ask the big questions.

Personally, I feel that Crowley realized pretty much straight away that *Liber XV* could have a wider audience than just an OTO membership. Crowley certainly invited non-members to Mass; he performed it and other rites in public, and encouraged the early OTO organizers of his M∴M∴M∴ to do the same; at one time he even seriously considered trying to get the USSR to adopt *Liber XV* as the Soviet Union's official state ritual! In his later years, Crowley worked closely with Agape Lodge members in the United States, to ensure that their public celebrations of the Gnostic Mass had professionalism and presence. Other than these (and many other) examples, we also have the Sacraments of the Church as provided for in *Liber XV*, some of which (in my opinion) were only meant for children—who again would obviously not be OTO initiates. This too suggests that the Church might reach out to a wider community, or at least could be inclusive of our families, friends and children. The questions these events and provisions pose—combined with the living tradition of our own history, experiences and ideas— will no doubt equilibrate and counter change in the alchemical cauldron of time, bringing forth new creations and directions for the Church in the future. But what all of this also suggests is that we have to stay open to possibilities in regards our sacred rite, in regards the Church which gives that rite its clergy, and in regards the Order which trains that clergy. We have to stay open to ourselves and to each other, and to where the rainbow coloured texture of our Light might lead us. In other words, I believe our Church is constantly evolving.

My 'plan' for the last few years had been to wait until we were a Grand Lodge before doing too much more with EGC. After operations peaked around the mid-late 90s, things have been kept intentionally low key. One reason for this was that it didn't seem wise to move too far forward while there was only one Bishop. That went against my management thinking for one thing (and still does), nor do I think it would have truly represented our diversity or brought out our potential. The buffer period also served another purpose; it gave a new generation of individuals and teams some time alone with the Mass without too many organizational pressures. In the past, some have rushed or been rushed into the public mass roles, with not always good results, whereas giving people plenty of time to discover and experiment with the Mass for themselves can be useful to experiencing and cultivating the sacerdotal spirit.

The fruits of these past and quiet EGC years can, however, be quite objectively judged—there has been an obvious Mass revival in Australia: we now have a number of active 'Mass teams' in our local bodies, we've had an increase in both 'novice' and 'ordained' Priests and Priestesses (in particular, Priestesses), and for the first time in our history, we now have a group of Bishops. The Mass is in safe hands (I say that with emphasis, for on occasion in the past our sacred rite has ended up in the wrong ones), with some very talented and dedicated clergy and novices. We're still undeniably a small EGC, with quite a low percentage of Order members actively officiating in the Mass. We have no permanent Temples, and putting on Masses, be they public or private, is a logistical challenge for our groups at the best of times (hiring venues, transporting equipment, setting up, etc.). But we manage to celebrate the Mass regularly, and with the creation of the Grand Lodge in April I feel that we're now in the best position yet to observe and help develop the EGC in our local bodies. I'm the eternal optimist in this regard: my eyes are set on exponential growth! And I think we've learned some important lessons in how the Mass evolves in the field, what is conducive to this and what isn't. My vision for the future is simple and straightforward: I would like to see the Mass celebrated as often as possible by as many as possible. The condition and expectation is unambiguous: 'Let the rituals be rightly performed with joy & beauty!' (AL II:35). So is the criteria: 'But ye, o my people, rise up & awake!' (AL II:34). Crowley's 'New Commentary' on these and related verses (see *The Law is for All*) is instructive for more technical detail and sage advice: '...when we take no pleasure, and find nothing to admire, in our work, we are doing it wrong.' (from the Commentary to AL II:35)

I am pleased to announce that as we start to better organize the EGC, Bishop Phoenix has kindly agreed to serve as our national EGC Secretary. In the first instance I'd like all existing Priests, Priestesses, Deacons and Novices to contact us for official Grand Lodge EGC recognition. Priests and Priestesses should advise which Bishop/s they are coordinating with; Deacons which Priest/s or Priestess/es they are working with; and novices which Bishop/s and/or Priest/s, Priestess/es they are training with, as is appropriate. This will help us to get a realistic picture of where we are at, and see where or how we can best assist and improve. Apart from the more organizational or bureaucratic nature of this call, by linking everybody together we also ensure the Mass in any one centre does not grow up in isolation. I've found that central to the success and continuity of Mass operations is our ability to consistently question and challenge our assumptions and idiosyncrasies in relation to the rite, to remain creative and open to change and challenge, rather than get bogged down in 'local traditions' or similar. I'd like to think that the inter-relationships we are now proposing will aid rather than hinder—just stay lateral with it and enjoy yourselves. In my opinion, if the relationships forged are creative and dynamic, so too will be our Church.

On my end its slow going right now, mainly as there are quite a few other things to deal with as we implement our Grand Lodge processes and continue with the ongoing legal issues. However, I am working on a number of new EGC publications. First, an officially issued 'practice/study' script of *Liber XV*, approved by the Patriarch and issued by order of the Primate, for use within Australia. This will include, for example, the complete list of current Saints (not forgetting the latest who was canonized by the Patriarch while in Australia—Frank Bennett), as well as clarify some ambiguities in the rubric. An EGC manual for the Grand Lodge also has to be prepared (existing clergy would be familiar with the *International EGC Handbook*—we now have to come up with our own), and at some stage I'd like to work on, in collaboration with Bishops here and elsewhere, an annotated version of *Liber XV* that gives suggestive guidelines on performance. I will try to get the 'practice/study' script out ASAP. In 2007, I'm interested in organizing an EGC Retreat specifically for our ordained and novice clergy. This has been a long time coming, but I think we're finally at a stage to warrant it. Our last EGC retreat (with Sabazius and Helena in the mid 1990's) was more of a general OTO gathering with workshops on the Gnostic Mass, rather than the specialist meeting of clerical and novitiate members I am now proposing.

I think the combination of all the above over the next 3 or so years will see our sense of what we can do with the Church—and the Mass—enriched, and the foundations of a new Church operational culture established. For now, I'm happy to see how things go and grow within this timeframe before firming my position on some of the more vexing questions ahead in regards our development and its supporting policies. But even so and at the outset of this new adventure, I must say that in my view the EGC and the OTO are one, and should be firmly aligned and considered as such. I don't see the Church as a separate or distinct organization to OTO, but rather, as an important, if specialized, aspect and expression of it. I'm not really interested in developing an EGC infrastructure or presence that appears in any way to be independent of the Order. The sacraments and mysteries of the Church are not only embedded into the Order's overall design, but you could even say they are essential to it. And amongst its many virtues, the Mass can be seen as the principle means by which we communally celebrate and participate in the mysteries of the Order, just as we individually partake of such through the process of initiation. The latter, as a gradual process, can also be considered the principle means by which the Order trains its clergy— by progressive initiation. As a result, some OTO degrees actually confer EGC office: the 'KEW' ordains the Priesthood (Priest or Priestess), and the Magus of Light sub-degree of our VII° ordains the Bishops; likewise the X° is made the Primate of the Church within a national section, while the OHO or XII° is made our Patriarch.

In 2004, when I was writing up the Australian Grand Lodge Bylaws (approved by the Areopagus in 2005), I further developed the mapping of OTO degrees to EGC office. Building on the natural resonance of First Degree to Baptism and Second Degree to Confirmation, I attributed the Third Degree to the Deacons: I believe the mystery of this degree warrants the attribution, plus it seems to fit in nicely with the overall scheme. It also makes clear the distinction between lay members and clerical office, requiring that further advancement to the Third Degree. This does not mean the Third Degree is an ordination as is the case with KEW or the 'Magus of Light', but only that we have an Australian EGC policy that further aligns clerical office in EGC to the OTO degrees. Third Degree is a requirement for appointment, as is the usual showing of vocation for the role. In our tradition, clerical office does require ordination, but in the case of the Deacons it does not occur by virtue of initiation. We can therefore see the

Deacon as a unique office where ordination occurs outside of initiation and in a special (for it should be) EGC ceremony. This serves to underscore the function of the Deacon as an assistant (the term Deacon comes from the Greek word *diakonos* meaning 'servant'), distinguished from the senior EGC officers where ordination is through initiation (Priest, Priestess, Bishop). That ordination is through public EGC ceremony also emphasizes the unique role the Deacon plays in our Mass as a bridge between the laity/congregation and our clergy. Public Ordination ceremonies for Deacons would have to be approved by the Primate working through the Bishops: I encourage interested Mass groups to develop their own rites in this respect.

We have not ordained Deacons in quite a while, so I'd encourage Deacons who have not been ordained to seek ordination and recognition by EGC.

To become a Priest, Priestess or Deacon, some members will ask: can I learn and do these roles if I am not of the required degrees? Yes, and that's actually preferable. In the EGC, those in training are known as the 'novitiate' (or novices), and the 'training period' helps demonstrate the criteria for outward formal recognition applied by EGC to Priest, Priestess and Deacon status—showing 'vocation.' It also builds up the necessary experience, and can serve as criteria for invitation to KEW (for the EGC minded of our members). If you are seeking entry to the novitiate (open to all First degree and higher members), contact your clergy, one of the Bishops, or the EGC Secretary.

The other question that comes up is: if I am of the required degree/s do I have to serve in the EGC? No, and there's no stigma attached to deciding not to be involved with the Church. It's not everybody's cup of tea, and that's cool. EGC office rests entirely on choice and vocation. These principles, I believe, are central to EGC thinking. As stated above I hold that our First Degree (Birth) resonates with the sacrament of Baptism, while our Second Degree (Life) does the same for Confirmation. In fact, I'd even say initiation into these degrees overrides any need or requirement for these sacraments, as OTO initiation is in and of itself a sacramental system, and the EGC is but a part of and included within that system. So in our Bylaws, I did away with the requirement for Baptism and Confirmation for OTO members (with the Patriarch's approval), and defined general membership in the Church ('the Laity') as this: "Membership in the Association [i.e. OTO] *automatically* grants Lay membership in EGC upon a member's own *cognisance, and intention to participate* in the Ecclesiastical congregation, activities and rites" (Section 10.08, my italics). As a First or Second, it is not so much that you have been 'baptized' or 'confirmed' into the Church (for this was not the intention of these initiation ceremonies) but that these sacraments are simply not required. Being an initiate in our Order, desirous of participating in our mysteries, is what matters. The efficacious quality and magical potentialities of

Initiation allow for the connection to be implicit and inherent, to be 'brought out' in each willing individual by intent and participation (the lay equivalents here to the 'choice and vocation' of clerical office). I think this implicit arrangement cuts out a lot of unnecessary dogma and division pertaining to OTO and EGC: 'The problem we have set for ourselves is to propagate the Gnostic Catholic Church without falling prey to the obvious and more subtle pitfalls that attend such a venture. The foremost in my mind would be a misguided attempt to graft Thelema to the vestiges of Christianity... occasionally one observes the unnecessary adoption of elements of Catholic belief into EGC work. I feel that as Thelemites, with our own sacred books, theogony, ethics and neo-gnostic ritual tradition, we have no need to borrow worn out customs and formulae' (Hymenaeus Beta, 'On the Gnostic Catholic Church', 1990). So mote it be!

The practice for some time here in Australia has been to not conduct rites of baptism and confirmation for OTO members. This tradition continues.

Now, if you look at *Liber XV*, it is however quite obvious that Baphomet intended for rites of baptism and confirmation to be conducted by the Church, and he made explicit reference and provisions for them in *Liber XV*. What are we to make of this? In my opinion, the answer is as simple as it is obvious—what Baphomet actually had in mind for baptism and confirmation was a series of sacraments for *children* rather than grown adults. His sketchy baptismal notes from his Cefalu diary (see www.hermetic.com/sabazius/bapnotes.html) are clearly written with children in mind. I believe the theological basis for this is AL II:41 (see the 'New Commentary' for instruction), rather than just mimicking the traditional sacramental systems, rules and regulations of the Christian Churches (although, like Baphomet I agree that 'with regard to the preparations for Sacraments, the Catholic Church has maintained well enough the traditions of the true Gnostic Church in whose keeping the secrets are', *Book Four* Pt III, Ch. 20 'Of the Eucharist'). I also hold that the 'true Gnostic Church' Baphomet is referring to is the OTO and its Sanctuary of the Gnosis.

As the OTO then, our 'sacraments' of baptism and confirmation are our unique ways to celebrate the feasts for life, fire and water—for children. And as 'sacraments', they emanate from the Sanctuary of the Gnosis and Thelema, not the symbolic meanings, liturgies and structures designed for the administration of Christian sacraments (which is not to say these shouldn't be studied and will not inform or inspire in some way those who do). When our demographic and/or circumstances require we have rites for children, as one day it will (and sooner rather than later I think), we will have to write them. We may even one day have children as *the Children* in our Mass! Such rites of baptism and confirmation for children will require the approval of the Primate working through the Bishops. More details on these and the other sacraments will be given in the *Grand Lodge EGC Handbook*.

Can adults who are not in the OTO take baptism and confirmation? I really do not think Baphomet envisioned that at all, especially if we apply the logic and formulae of the 'feasts' to the symbolism of these sacraments as practiced by EGC. Personally, I have to wonder what these sacraments would actually achieve for non-member adults, both for the individual and for the OTO, and why someone would desire these sacraments of our Church but not seek initiation into the Church's Order. It seems, frankly, like a cop out. Personal opinion aside, from a purely strategic angle I think we're at a stage where we need to gather our forces and not spread ourselves too thin in regards EGC work. Right now, I don't think we're in a position to meet the demands and responsibilities that non initiate 'adult' members would place on us. One day some of our Church centres will qualify for ministerial status and we can review this approach ministry by ministry based on public services, clerical skill and experience, congregation, and the relevant legal registrations. For now, I think these sacraments are for children only. I don't want to extend it beyond that to non-member adults until we have thoroughly studied the subject, and have a better understanding of what we are doing and where we are going in this regards. But I think clergy qualifying for ministerial status the essential criteria for this to be considered any further. I do, however, fully encourage non-initiates to attend Mass and join our congregation in those areas where EGC groups opt to celebrate public masses. Fellowship with us beyond that, however, is a case of taking initiation.

Finally, we have not done 'public' ordination rites for priests or priestesses for some time either, and this too will continue. I do, however, understand that some groups and individuals may still feel the need for public ceremonial in an EGC setting to recognize achievement/s from 'private' initiation/s (for example, if you've just been recognized as a Priest/ess after KEW), and to present the new Priest or Priestess to their congregation. For those of you that were there, I had my own version of this on Easter Sunday this year. In similar fashion, I class such rites as 'celebrations' rather than as ordinations per se (given these are initiations), and you are at leave to develop appropriately modified celebratory-styled Gnostic masses for such occasions. These rites will, however, require the approval of the Primate working through the Bishops.

What I hope to see emerge with these changes are new approaches to the way the Church can operate, view itself, and articulate its sacramental practice, while engaging in a new and creative magical liturgy aligned entirely with and within the OTO system. This outline gives an overview of the immediate direction and activities ahead for the EGC. It obviously differs in parts from how our Sister Grand Lodges are working the Church, but I think it magically grounded, suited to our own unique conditions and outlook, while ensuring the promulgation and celebration of our Mass, and the continued development and evolution of our Church in accordance with the law of Thelema and the doctrines and teachings of the OTO. We are a magical, Thelemic Church of initiates—so let's be that and do that. I encourage the interested to participate in our Mystery of Mystery.

OZ 1 ANNO IVXIII - 21 AUG 2006 E.V.

'NEW COMMENTARY' THEOLOGY - PART II

The abode of peerless purity whose lamps are the Stars

GRAND MASTER SHIVA X°
(PRIMATE, ECCESIA GNOSTICA CATOHLICA)

In the first issue of Oz, I offered some 'notes' for reorganizing the Gnostic Catholic Church (EGC) in Australia. I also gave my reasons for not moving on this prior to the chartering of the Grand Lodge. Looking back at that article now, I think it had way too much information for our new members, and probably raised more questions than it answered for others. To be honest, some of those questions still don't have answers—but that's all part of it, and we'll work it out as we move along. Our Frater Superior once described the OTO as an "experimental research organization", and what we're about to embark upon is just that. In my view the EGC is an integral part of the OTO experience and 'experiment', with the ability to awaken nascent spiritual and social dimensions of our unique laboratory. So, I don't think we need to pretend we have all the answers when we don't.

I also don't think we need to be 'different' just for the sake of it, or for that matter, to follow pre-existing EGC models without carefully examining whether they are right for us. We have our own Nature to explore and enjoy, and I think we've already learnt a great deal about what works and what doesn't in our particular environment. This being said, the first practical steps towards developing the EGC along the lines I suggested begins at this year's ANA. (Annual National Assembly) in September. I thank those of you who have already started things off by working with the Bishops. Stripped of the organizational detail (which we'll go through at the ANA), underlying my first address was a vision of an EGC that was truly configured for 'the PEOPLE' (vide *Liber XV*) and not just for ourselves—to identify that polarity, think about what it means, and initiate and invite its interplay. From there, let's see what happens. For most if not all of you right now, 'the PEOPLE' at your Masses — your EGC congregation—are your OTO brothers and sisters, give or take some family and friends. That of course is fantastic, and a realistic reflection of where we are at developmentally. Down the track I can also see a time, perhaps no time soon, where although OTO brethren and bodies remain the backbone of our congregations, 'the PEOPLE' becomes a wider community that looks to the Order for its Church, clergy, and celebrations. In other words, as we develop and grow, so too will 'the PEOPLE' of the EGC, and this seems a natural extension of our socio-spiritual dynamic. It also gives us an important insight into the role of the Church, and perhaps one that ensures we never get too insular: to promulgate and celebrate the Law of Thelema in the world through the rites and sacraments of EGC. Although some aspects of our Bylaws require revision in regards EGC, we already accommodate for this 'bigger picture' in things like 'ministerial' status, which one day some of our Bishops, working with Priests and Priestesses, will have.

So, natural and self-organizing growth is an embedded concept—a seed if you like, from which the Tree of Gnosis grows. 'Glory and worship be to Thee, Sap of the world-ash, wonder-tree!' In the above sense, the EGC can be looked upon as the public face, public worship and public service of an otherwise private OTO organization, whose rites and teachings are generally reserved and preserved for members within the security and sanctuary of temple precincts. So, while the EGC has—or will have—its 'public' congregation so to speak, keep in mind that its clergy are OTO only. In the authorized popular commentary to The Book of the Law, Crowley taught 'There are to be no regular temples of Nuit and Hadit, for They are incommensurables and absolutes. Our religion therefore, for the People, is the Cult of the Sun, who is our particular star of the Body of Nuit, from whom, in the strictest scientific sense, come this earth, a chilled spark of Him, and all our Light and Life.' From an OTO perspective, the EGC can be viewed as our particular vehicle to inculcate this, for the People, with Love and Liberty. Love and Liberty are attributes of the All Father,

CHAOS, celebrated in our Mass as the 'sole viceregent of the Sun upon the Earth', whom we worship with 'the Mother of us all', BABALON. To play on Crowley's comments above, here is our regular or public temple. And while CHAOS and BABALON are to be worshipped in public (as distinct from the private worship of our incommensurable dyad), as the Father and Mother of us all, we've all got to develop our own personal relationships with them, each to their own. I believe the Mass helps us get there, individually and collectively, for the celebration of what Crowley called above the 'Cult of the Sun' highlights the universal and yet personal nature of the Lord of the Aeon, Ra-Hoor-Khuit. Crowley taught that RHK was a Solar-Phallic deity, but obviously not of the Dying God type. RHK, he said, is 'the Crowned and Conquering Child' in ourselves, our own personal God. He applauded Freud and (moreso) Jung for identifying this 'Child' with the psychoanalytical Phallic consciousness of full genital organization in men and women, and for making 'the connection of the Will of this "child" with the True or Unconscious Will, and so for clarifying our doctrine of the "Silent Self" or "Holy Guardian Angel."' These mysteries and meanings of the Great Work and our cosmogony are for each of us to get our heads around and ultimately attain to. They underscore that 'Baptism of Wisdom whereby we accomplish the Miracle of Incarnation', and in my opinion that thaumaturgical and Eucharistic mystery we celebrate as the 'Miracle of the Mass'.

The 1918 edition of the Mass noted that *Liber XV* was 'edited from Ancient Documents in Assyrian and Greek by The Master Therion', Hymenaeus Beta commenting in *Book Four* that '"Assyrian" probably refers to the Syrian, Chaldean and Jacobite liturgies rather than ancient Assyria.' Reference to this 'editing job' by 'Therion' in an official publication of our central rite quite possibly also demonstrates the charge given to the Beast in The Book of the Law II:5 'Behold! The rituals of the old time are black. Let the evil ones be cast away; let the good ones be purged by the prophet! Then shall this Knowledge go aright.' Crowley commented, 'The "old time" is the Aeon of the Dying God. Some of his rituals are founded on an utterly false metaphysic and cosmogony; but others are based on Truth. We mend these, and end those... The schools of Initiation must be reformed.' I think it's plausible to suggest that in a magical sense Therion 'mended' the Mass of 'the true church of old time' and left it for those who would claim the heirship, communion and benediction of its Saints: the OTO. And the 'Knowledge' that is to go aright, what Crowley considered 'the initiated Wisdom of this Aeon of Horus', in my opinion includes that particular Gnosis preserved, taught and celebrated by the OTO. In public celebration of this we are enjoined by our Deacons speaking the words of Hadit; 'But ye, o my people, rise up & awake!' (AL:II:34) and to 'Let the rituals be rightly performed with joy & beauty!' (AL:II:35). The 'new commentary' to the verses that follow outlines the basis of a possible public celebration, liturgical calendar and sacramental system that can easily (in my view) be adapted into an EGC framework. This hypothesis will have to be tested, observed and experienced over time, and eventually we'll have to draw our conclusions. Primates I can assure you are not infallible, but I think we should give this a go, with open minds, yet mindful not to fall into old dogmatisms. Joy and Beauty are essential ingredients of our celebration. Crowley used these words passionately in their ordinary sense in his teachings, and also employed them as technical terms in his extraordinary art and science of religious ecstasy.

In what I think our philosophical equivalent of ontology (the science of Being)—what I call 'Ireology' (the science of Going)—joy and beauty are probably the transformative agent of genius; the jet propulsion, disintegrator and transmuter of 'knowledge' that enables Microprosopus (the conscious mind) to reach to Understanding (Binah/BABALON) and Wisdom (Chokmah/ CHAOS), the supernals that in turn 'reflect respectively Nuit and Hadit from the Ain and Kether'—or in day to day magical terms of enflamed prayer, the means by which mind informs understanding, understanding presents a simple idea to the Will, and the Will issues its unquestioned commands. Crowley felt that spontaneity was a key indicator of Beauty and precursor of creation, evidence of what he termed 'magnetic intensity' (Joy?) and requiring absolute freedom from obstacles, internal or external. In terms of our circumstances and public orgia, it's pretty hard just right now for us to have spontaneous Gnostic Masses, and for most of you, organizing and putting them on is full of obstacles! But we do it, and I think we have 'spontaneous' realizations and feelings in the process—for each other, ourselves, our Gods and our Mystery. This too is part of the course of 'Ireology': progressive assimilation of the experience of joy and beauty whereby we learn more about our own Star. 'Experience is the great Teacher' wrote Crowley, 'and each of us possesses millions of years of experience, the very quintessence of it, stored automatically in our subconscious minds.' The release of this 'venom from hell' is something I think our Priestesses and Priests develop an intuitive awareness of, when with joy and beauty they celebrate the human, cosmic and cosmogonic interplay of sexual polarity in our Mass. I find these words by Crowley fitting, although he was not referring to *Liber XV* when he wrote them (see the 'new commentary' to AL:II:26): 'This awakes the earth to rapture; not until then does union occur. For, in working on the planes of manifestation, the elements must be consecrated and made "God" by virtue of a definite rite.' One thing we do manifest is rapport and rapture in working the Mass with each other and for each other: natural, spontaneous and magnetic. Priests and Priestesses working together develop a particular sensitivity and 'knack' for this (something once described to me as 'magically falling in love'), but I think it applies to all who can truthfully 'rise up & awake'. It is the best teacher in matters ecclesiastical you can have, and to be open to it is an approach to participation in our celebration that I encourage. In a sense it becomes an acquired skill, and the harbinger of genius (defined in our context as the ability to 'administer the virtues to the brethren' but using Crowley's words: 'a genius in this sense being one who has the Idea, and is fortified with power to enflame the enthusiasm of the crowd, with wit to know, and initiative to seize, the psychological moment'). Technical proficiency helps clear the obstacles and frees up the channels to let this flow. As Crowley wrote, 'Joy and Beauty are the evidence that our functions are free and fit; when we take no pleasure, and find nothing to admire, in our work, we are doing it wrong.'

'Let the rituals be rightly performed with joy & beauty!' AL II:35

Admire each other! Enjoy yourselves!

OZ 4 Anno Ivxv - 21 June 2007 e.v.

From the GM (AUGL in Japan)

Grand Master Shiva X°

Firstly, thank you very much for having me over this weekend. It's great to be here again. OTO Japan has really become something of a home away from home for me, and being here with you is something I've been looking forward to. This is my fourth visit in as many years, and I must say, that as an outsider, it has been remarkable to see how you have come along. I have been watching your transition from being a predominantly local body organised to having a national administration that is giving 'OTO Japan' meaningful identity. And I have also been watching how you have been handling the leadership changes we have had here, and addressing your unique multicultural challenges and synergies. This weekend I have talked with your national Officers - your Frater Superior's Representative for Japan and his team - about things like strategic goals, national development, translating our rites into Japanese, and future directions. These are all on OTO Japan's agenda these days, and are discussions we could not really have had with any depth, four years ago. So, I would like to take this opportunity to first of all applaud and commend your work and progress. I mean it. You've come a long way in a pretty short time. I also want to thank you for Mass. This had extra special meaning for me, as a little earlier we worked the KEW or Knight of the East & West degree of OTO. I don't get to work this anymore in Australia, and so I had a lot of fun. As you may know, the KEW is the first of the invitational degrees of our Order, and it has a particular significance for the Priests and Priestesses of our Church. It was fitting then, that Brother Hiroyuki has also asked me to round off the weekend by speaking about the EGC - the Ecclesia Gnostica Catholica or Gnostic Catholic Church, and *Liber XV*, the OTO Gnostic Catholic Mass. Usually I prefer to talk pretty much spontaneously rather than lecture, but for translation purposes tonight I have prepared this pre-written speech. So, just be warned that I am definitely out of my comfort zone style-wise, though I hope I can still give you something of interest and perhaps something a little different to what you may have been expecting.

Before I start could I point out a few things:

Firstly, as you know I am the Primate or Presiding Bishop of the EGC in Australia. Much of what I say will no doubt be coloured by an Australian perspective and the particular office that I hold. Please keep that in mind, as some of the things I might say would not necessarily apply to the situation here in Japan. What we will see emerge here given time, and what we are working towards, is a uniquely Japanese expression of our Mystery of Mystery and ecclesiastical structure, one that gives sustenance and meaning to your own spirit, culture, community and environment. So, don't take what I say as gospel, but rather, as suggestive of the possibilities and directions your own

Ecclesia might take based upon your own needs and priorities.

Secondly, I think that some recent publications have given the impression, intentionally or unintentionally I cannot say, that the EGC is a separate organisation to OTO. I do not share this view. To the contrary, I hold that the EGC is central to the OTO, in the same way that our Mass, as Crowley described it in his Confessions, is the central ceremony of our public and private celebration. In Australia for example, our long-term vision is to have the EGC sufficiently developed in all of our operational centres so that it can serve as a public vehicle and public service of the OTO - taking our Mystery and Thelema out into our society and communities, and expanding our outreach and congregations beyond just Initiates. Now, while we may easily enough interpret 'public and private celebration' by plain English or even magically, please note that these are also very precise philosophical constructs of the Western Canon. I think Crowley was aware of this. The relationship between public and private worship has been a discourse that runs through the religious narrative of the West since late antiquity. Theologians, lawmakers, and others have constantly looked at how private worship and domestic religious activity were informed or could be informed by an institutional public worship from centralised, episcopal sources. This in turn has contributed to the development of western thought and society. You still see this in the varied ideologies we have today concerning Church and State. I would propose that any serious study of our constitutional model - even for you here in Japan with a much different historical, cultural and spiritual backdrop - has to consider what this dialectic means for the OTO - how for example our private Mystery informs public celebration, and how the public celebration of our Mystery in turn informs the private and public lives of our Congregations and our Order.

This leads on to my third point, as it has also been suggested that no authority other than Aleister Crowley needs be recognized in relation to the performance of the Gnostic Mass. I don't share this view either. While I do believe that we must all engage with the Mass upon our own inspiration and endeavour, and that we must study *Liber XV* very, very carefully, I hold that ultimate authority on OTO doctrine (and therefore also on EGC and the Gnostic Mass) rests with Baphomet's lineal successor, the OHO or Outer Head of the Order, at present Frater Superior Hymenaeus Beta, the Patriarch. In similar fashion, I hold that the OHO alone is the executive editor of *Liber XV* - a task and role that directly and indirectly informs how we interpret and enact performance. Gnosis in my view is not only received, but transmitted, and that is a Mystery of the OTO and our continuity that need not detain us here. So to commence our discussion keeping in mind the points just raised, let me say that first of all I don't think you can discuss the EGC without looking at the OTO. The Order as you know is broad and multi-faceted, but there are a few things pertinent to our discussion that I would like to raise here.

Firstly, we now know that early on Crowley initially, albeit privately, saw the OTO as a useful vehicle for organising groups and for group work. As Magister Templi organising the A∴A∴ movement, he was frustrated that Aspirants to the Great Work were not sticking to the solitary syllabus required, and were meeting and socialising together. Crowley's thinking was pretty much, if you cannot stop them meeting, control how they meet and what they do and learn when they meet. In other words, make group organisation an instrument for the Great Work and avoid the potential for slackness, idleness and gossip that comes with any group venture. To this end, you may be interested to know that many features embedded into Crowley's approach to the OTO have only been identified in the past 30 or so years as key concepts of adult learning, where group work is now an important feature of educational design and assurance of learning practices. Crowley wrote in the *Blue Equinox* that the OTO trains groups by way of progressive initiation. On the other hand I would say that the A∴A∴ trains individuals. It was from this group perspective that Crowley began to formulate his vision for the OTO, which he considered, to quote him, a 'complete system of morality.' In other words, a collective Moral System - the ethics and rules of right conduct - that might complement and support the individual Magical System offered in A∴A∴. Note also the emphasis on being a complete system of morality - Crowley's wording is intentional, and distinct from the 'peculiar system of morality' by which regular

Freemasonry describes itself. Some people knee jerk when I start talking about morality rather than something that sounds much cooler, like Magick or Occultism. If however you look at our foundational papers, *Liber 52* for example, you will see that what Crowley was looking for in OTO initiates, as we still do today, were essentially moral attributes, such as courage, honour, virtue, devotion and zeal. In his *Confessions* Crowley writes that he revised and composed the OTO rituals by asking himself 'how do I bring out what is best in a man'? Our moral virtue, however, be it nature or nurture, is also an evolving individual and collective psychic process, and on one level at least emanates from how we see and understand our world and universe, how we see and understand ourselves and our place in the world and universe, and how we best co-exist as the human race, and indeed, survive. Our morality reflects our understanding of existence itself. For the religiously minded throughout the ages, such has been spiritualized, celebrated and observed in belief, rites, and customs. On that score the OTO asks the big questions and teaches the Mysteries of existence. Crowley therefore also described the OTO system as the mystery of incarnation and Path in Eternity, fixing our goals firmly upon a fundamental belief in the Brotherhood of Man. To this end as you all know, we have embarked upon the humanitarian mission of promulgating the Law of Thelema around the world. Paradoxically therefore, a moral system is no less magical, and you cannot have one without the other - it's a matter of context. Crowley taught that the OTO conferred the magical secrets that made one a Master of Life and in relation to which he considered the Central Secret of the OTO of profound import and value to humanity. He writes about this in a number of places, and in *Liber Aleph* describes it as the true formula of the Magick of the Aeon, acknowledging Theodor Reuss and the OTO's role in tutoring him. After attaining the Grade of Magus, Crowley's vision for the OTO further expands, emerging as the principle vehicle by which the Master Therion could preach his Law unto mankind, and as a social model of initiated Kingdoms organised in accordance with the Law of Thelema. As an example, we see this in the *Blue Equinox* OTO papers, that still inform our work today.

Putting these points together, in a sense the OTO can be seen as suggestive of an Order formed by an adept and organised along the lines of the Orders of the RC and GD, to cover a specialized method of a) illumination and b) emancipation, as provided for in *One Star in Sight*. So, I don't think we can really look at the OTO without considering the A.'.A.'., from whom our Law came. Our rites and ceremonies - including our Mass - need to be considered as allied and aligned to the Great Work. It is my belief that from this apocatastasis fresh insights and realizations about the OTO. System and its potential are possible. What we also see here, and I think this is important, is that our vision of the OTO may broaden over time. It evolves. This didn't just happen to Crowley - it occurs in each one of us as a matter of personal progress, and happens on both individual and collective levels. The Gnostic Mass is actually an excellent example of this if viewed historically. It is easy for us to take the Mass for granted these days, but imagine the significance of the rite at the time it was first written? Consider how it might have been received by the OTO demographic at the time - young middle-class men down from Cambridge or Oxford, or esoterically minded Freemasons and Theosophists. This was an entirely new religious experience and Gnosis offering a revitalized appreciation of the divine, and not least of all, the feminine. Who else was worshipping the Goddess in a western religious context? Who else even had priestesses? These days we don't think too much about publishing *Liber XV*. It is on the net, in print, on YouTube. In many countries, this won't create any major stir. We are a long way from the 1919 *Blue Equinox*, which was seized in the USA under obscenity laws for printing our Mass. In many countries today a disrobed Priestess may not exactly be considered mainstream religious practice, but it is certainly not considered obscene. In Australia for example, where we had to fight in our courts against claims Thelema and OTO were unlawful, independent expert witnesses examined the O.T.O., including our Mass. These witnesses and our courts rightly found OTO to be a lawful religious organisation and therefore Thelema a lawful religion and philosophy. Times have changed. Consider the influence the Gnostic Mass has had, explicitly and implicitly, on the religion of Wicca; look at how that movement has grown around the world, and the influence it has then had on neopaganism, the goddess movement, popular culture, and certain schools of feminist philosophy. I am probably about as far from a Wiccan as you could get, trust me, but I want you to see how, right now, we respond and engage with the holy and sacred office of Priestess in all of her varying guises, once again functioning in the world and its people.

And who kicked that off? If social change is moulded by psychic content, then I feel the OTO has had its own particular part in it, albeit under the radar and by six degrees - or is that nine degrees - of separation. Although this appears to be a wholly endogenous viewpoint, I would say that these are actually the new offerings and consequences of the dialectic of private and public celebration I talked about before, wired to an unfolding new Aeon. My gut feeling is that it is through the Office and in the persons of our Priestesses that this process takes shape and form. In fact, my prediction is that the 21st century will be the century of the Priestess. Crowley covered the Priestly formulae with initiated insight, illumination and genius, but I honestly think our Sisters are going to open us up to a new awareness of sacred and psychic space, with its associated perspectives and approaches and techniques, and new ways of living, loving and learning. Our Mass is one of the vehicles for this. It is one of the reasons I feel Crowley once described the OTO as involved in work of a cosmic scope. And I further hold that as society continues to evolve into the future and way down the 21st century, the possibilities and practices related to our Mass will both inform and be informed by this ferment. Now, what Hiroyuki actually asked me to speak about tonight was Thelemic and qabalistic symbolism in our Mass, and in case you haven't already noticed, I have been doing my best to dodge the subject. For one thing, there's no doubt the Order has some esteemed brethren out there who are much better than myself at such expositions and enjoy doing them. I do not, and my own modus operandi quite honestly isn't really all that technical or theoretical, which is what I suspect may have been getting asked of me. What I encourage first and foremost is individual participation in the mystique of our symbolism. This can be achieved over time through honest participation, collaboration, aspiration, dedication, meditation, imagination, initiation, and the joyful and beautiful celebration of our rite. In other words, enflame yourselves in prayer. And don't stop, for this is an ongoing process - each to their own and at their own pace and in their own style and to their own nature. You will learn things when you least expect it, and what you may find is that participating in the mystique of the symbolism - the Mass as a living symbol in itself - opens you up to the image making faculty of self, and on some level experiencing this transpersonal wonder through the ritual, symbolism, structuring principles and sacramental impulse of Thelema. These types of personal experiences are vitally important when it comes to matters EGC, but when the transpersonal is transmitted into consciousness the risk is that such encounters get located, fixated or translated solely by the intellect. So you have to be really careful in that regards in terms of your own work, and in regards who you are listening to. For that's how we can get our qabalah and our magick all wrong, and it can also lead to petty sectarianism and dogma - something our Church needs to avoid - where the essence of our public celebration remains unconscious as a private, psychic factor. I long wondered how I might define an 'Oriental Templar' in a manner that struck deep with me. Borrowing from Edinger, I arrived at the Oriented Ego, that is, the ego directed or oriented towards the transpersonal self; that which can equilibrate the East and West of inflation and alienation and attain the Royal Art. I believe that the Miracle of our Mass directly assists us to strip away at our psychological veils to make this happen. The word 'Mass' comes from the Latin word 'Missa', meaning 'dismissal'. This word was used in the old Christian liturgies to signify the end of the rite - 'Ire, missa est' ('Go, this is the dismissal'). I am going to hijack Romish liturgy here and say that this is what I mean by stripping away our psychological veils - dismissing them, which is to Go, Ire, the fifth power of the Sphinx. And you see this adumbration in the Priest's final words and blessing in our Mass, and in the final Collect appropriately called 'The End', both of which relate to accomplishing the True Will. For, as Magicians we are experimental researchers of the psyche, and as Jung said about experimental researchers, our ethics must admit where our conscious knowledge comes to an end, for that end is the beginning of True Wisdom.

Let's talk a little about the Mass proper. Our Patriarch once described the Mass as 'a celebration of the sexual polarities and their cosmic and natural interplay,' adding that the liturgy was structured from the male standpoint, in that the male has the largely active role, and *Liber XV* was after all authored by a male. I don't think you could describe the Mass any better or more briefly than that so I'm not even going to try. And with that description in mind much of the symbolism of the Mass, cosmic and natural, unfolds. (By the way, the Patriarch also suggested in that address that perhaps one day a woman adept of the Sovereign Sanctuary might write a Mass where the woman plays the largely active role, as with Siva and Sakti). Crowley wrote that our Mass corresponds to the Mass of the Roman Catholic Church, and elsewhere that the Roman Catholic Church had done an okay job in preserving the method of preparation of the Sacrament. He was alluding to the OTO's possession of these secrets in our Sanctuary of the Gnosis, and it can be said plainly, I feel, that the Canon of our Gnostic Mass celebrates them in dramatic and public form. After Crowley's expulsion from Cefalu, he recorded in his diaries that the Secret Chiefs had told him to use the Roman Catholic rituals for the Great Work, to benefit from their accumulated and ordered energies for magical advantage. Much later, in the 1940s, when he issued the Manifesto of the Gnostic Catholic Church, it declared '... the Masters have decided that the time has come for the administration of the Sacraments of the Aeon of Horus to those capable of comprehension. The sexes are equal and complementary. 'Every man and every woman is a star' AL I.3: 'The priestess must now function as well as the priest.' Putting these threads together, our Mass can be seen as an example of Crowley purging a ritual of the old time (see AL II:5 in this regards). Perhaps that is why the 1918 edition of the Mass carried the credit 'edited from the Ancient Documents in Assyrian and Greek by the Master Therion.' We may also note in this regards how we claim heirship, benediction and communion with the 'saints of the true church of old time' in our celebration. The Patriarch has described the Saints we call upon in *Liber XV* as a list of men and man-Gods that understood the divinity of women, something we too understand, celebrate and elevate today. About the same time as the diary entry I mentioned earlier, Crowley also wrote - and this is very important I think - that the formula of the Dying God was not abrogate, but rather, had been absorbed into a more complete understanding of Nature. It is with that more complete understanding that the Operations of our Mass work.

Crowley taught that there was a true connection between the Creative Force of the Macrocosm and that of the Microcosm - this is what he is getting at in regards the more complete understanding. He said the study of Nature is the Key to the Gate. In our Mass we celebrate Nature from that perspective. In fact, I would say that the Sacrament is one means whereby we purify and consecrate our Microcosms in order to make that connection, in the experience, identification and Unity of congregational and divine wholeness: 'there is no part of me that is not of the Gods.' The obvious spiritualization of sexual polarities and symbolism in our rite reiterates that the old dying god Tragedy of the bloody sacrifice which constructs Romish liturgy (with its informing archetypes of ritual regicide, renewal of deity through human sacrifice and the totem meal of ancestor worship) has given way to the Comedy of Pan and the continuous curve of the sexual sacrifice. Our Mass is also described in the *Blue Equinox* (but see also the OTO curriculum in *Book Four*) as representing the original and true pre-Christian Christianity. That might sound weird, but keep in mind what I have been talking about in regards the 'old time'. By one measure anyway it relates to the timeless truth of the doctrine of the Trinity, of the link between macrocosm and microcosm, of Our Lord in the Universe the Sun and Our Lord in ourselves whose name is Mystery of Mystery. This doctrine is taught progressively within OTO and is celebrated in our Mass.

I would now like to talk about our Saints. I want to speak of their essence though, not of their history and who they may or may not, have been. I have been using the word sacrifice tonight in its sacramental sense. We use this word in our Mass - the sacrifice of life and joy - and it derives from sacrificare, 'to make sacred' or 'to consecrate.' In dogmatic theology two aspects of the sacrifice of the Mass are the

Deipnon and Thysia. Deipnon means 'sacrifice' or 'slaughter', but also refers to 'blazing', as in the smoke of a burnt sacrifice rising up to to God. It is therefore a spiritualized form of food-offering that by psychic association implies a pneumatic transformation of substance. Note here the pneumatic words of our Priest during the *Mystic Marriage and Consummation of the Elements* part of our Rite. Thysia means meal and relates to the idea of a sacred or consecrated meal. Both are highly evocative, not only in terms of their primitive resonances stored deep in our psyche and recorded in mankind's history, but also in relation to our own Eucharist, the instructions for which includes both burnt offering and consecrated consumption. So far as the Mass goes, in this day and age the Deipnon and Thysia have been rationalized as much as they have been spiritualized. Advances in comparative mythology and psychology mean we understand them a lot better in terms of the doctrine of the Aeons. It seems to me that in light of this there is less Mystery and mystique, and more acceptance and rationalizing of the symbolic act. It's a lot easier to explain away, to label and categorize.

Look at how matter of factly the elements are described in our Creed - only forasmuch as they are transmuted in us daily do they mean anything so we can profess belief. While this is not to say that in our celebration a spiritualization or psychic transmutation cannot take place in our hearts and minds, it does suggest that something further is needed to perfect our feast. The elements by themselves, while transformed into the essence of the life of the Sun and the joy of the Earth, from a human perspective represent the best we have to offer of human endeavour; they celebrate our labour, our culture, our inventiveness, our humanity and vitality, of the Earth and under the Sun as it were. Our Cakes of Light are something altogether more really, incorporating sustaining, magical and curative virtues, and the subtle principle of animal life. The Roman rite is sometimes referred to as the 'bloodless sacrifice'. Not so with us, and our Cakes need to be carefully studied in *Book Four* and our Holy Books. Yet in our rite, even given the virtues of the Cakes, we still need our Saints in their essential presence to, as our Deacon intones, perfect our feast. Note that the Saints appear before the transmutation clause in our Creed, which may suggest they are necessary for that Miracle. That we call upon them in a public celebration affirms how each one of us, as active participants in the miracle of incarnation and conscious of the same, confesses - which means to acknowledge - our starry heritage, and therefore theirs, that we might be in their company and partake of their communion. By acknowledging our starry heritage, we have turned towards the Aeon, also signified by the sacred rather than physical East of our Temples, our orientation, our qiblah.

This is all necessarily a Mystery of Mystery, to be experienced rather than explained, but I feel the association is to a sempiternal company of Saints whose puissance, potency and presence rends the veil - at least for a moment -

of our ordinary temporal and spatial limitations, and indeed the limitations of consciousness itself. And it is this that perfects our feast at the moment of transubstantiation, for at that moment they are present in space and time, and with us in our communion, the communion of saints, and in us. There is certainly a spiritual continuity here with the eternal priesthood and perpetual sacrifice of dogmatic (and pneumatic) theology, but it now suggests the blood or perpetual sacrifice of the Saints offered up to and mingled in the Cup of Our Lady. It seems to me that in a manner that defies rational explanation but invites intuitive perception, our blood mingles with theirs in a type of mystical contagion if you like, and in that death is a new life that is the Covenant of Resurrection. For in our Mass, as you may know from the Creed, we worship Babalon and Chaos, and in a very human way, natural and symbolic, we offer those aspects of Babalon and Chaos within, by which we may approach them and celebrate them. The mysteries of Chaos and Babalon need to be studied, in the *Vision and the Voice* and elsewhere. While that is a personal and private matter, I do feel that in our public worship of togetherness Our Lady spills the blood of saints in every corner of the earth, manifesting the glory of the All Father in the world and its people. Babalon too, I feel, is invoked in our rite, and in this celebration of love we overcome evil - as described in *Liber 150* and elsewhere - thereby honouring and serving she who is the Redeemer and Guardian. Perhaps one reason we can truly celebrate this Supernal wonder is that, as I mentioned before, we also confess or acknowledge our starry heritage in our Creed, in its eternity and in its return. To acknowledge something is also to take ownership of it, and if you own something you can also give it away without expecting anything in return, or if you like, without lust of result. That's a real sacrifice. This is what we do so far as our ordinary consciousness is concerned in the Miracle of Incarnation (a sacrifice of labour and heroism), and also what we do in the Miracle of the Mass (a sacrifice of life and joy). By offering All that we are in the descent into Hell, we become all that we are Not and ascend to the heavens. And this is the Comedy of Pan that is the Brotherhood of Man: there is no part of me that is not of the Gods, and there is no God but Man. We can become more than ourselves, becoming conscious of That which was unconscious, the darkness that is Light, crystallizing in our blood. Language is limiting here, so I would like to quote from *Liber CCCLXX*, speaking the words of Baphomet: 'Therefore lift up thyself as I am lifted up. Hold thyself in as I am master to accomplish. At the end, be the end far distant as the stars in the navel of Nuit, so thou slay thyself as I at the end am slain, in the death that is life, in the peace that is mother of war, in the darkness that holds light in the hand as a harlot that plucks a jewel from her nostrils.'

Carl Jung, who was a great student of the Roman rite, said that the Christian Mass for the western psyche was the rite of the individuation process, transforming the soul of empirical man into his totality of full consciousness, and a repetition of the whole drama of Incarnation. We are back to the two miracles in our Creed once again. The individuation process, taught Jung, not only represented a new unity, but a new revelation, where the self is both the father or creator of ego, but also, as it is begotten by the ego entering into relations with our unconscious contents, the son. In a similar sense I feel our Mass is the rite of the initiation process, the process of Going, a journey. Crowley taught that a Eucharist of some sort should be consummated daily by every Magician, and it should be regarded as the sustenance of one's magical life. And in Liber Aleph he states 'Neglect not the daily Miracle of the Mass, either by the Rite of the Gnostic Catholic Church, or that of the Phœnix.' For this is the way, little by little and day by day, of internal lustration by God. While we may not yet be in a position to celebrate our rite together daily, we do have a liturgical calendar, which is given in AL II and commented upon in *The Law is for All*. In *Liber 837* Therion openly declares that in the relevant verses of AL II is a Calendar for a Church. In Australia, we have organised the Gnostic Catholic Church in accordance with Crowley's popular or public commentary to these verses, and while early days in terms of our own organisational readiness, it presents us with opportunities for times when our rite can be regularly celebrated to a liturgical calendar that will see us into the future, and support future growth. *Liber XV* provides not only our rite of public celebration, but is also a blueprint of how the EGC might be organised, in that it provides for various sacraments such as birth and confirmation. In Australia, we have also aligned this sacramental system with some of the feasts given in AL II, as commented upon by Crowley, giving us new sacramental feasts - a new Thysia if you like - to offer the People through the miracle of incarnation and life's critical and consecrated stages and events.

Hiroyuki asked me to make mention of training in EGC. What should you be reading and doing? In Australia we are still a long way off from developing a general syllabus, and I tend to be very, very cautious about such initiatives as I do not believe we are a one size fits all organisation, nor do I think carbon-copy clergy a desirable outcome. What I can say now, however, is that I am utterly convinced that one function of the OTO was to train the clergy of the EGC by way of its system of progressive initiation and related curriculum. I would add that in Australia I insist upon every Priest and Priestess working with a Bishop or Bishops, who in turn work with me, so that to the extent that we can in life's twists and turns, we stay connected, in tune and in touch, and start to really organise our Church. We should also recognize that fundamental to the OTO experience is that we celebrate and work with the Lord within and without, something entirely different to say the Christian theological approach which has focused on an allegedly historical but no doubt metaphysical entity at the expense of the 'Christ' within. Jung thought that was a wise idea, thinking were there a widespread recognition of Christ as a psychic centre, the greater the threat of ego inflation and a catastrophic 'psychic epidemic.' We however are Initiates of the New Aeon. Nature is no longer viewed as catastrophic. What I am getting at here is that a lot of our training is personal and if honestly pursued, somewhat challenging, as we work through our complexes, and this underscores our celebration and relationship with the Lord of the Aeon, equally universal and personal. We must walk humbly, support each other, and have the utmost and profound fraternal respect for the different means by which we individually prepare ourselves as priests and priestesses, albeit within certain obvious and in my opinion common-sensical ecclesiastical guidelines and requirements. We should also acknowledge that the preparation of clergy is fundamentally different from the point of view of Catholic and Gnostic Catholic (OTO) doctrine. The Roman Catholic Priest serves as a minister due to the belief in the efficacy of the Christian apostolic succession. Crowley addressed the magical viewpoint in *Magick Without Tears*, to which I quote: 'Our own authority came to Us because it was earned, and when We confer grades upon other people Our gift is entirely nugatory unless the beneficiary has won his spurs. To put it in slightly different words: Any given degree is, as it were, a seal upon a precise attainment; and although it may please Us to explain the secrets of any given degree or degrees to any particular person or persons, it is not of the slightest effect unless he prove in his own person the ability to perform those functions which all We have done is to give him the right to perform and the knowledge how to perform.' That too describes Our approach in Australia, and it again places an emphasis on personal aspiration, vocation and effort. I have overheard it said that if this is the case, then the only real Masses are those performed by high degree members who must have proven themselves to get where they are, and given their degree they must obviously know more. I think that is absolute rubbish and confusing Crowley's message. I believe I have Crowley on my side here, who also said that in relation to the Mass and this very suggestion, 'Besides, quite Low Initiates can do this work.' Now, I think Crowley is alluding to a few different things here, but it is also a very practical instruction and I would take it as words of encouragement and approval. What matters is that we congregate and celebrate with joy and beauty, not what Roman Numeral with a degree sign happens to be after your name. That we align some of our degrees to clerical office highlights the training clergy receive from OTO initiation, with related responsibilities, but it all still boils down to our own efforts, experiences and service, assisted by the Order. As Therion said in *Liber 837*, 'All you have to do is be yourself, to do your will, and to rejoice.'

I need to end up now so I would like to return to where I began, and the notion of the OTO in service to the Great Work of A∴A∴. If the Gnostic Mass is our central rite, then it must be central to that service. That is probably a talk in its own right, not that I am claiming to understand all of it by any means. But to be brief and in regards our public celebration, recall my earlier comments, quoting Crowley, on the virtues of a regular Eucharistic celebration. Crowley cited the Gnostic Mass specifically, and expands upon these virtues in Chapter XX of *Book Four Part III*. In this Chapter he also says of the Eucharist that it 'is the most important of all magical secrets that ever were or are or can be. To a Magician thus renewed the Attainment of the Knowledge and Conversation of the Holy Guardian Angel becomes an inevitable task; every force of his nature, unhindered, tends to that aim and goal...'. This attainment is the Next Step for humanity, and our celebration helps prepare humanity, I feel, little by little and day by day, for that aim and goal, thereby serving the Great Work. Finally, I want to thank you all for the opportunity of talking with you and I hope we can do it again some time. There is much more to say, and visits like this force me to say it, which I'm hoping is a good thing. But actions speak louder than words, and for those of you who pursue an active involvement in EGC I can only express to you my deepest respect, admiration and encouragement, and offer you from a distance whatever assistance I am able to give. I think you have really interesting work and times ahead of you. I have spoken quite intentionally today from a very western viewpoint, and a western male viewpoint at that. But you are Eastern, whether you be Japanese, or on another level, American, Canadian, New Zealand or Italian Japanese. Japanese culture is not structured upon the premises or ways of thinking most of what I have talked about are. It is different, and it is your home. And in saying this, we have not even begun to explore the sexual and gender polarities here, which we've candidly talked about on other occasions, how they apply and play themselves out, within the Order and outside of the Order in this culture. When I am here I feel like I am truly in the company of the Knights and Dames of the East and West. It is a unique OTO experience that I imagine there are few places in the world where you can actually experience it, but that also means you have your work cut out for you. Let me assure you it is Work that will take us to new experiences and new understandings of our System, and indeed, of humanity. It is new ground. I have to admit I am somewhat envious - I grew up in the West, was born in the East, am a child of both, and culturally and psychologically am simply not strictly wired to one or the other. In a sense I can relate to your challenges - even the ones you might not see coming just yet - but more importantly I see and feel your potential. It's one reason I easily feel at home here. We are the Oriental Templars, a unity of East and West, and you my friends, are at the vanguard of this experience. So mote it be, and I am blessed to be a witness. I would like to close off by reading a Chapter from The Book of Lies that touches on some of the themes from today's talk:

THE BLIND WEBSTER

It is not necessary to understand; it is enough to adore.

The god may be of clay: adore him; he becomes GOD.

We ignore what created us; we adore what we create.

Let us create nothing but GOD!

That which causes us to create is our true father and mother; we create in our own image, which is theirs.

Let us create therefore without fear; for we can create nothing that is not GOD.

OZ 17 ANNO IVxviii - 22 September, 2010 e.v.

Toiling the (Local) Fields of Our Lord

Grand Master Shiva X°

First of all I would like to thank all of the Man of Earth local bodies and the Electoral College for keeping things running smoothly while the Grand Lodge has been settling in. This secular year has gone really quickly—it still seems like the Easter weekend was only yesterday! But since then, I'm pleased to see that initiations and Gnostic Masses have continued at a steady pace, and to know that within our ranks is the first generation of OTO members initiated under the auspices of the Grand Lodge. AUGL now has most of its front line talismans in place: new pledge forms, certificates, charters and other authorizations, this newsletter and the website. We'll get to the rest throughout 2007. The Frater Superior had joked to me that 'Patience' was the Word of the X°. I am beginning to understand what he meant! At the AGM and joint meeting of Governing bodies in August, I finally gave in to our GTG Brother Chris who had earlier requested a 'vision statement' for the Grand Lodge. Don't cringe just yet—'Magick Wong' as he is known can ably put a magical twist on management speak (and mean it): think 'imagination' (vision) and 'will' (mission), the yin and yang of magical practice. I gave Chris and the others present 6 words:

- Duly Constituted
- Truly Consecrated
- Fully Congregated

I wouldn't call this a vision statement 'proper' as there's nothing particularly visionary about it—it's more an Obligation and not a new one at that. On the one hand it's our 'bottom line' of what the OTO should be doing as a given, but on the other hand it also looks ahead to loftier organizational aspirations. It's become a sort of mantra for me—an easy way to evaluate what we are doing and where we are going. If I cannot justify the numerous projects and processes we're planning/preparing for within these terms, they're either put on the back-burner or on the chopping block. You could probably do the same locally. A vision/direction/plan or a magical obligation swells in potency if you can square the circle and put it to a time frame, so I kind of did that as well. Our obligation to acting upon the 6 words above is being strategically planned in 11 year cycles—a time frame not without precedent in our organizational make-up (See *Liber CXCIV* on the Electoral College and the Revolutionaries, for example). Every year at the annual get together of Executive and Governing members, we are going to intensively and critically assess our actions, plans and progress, report on the past and initiate the future, mapped in a sense to the 'Triple C' mantra. Our obligation to working this is straightforward — Government really is service around here, we're here to stay and built to last, and 'all must be done well and with business way' (AL III:41). 'Patience'. The Triple C has both generalist and specialist applications, and will mean different things to different people at different times.

Here are some basic ideas:

- Duly Constituted: that to the extent possible, practicable and legal, we strive to establish in full every functional component of the OTO Constitution in accordance with the direction—and with the approval—of International Headquarters and our Frater Superior.

- Truly Consecrated: that in seeking to develop and expand the Order, we never compromise our spiritual integrity, rites, teachings and mysteries, and ensure that these are practised, preserved, taught and passed on with 'initiated' excellence and gnosis.

- Fully Congregated: that the above two points work together to ensure that members continue to be admitted to, and advanced through, the degrees of the OTO.

In the real world, a 'vision statement' is usually expounded in the aims and intent of a 'mission statement.' We don't have one of those explicitly, but we do have a legally required Statement of Objects/Objectives (posted on our website) that is 93% 'borrowed' from the US Grand Lodge 'mission statement'. In the years ahead I imagine that we will be better qualified to write new and original Objects that better express the AUGL culture as it emerges. While dressed in the language of organizational formality, it gives a good if at times veiled synopsis of what the OTO is on about. A few months back I asked our EC President Brother Phil to conduct a 'pulse' check on Man of Earth operations. He gave each local body a few simple questions requiring numerical responses, and then averaged out these scores to arrive at a final number. As a statistical measure this may be misleading —surveys don't allow for situational / localized explanations and context, and on that level the OTO really is a local beast—but it's still interesting. Also, of the 5 bodies contacted 1 didn't respond (in itself an indicator, e.g. 80% response rate instead of 100%), so that affects the averages tallied. I have to admit that some of these responses surprised me. By one scenario from the above, it could take over 3 months (101 days) just to get our candidates into Temple. Roughly speaking, dividing questions 3 and 4 by 3 and 5 by 2 gives an idea of what I'd call our idealist '93%' optimum. Times may have changed, but just remember that we've done more with less in the past, and that was before email and the Internet were around to help.

I also pulsed our Initiation Secretary, Brother Adam, and grabbed what stats he could gather on the fly. This secular year there were only 2 late Quartermaster orders, 4 requests for waivers to the processing period, and no incorrect pledge forms. The waivers were mainly the result of local offices losing or forgetting to mail in forms, and we'd like to see that improved. Even so, I'd say this is quite positive feedback from our GISG. It's not only a testament to our local offices, but also to Brother Adam, who over the years has magically forged his hybrid office of Initiation Secretary and Quartermaster into a living and vital part of our community and practices. Finally, there were some aspects of SGIG reports to my office that are worth sharing with everyone. First, on more than one occasion I've heard that our local body Masters are having to cover one or more subordinate positions (Secretary and/or Treasurer) themselves due to lack of willing and/or able assistants. Secondly, there are some common catch 23 conundrums being reported: young members dropping off as (their impression is that) nothing is happening locally, local bodies organizing events that are poorly attended by just those members, and an over reliance on the 'usual people' for 93% of local body logistical work in organizing / hosting Order events and meetings. Sound familiar? These are some of the big and important issues that we will need to heart and brainstorm, and act upon, in the field and at our Middle.

In the meanwhile, I want to thank those of you who right now are working above and beyond the call of duty to keep things running. I'm also aware that with the creation of the Grand Lodge many of our 'Grand' appointments have less time to do things in their local bodies and that this has created a few 'staff' shortages. We pretty much expected that, but time and momentum should fix it up that —nature abhors a vacuum. These are early days. What I've wanted to show in this article is that from the SGC and Executive right through to your local body we all still have our work cut out for us. It should hopefully be equally clear that we are all connected, we are all in this together, and anything affecting one group inevitably affects us all. One thing I've learnt is that successful and sustainable OTO groups tend to find their right balance between running efficient transactional processes of OTO 'business' (communication, administration, treasury etc.), and being effective transformational agents—transforming and in-spiring ourselves, each other, our Order and the world—through the rites and teachings of the OTO and its mission of promulgating the Law of Thelema. You may be successful at one or the other, but without both in harmony there's no sustainability. That's what we're working on building up— equilibrium. So, keep up the wonderful 'Work, & be our bed in working!' And it helps to have a few other beds out there as well!

OZ 2 ANNO IVxiv - 22 Aug 2006 e.v.

'YOU WILL ALWAYS BE A LONER'

Remembering Parsi Krumm-Heller

11/02/1925 – 17/06/2008 e.v.

GRAND MASTER SHIVA X°

Parsival Krumm-Heller died peacefully on Tuesday 17th June in Sydney, Australia, after an ongoing series of illnesses. In recent years he'd had a triple bypass, and two aneurysms. After having his family around him in his final days, he died the way he wanted to: on his own. He confided in his son, Rainer, shortly before his death that this was his preferred way to meet his final earthly Mystery. The son of noted German author, occultist and mystic Arnoldo Krumm-Heller (Frater Huiracocha, 1876-1949, founder of the FRA or Fraternitas Rosicruciana Antiqua), Parsival, or Parsi as he preferred to be known, was born in Mexico and then schooled in Germany. He quite literally grew up in the European occult scene of the early 20th century, getting to know many of its historically important figures - his 'Uncles' and 'Aunts' - such as Karl Germer, Martha Kuntzel, Peryt-Shou, Hermann Metzger and Friedrich Levke, and many others. A dedicated Thelemite from an early age, Parsi would become a teacher in his own right. While in the English-speaking world Parsi is largely known for training a young Marcello Ramos Motta, before passing him on to Karl

Germer for further training in A∴A∴, his accomplishments in Europe and South America were many - advising, teaching, and authorizing many lodges and groups associated with the FRA, tirelessly working with a network of people and groups that continued Arnoldo's curricula, legacy and lineage, and advising various Rosicrucian and occult movements in Europe. He preferred to live in relative silence and privacy, never seeking the spotlight or a name for himself. First and foremost Parsi's focus was to preserve his father's teachings and legacy. In 2005 Parsi's English edition of Arnoldo Krumm-Heller's *Logos Mantram Magic* was published by the Australian OTO, with ongoing plans to make more of Arnoldo's works available in English.

When I first contacted Parsi in the early 1990s the first thing he asked me about was how Motta was getting along. Unaware that he had died in the late 80s, I filled him in on the SOTO and other goings on that had occurred in the eventful times leading up to Motta's death. Many years later Parsi confided that Karl Germer and himself had done an analysis of Motta's chart and determined that while he had potential for enormous good, he ran risk of bringing about his own downfall. As time went on we were able to put Parsi in touch with some of Motta's former A∴A∴ students, which I think he appreciated. Parsi had an adventurous and accomplished life with enough stories to fill a book. During the War he served in an elite section of the German navy doing secret mini-sub missions. He was captured a few times, had a knack for escaping, and was even interrogated by British Intelligence. I cannot remember the exact story anymore, but he was either the last German POW released after the War, or the last German POW released from North Africa. The German naval flag draped his coffin at his funeral. One of Parsi's fondest stories was meeting Aleister Crowley. Parsi was five years old and Crowley and Germer were coming to the Krumm-Heller household for a meeting with Arnoldo. Parsi told me how everybody was running about frantic as 'Therion' was visiting. When it was explained to him that a 'Beast' was coming to the house, he said he was quite scared, as he didn't know who, or what, the Beast was. It was at this meeting that Crowley walked straight up to young Parsi and said to him in broken German 'you will always be a loner.' It proved to be the case, and Parsi held a fond affection and respect for his 'Therion' (as he preferred to refer to Crowley) for the rest of his life. Parsi's primary magical interest was in his father's unique synthesis of western magic, qabalah, yoga, and South American shamanism, astrology and medicine. He knew Arnoldo's System thoroughly. Although never a member of the OTO, Parsi (like his father) held the Order in high esteem. He would stress to me the importance of the IX° for humanity and the world, yet for all that, eloquently if cryptically articulate the differences between the Order's application of these Mysteries compared to his father's System. According to Parsi, it was his father who taught him to appreciate and respect the work of the OTO. He said that his father's Order, the FRA, was initially set up as a 'training ground' of sorts for Spanish-speaking aspirants, and that Arnoldo hoped the best students would then 'graduate' to the OTO. I never really pursued our discussions on this, but I think this refers to the OTO under Reuss, who Arnoldo knew well.

In the early-mid 1990s at my first face-to-face meeting with Parsi he was interviewed by US Grand Master Sabazius, on one of Sabazius and Helena's visits to Sydney. He enjoyed the interview and would continue to mention it every now and then. It marked his reconnection to the OTO and I think fired up his interest in various avenues of research. It was also the first time in quite a while that he'd really spoken about Crowley, Thelema, the OTO and the various interrelationships with the Krumm-Heller history. Over the years many OTO brethren would assist Parsi's research. In his final weeks he was still requesting info from the AUGL OTO archives, and I was arranging for him to be interviewed by one of our Italian brothers. In 2006 when the OTO Areopagus met in Sydney, the Krumm-Hellers hosted a dinner for the Frater Superior and other senior members of the Order. Parsi took great joy and pride in the event, formally greeting everyone individually, and amidst the celebrations and conversations that followed there was a real sense of fraternity and collaboration, a unity of purpose, and of history, as two great lineages came together for the first time in decades, in recognition and acknowledgement.

After the death of Arnoldo in 1949 and on the advice of Friedrich Levke, Parsi moved to Australia in 1954, following attacks on the Krumm-Heller name and teachings by a certain Christian Religious Order. He settled with his family on the northern beaches of Sydney, working hard to build a new life in Australia. He studied and earned a Diploma of Management, and held various managerial positions throughout his working life. Parsi's exact words to me on moving to Australia was that he took a fifty year 'vow of silence' on the advice of his Superior, Levke. When I started corresponding with and meeting Parsi in the early 90s for a while there I used to think he was a little annoyed at me for blowing his cover ten or so years too early! Note that our English edition of *Logos Mantram Magic* came out in 2005, fifty one years after his move to Australia. I don't know whether that's just a coincidence. Parsi's Foreword to that edition is almost certainly the most substantive public document he has written about his father in English. Parsi has, however, authored two other books. After retirement Parsi's focus returned to more arcane issues, such as the promotion of his father's books and the advancement of the FRA In more recent times he appointed an ambassador for the FRA to promote the teachings of his father throughout France, as well as other Latin American countries. Parsi continued to correspond with various individuals, and has passed on an extensive legacy and heritage to his son, Rainer, who will continue his work. One of my favourite recollections of Parsi was visiting his home sometime in the early 90s. After a delightful breakfast he showed me a painting - I can't recall it greatly, but it might have been a Macroprosopus and Microprosopus arrangement - and told me that it was painted by none other than Papus (Gerard Encausse), a gift to his father. Seeing I was suitably impressed he then asked how good my Hebrew was and wanted me to translate the Hebrew for him. I was being examined, and that wasn't in my game plan for the day! Other than a few obvious words I think he found my lack of Zoharic translation abilities amusing. After then showing me various archives and generously passing on some Crowley archival materials, he asked if I could read German. I said 'no', which seemed to strangely please him, and he then proceeded to show me a stack of his magical papers - A∴A∴ examinations and the like - all written in German. Next came (what seemed to me) his pride and joy: his Stele of Revealing - I think he told me it was hand painted by himself, but perhaps it was one of Levke's, I'm not sure. Feeling suitably deflated from my lack of language skills, I gleefully pointed out that his Stele had a 'typographical' error in one of the hieroglyphs. Memo: bad move on my part! Many years later Parsi gave me a big, ornamental decorative plate from India, with a type of wheel of life design on it. It belonged to his father. Parsi told me it was his father's favourite, and was always placed in his study. I could imagine Arnoldo staring at it and thinking while he was doing his work, and the plate certainly has a talismanic aura. I use it in a similar way. I will remember 'Parsi' for his generosity, humbleness, dedication to the Work, and stern yet always sage advice; and most importantly for his friendship, encouragement, guidance and counsel in regards my work for the OTO. His wry fatalism in later years (as it was once described) perhaps a true sign of his Grade. The last thing I passed on to him, about a week before his death, was a copy of his friend Peryt-Shou's version of the Egyptian Book of the Dead. His passing marks the end of an era. A man of mystery and privacy, in my own way I will miss him dearly.

> 'Unto them from whose eyes the veil of life hath fallen may there be granted the accomplishment of their True Wills; whether they will absorption in the Infinite, or to be united with their chosen and preferred, or to be in contemplation, or to be at peace, or to achieve the labour and heroism of incarnation on this planet or another, or in any Star, or aught else, unto them may there be granted the accomplishment of their Wills; yea, the accomplishment of their Wills.'
>
> - *Liber XV*.

I thank Oceania Lodge for the memorable Mass celebrated in Parsi's honour. I represented the Order at his funeral service - a small and private affair - a few days later.

OZ 9 ANNO IVxvi - 22 SEPT 2008 E.V.

'Initiation in the Aeon of the Child: the Path of the Great Return'

Introduction to J.Daniel Gunther's 'Initiation in the Aeon of the Child: the Path of the Great Return'

Lecture series in Sydney, October 2010 e.v.

Grand Master Shiva X°

'I know not who I am; I know not whence I came; I know not whither I go; I seek- but what I do not know; I am blind and bound, but I have heard one cry Ring through to Eternity; Arise and follow me!'

And so begins the Path of the Great Return. No sooner has the Aspirant set off on the Path, passed the Guardians of the Gates and been gilded by the Light, made Master of Fate and wholly Initiate, then he or she will encounter, if they have not already, the dryness that is the dark night of the soul. And you can rest assured that it is not much fun. But somewhere and sometime during the anguish of the night, when you are beyond thinking and feeling and hope, there might come a Vision, and a kiss, from the Beloved. And in that moment a new zeal is inflamed within, unexpected and unexplainable, bringing with it the ecstatic yet stark realization that that there is no turning back! And should the Aspirant have ears to hear, a sweet Voice guides and beckons them to the bridal chamber. And so on it goes unto the Mountain of Initiation. On this arduous and often painful path we are taught to be lamps to our own feet, but today I am truly honoured to be introducing J. Daniel Gunther, a man who has worked silently for decades to clear that path, to polish the old signposts, and put up a few new ones, for those who embark upon the Inward Journey. His first book, *Initiation in the Aeon the Child*, introduced the A∴A∴ System of Initiation to a new audience, and further instructed an old one, in many cases making public for the first time what the Frater Superior of the OTO, Hymenaeus Beta, called the 'transmitted doctrinal insights' of Thelema. I know that many of you are here because you have read that book. For those of you who have not, and might be interested, we do have some copies available at the door. Over the next two days, not only will Daniel be expounding upon many of the themes found in Initiation in the Aeon of the Child, but I'm excited to say we'll also be hearing new lectures that draw from Daniel's forthcoming book, *The Angel and the Abyss*.

The Angel and the Abyss not only describes the critical stages in an individual's passage in A∴A∴, but also, in my opinion, the collective spiritual evolution of humanity in the New Aeon. As some of you know, I am presently working on the new, official OTO edition of Aleister Crowley's *Magick Without Tears*. During this work it occurred to me that on top of everything else that Aleister Crowley was, he was also a great pragmatist. He did all he possibly could for the Great Work, and left the Mysteries out there for those that follow, and for those who would pick up where he left off. Knowing what he would be able to realistically achieve in his lifetime, his magical focus was to guide humanity to what he called the Next Step, the Knowledge and Conversation of the Holy Guardian Angel. I think Crowley realised that it would fall upon those who came after him to carry out what the Secret Chiefs also wanted him to do - to teach humanity how to Cross the Abyss. After I first read *Initiation in the Aeon the Child*, I realized that this time had now come, and that what had once seemed a wishful but unattainable ideal, was now an actual possibility for mankind. It can and will be done. And I credit J. Daniel Gunther with inaugurating this tremendous shift in the consciousness and initiatic impulse of living Thelema. This is something I obviously cannot and do not say lightly, and I think that after the next two days you may have some appreciation of what I am saying, and perhaps your own opinion on the matter, each to their own. When Daniel accepted my invitation to come here, I got a little over-ambitious and totally unrealistic in terms of how many lectures we could schedule each day, so we've had to make some slight adjustments to the program. We are now looking at 4 lectures a day, and both days will conclude with question and answer sessions. So if questions pop up during the talks, just make a note of them on the pads provided and raise them with Daniel during the Q & A time. The verse by verse exposition of Liber 65 Chapter 1 scheduled for this afternoon is actually 2 lectures, and you should have had a booklet copy of Liber 65 left for you on your seat. Give or take 15-20 minutes, all the lectures should go for about 1 1/2 hours each. Some elements of the two lectures we've had to cut, Twin Warriors about the Pillars of the World - the Sevenfold arrangement of Hoor, and Fruit of the Just - the Revelation of the Thelemic Pentagrammaton, have been absorbed into the content of the other talks. I'm actually glad we've had to cut some content - it gives me an excuse to invite Daniel back sooner rather than later. We also have a surprise for you at the end of Day 2 that is not listed on the program, but is the fourth 'lecture' if you like. So please, don't hold back & make the most of our time together. Some informal time is also scheduled, where I'm sure Daniel will be happy to do any book signings and the like, and of course for those who opted in for it, we have the banquet tomorrow night. Please note that we are here, first and foremost, to learn - & in that regards this is very much an intensive. To fit everything in comfortably, the tea breaks are limited to 15 minutes and lunch 30 minutes and I'd ask you to be prompt returning so you don't miss out on anything or disrupt proceedings, for we've been waiting a long time for this. Now, I don't just mean waiting for Daniel's book to come out, although some of us were waiting quite a while for that, or waiting for

Daniel to get here, but we've been waiting a long time for this. I have read the letters in our Grand Lodge archives, from my predecessor Frank Bennett, who in the early 20th century tried unsuccessfully to get Aleister Crowley here to Sydney for lectures. As the first official Grand Lodge sponsored public event, I am pleased to finally make good of my Uncle's vision, and with the rightful and only person who could deliver those lectures today. So Brothers and Sisters, friends and welcome guests, I thank all of you for making the effort to come along; I know that for many of you this has meant taking time off work or otherwise juggling your everyday commitments and your wallets, and that a number of you have come here from interstate and overseas. As we spend the next few days together, consider that in this room we have attendees from New South Wales, South Australia, Victoria, Western Australia, Queensland, New Zealand, Hong Kong, Japan, Italy, the United Kingdom and the United States. I encourage all of you to make the most of this learning experience brought to you by Ordo Templi Orientis in service to A∴A∴; again - please don't feel shy about participating in the question and answer sessions; in all honesty we have put this on for all of you and not for profit, and so let us proceed with a spirit of enquiry, engagement, openness, mutual respect, and collegiality. I am very pleased and very humbled to see the OTO carrying out its traditional function of practically supporting and assisting the Great Work of A∴A∴; and so without further ado, I'd ask you all to put your hands together and welcome Dan and his partner Gwen to the floor.

OZ 18 ANNO IVxviii - 22 December 2010 e.v.

VENI COOPER-MATHIESON

The Land of the Dawning

FRATER HERMELLYON

On the original Australian OTO Lodge charter issued by James Thomas Windram and L.B. Yardley on November 15th 1915 e.v. there are two signatories: Frank Bennett (Fr. Progradior, a Saint in our Gnostic Mass, about whom much research has been done[1]) and Veni Cooper-Mathieson.

Veni Cooper-Mathieson was born Amanda Melvina Cooper in Maitland, New South Wales on the 4th October, 1867 to parents Thomas Henry and Letitia Anna (née Dudgeon) Cooper. Amanda's father was born in Stockport, Cheshire, England, and was a Crimean War veteran who worked as a blacksmith. Her mother was born in Antrim, Ireland. They were married in Brisbane on March 25, 1864. Amanda had two younger siblings, Albert and Oscar.

If you google her you'll find that she was a bright star in the world of New Thought, beginning in 1903, she published

---

[1] *Progradior and the Beast*, Keith Richmond, Neptune Press, London 2004.
The Magical Record of Frater Progradior and other writings by Frank Bennett, Keith Richmond (ed), Neptune Press, London 2004.
The Progradior Correspondence, Keith Richmond (ed), Teitian Press, Maine, USA, 2009.

voluminous amounts of material; novels, tracts and essays, as well as editing her own periodicals *The Truth Seeker* (1910-1913) and *The Revealer* (1915-1917)[2].

Her most famous adage is 'The positive thinker repels disease: the negative thinker invites infection.'[3]

On the subject of sin, Soror Veni wrote, 'Sin means "missing the mark" or falling short of the higher ideals of life which you have set up for yourself, and know to be your soul's true goal. To do or be, less than you are able or capable of doing or being, is sin.'[4]

She considered Australia 'the land of the dawning'[5], untainted by the bigotry of the old country and ripe with boundless possibility. Like all New Thoughters, she taught that 'every thought is a living force.' 'When you think a thought, you give life to a created idea. You have used the essence that brings forth a Word; then the Word becomes flesh in the earth of your being. It must produce according to its quality and character.'[6]

---

[2] *The Revealer* was based out of "The Truth Centre", I.O.O.F. Temple, 138 Elizabeth Street, Sydney where the OTO held monthly meetings, and Frank Bennett delivered weekly lectures.

[3] *The Universal Health Restorer or, The Great Physician Within*, Veni Cooper-Mathieson, Universal Truth Publishing Fellowship, Sydney 1929.

[4] See AL 1:41-45

[5] *Australia! Land of the dawning.* Veni Cooper-Mathieson, Truth-Seeker Publishing Company, Perth, 1904

[6] *A Marriage of Souls: A Metaphysical Novel.* Veni Cooper-Mathieson, Truth-Seeker Publishing Company, Perth, 1914

She was engaged in newspaper work before her pioneering New Thought mission began in 1903, where she began lecturing on social and sexual reform in the Domain in Sydney, under the auspices of The Woman's White Cross Moral Reform Crusade. The society was founded by Veni to promote celibacy among young women (a companion group for young men was less successful). She told a group of men at a Sydney meeting that, by engaging in sex, they were degrading and abusing their bodies and disgracing their 'manhood'. She advocated that men utilise their 'glorious pro-creative power' in more positive ways so as to live more spiritually attenuated lives. At least part of her concern related to venereal disease. In a lecture titled *Purity* given at the Sydney Domain on Sunday, October 4, 1903, she said:

> 'Men and Brothers!... Curb your wilful, ungovernable passions; keep them on a leash as you would a vicious and ravenous dog. Subdue and conquer them, or they will conquer you in the end, and dire disaster must be the result.'

Eccentric, but highly influential in her sphere (widely published in New Thought Periodicals in the US and UK) this metaphysician, healer and writer, like most New Thought types moved around a lot.

She did a stint in the UK and USA between 1906-1909, studying metaphysics, before returning first to Sydney then Perth where she set up several New Thought centres and The

Universal Truth Publishing Company. Travelling back and forth between Sydney and Perth between 1907 and 1914, she eventually 'settled' in Sydney for long enough to establish a new base of operations for her publishing endeavours, and co-sign the charter that began the first current of OTO in 'the land of the dawning'.

There's a big gap in the record of her life from that signing to her turning up again in Mount Victoria in the Blue Mountains west of Sydney in 1927.

Careful reading of her later tracts and essays shows that it's unlikely that she fully got with the program and entirely dispensed with her Old Aeonic point of view. While it's doubtful she embraced the Law of Thelema, her work following her involvement with OTO expresses the identity of God and Man ('Thus civilisation is inseparable from Man's highest expression of himself - individually, nationally, and universally- so is Man inseparable from his One Cause: THAT which expresses Itself through Man to his highest perfection, and in this manner the seeming two are united; God and Man are ONE.'[7]), and the ability of every man and every woman to make contact with the Divine (her descriptions of 'The Child-Christ' to be found within, ring of the same language of The Holy Guardian Angel in our own doctrines). Importantly, the strict encratism of her early work is missing from her later tracts,

---

[7] ibid

and she embraced the possibility of the Holiness of sexual union. It's highly likely that she conflated celibacy with the goals of the burgeoning women's liberation movement of the time. Many of the early tracts dealing with sexual propriety were couched in the language of Woman's emancipation; notably, *Thoughts on the Marriage Question*, published in 1904, but written in 1896, *The Heart of God* and *Mirrors of the Infinite* from 1907.

Between 1928 and 1930, she moved between Macquarie, Blackheath and Darling Point. It's difficult to tell of her contact with OTO during this period. It's likely she drifted away from it, perhaps attracted in the first place to its co-masonic nature.

The periodical she edited during the time of her involvement with OTO, *The Revealer*, has a particular Temple language that is informed by Masonry and Rosicrucianism. She also delivered a series of lectures on Rosicrucianism, 12 of which were published as *A Series of Rosicrucian Lectures on Spiritual Evolution*[8] Another course of lectures, *The New Creation*, is particularly informed by her contact with the Order.[9]

---

[8] Universal Truth Publishing Company, Mt Victoria NSW, 1915-18.
[9] Given the shambolic beginnings of the OTO in Australia (largely due to the vacillations and incompetence of Ernest Dunn, our first national head), and the fact that Baphomet was revising the M∴M∴M∴ rites during this time, it is highly unlikely that these insights were formally transmitted, but rather came through her close friendship with Frank Bennett. Although both Veni and Bennett were given Honourary VII° degrees to allow them to sign the National Lodge Charter, this in no way suggests that they had made their way through the complete system as

She later advocated what she called 'free unions' (or 'spiritual marriages'), outside the control or legal sanction of the State, in which the children of love matches would be raised in a spirit of genuine affection, and which the couple could dissolve easily if they concluded that theirs was not, in fact, a 'spiritual marriage' in the eyes of God. She wrote that unless a marriage was a 'true spiritual union there is no marriage in the sight of the most High God, for He deals with us purely as spiritual beings'.[10]

She spent a year in the Katoomba, before turning up (like all bad pennies) in Hobart Town.

Departing Sydney 8th March, 1933 and arriving in Hobart on the 10th. She continued her nomadic run; couch-surfing amongst the New Thought scene in Hobart before finding digs at 9 King Street, Sandy Bay in 1934.

Soror Veni is said to have been assisted for some 30 years by an 'Indian mystic'. The so-called 'Indian mystic' was probably the non-Indian, American-born Brother Ariel [Ariel Herman Adam] (1881-1952), who was Sr. Veni's secretary and house servant (also the secretary of *The Order of the Prince of Peace*, an esoteric order founded by her). He assisted Sr. Veni in her metaphysical work and other

---

we know it today.

[10] She was married twice herself first to Scottish-born inspector of police, Samuel Matthews Jr (married, Brisbane QLD, February 29, 1884, when she was just 16 years old); and then again to barrister and solicitor, Earlam Joshua Gibson (in Perth WA, 1902).

activities right up until her death in 1943. In an article published in *Smith's Weekly* on May 3, 1919 Randolph Bedford described Brother Ariel as 'sleek' and 'indefatigable', 'a little man, all Christian-Israelitish air, and Nazarenic beard', 'an Aminadab Sleek with a nasal drawl'.

She was scarcely off the boat before she drew heat from Hobart authorities, and in May 1934 she was arrested for 'practising as a physician', prosecuted and fined £2, with costs, in the Hobart Police Court. According to newspaper accounts at the time, she claimed that she had Divine powers of healing through breathing on patients and could detect inward physical growths that X-rays wouldn't reveal. She refused to pay the fine, demanding the court to present any of her clients who had cause to complain about her treatments.[11] None could be found, but the humiliation of cross-examination, in particular, being forced to describe a visitation of God in her teens, and the ridicule of the newspapers took its toll and she wound up in the remote southern village of Franklin, Tasmania in 1936.

Listings in the 'Church Services' section of *The Mercury* (Hobart, Tasmania) reveal that Sr. Veni continued to lecture on Sunday and Wednesday evenings at the Metaphysical Lecture Hall, in Moran and Cato's Building, 107 Elizabeth

---

[11] It's unclear if she (or someone else) wound up paying the fine, as there is no evidence she did any time for the offence. She represented herself in the Court proceedings, stating to the Court that she was her own solicitor with Jesus Christ as her counsel.

Street, Hobart until at least January 1936. The title of her talk from Sunday January 5th, 1936 was *The Great Pyramid Prophecy Concerning this Wonderful Year, 1936*. She lectured throughout January 1936 on *The Message of the Great Pyramid*, and the talk for Sunday, January 12th, 1936 was called *Warnings for the Present Age*.

Finally she moved to the township of Alonnah on Bruny Island on the D'Entrecasteaux Channel, where she died on 6 June, 1943 after a fall, at the age of 75.

> 'The real self, the Divine Man in each of us, never dies. ... These forms are but the fleshly tabernacles in which the Spirit of the Lord manifests Himself to grow to greater and greater perfection.' [12]

> 'Unto them from whose eyes the veil of life hath fallen may there be granted the accomplishment of their true Wills' - *Liber XV*

OZ 49 ANNO VIV - 23 SEPTEMBER 2018 E.V.

---

[12] *A Marriage of Souls*.

Woman Girt With Sword

Retreat address

Grand Master Shiva X°

Sisters of Thelema,

> Do what thou wilt shall be the whole of the Law.

It's good to be one of the girls tonight as one thing you learn quickly in my job is that you can no longer be 'one of the boys.' That's making light of it, but the truth is I'm really honoured to be here and to get some dedicated private time with you. I was asked if I was scared about turning up. I'm pretty sure that was a joke, although I can admit to being intimidated by the range of topics a keynote might explore, and confused by the depth and variety of feelings, opinions, topics and experiences that came out of my own head when I thought of addressing you. I've also just come back from doing a number of lectures in the USA and with them fresh in my head, I was surprised at just how much of their content spoke specifically to or about the feminine in our System. I wanted to share all of that with you too, and I realised all of this would take a one week retreat not a brief opening address. What I think this suggests is that we have a conversation here that has to keep on running, of which this is the start, but the trick tonight as always is to think more about you than me. So I will limit myself to what I think the most important.

It was telling that on my work slate this week - totally unexpected with a very short lead time to deliver on - was writing an endorsement for the publisher Inner Traditions about a book by my colleague the religious scholar and Crowley biographer, Tobias Churton, called *Gnostic Mysteries of Sex: Sophia the Wild One and Erotic Christianity*. It made me think of all of you wild ones, but maybe not in the way you're thinking. You see, I didn't get time to finish the book. And that's what you are to me in one sense. Unfinished business. An unfinished book full of Mystery and wonder and holy awe - wild and erotic and radically gnostic. Unfinished, as it's a book that is still writing itself. For in my view the Mystery and wonder and holy awe of womanhood in Thelema - its innate potential - as revealed in the sacred writings of Thelema, our Holy Books, while constellated, is I think yet to be fully understood and manifest in the operational sense. I don't think we are anywhere close to that just yet, and that's one reason why some years ago I said the 21st century would be the century of the Priestess. It's your time. Not just any Priestess mind you. Not the popular image or ego or projection from pop culture, pop paganism, the alpha babalons or the occult ghetto. I am talking about Priestess Adepti schooled in the way of the Sanctuary. Virgo Intacta, specially dedicated to the service of the Great Order.

Now, this is not to say that we on high have so much secret stuff to teach you if and when you make it up to us - although to be honest, there is a bit of that - but rather, through your aspiration, attainment and advancement, when the System gets put through the dynamics of your own bio-energetic and psychic network, what have you to teach us about our Mysteries? For I believe we have a lot to learn from you. It's time for your gnosis to function. I don't think it's fully functional yet. Not by a long stretch. Carl Jung said the encounter with the Unconscious is the revelation of the unknown. I believe there is a new encounter happening right now, a new encounter with the hidden spring, of which you are ordained oracles and teachers. That's the experiment before us. At Grand Lodge and even before then, we've spent at least 20 years now working hard to ensure the pathway to advancement to the middle and upper levels of the OTO could be free flowing and considered, through educational and organisational development. There's a long way to go and I need as many of you to jump on board and help out as possible, but we're getting there.

Recently we had our first Sister since Leila Waddell enter the Hermit Triad. I wouldn't underestimate the vibration in the waves of aethyr that has initiated and its impact on our egregore. Trust me on that one - I live in that space. I not only hope, but fully expect, some of you to follow suit. As many as possible. But let's be under no illusions here. You'd have to earn your stripes - no one gets there easily.

Not on my watch. But it's worth the effort. Not for yourself, but in service to those Sisters who will follow you. Not for yourself, but for the Holy Order. Not for yourself, but for humankind. If I have one message for you tonight, one hope, one appeal, one wish, one dream, one challenge - it's that you aspire to just that. The Sanctuary needs more of you. The world needs more of you. The Secret Master needs more of you. The experiments must continue, and we don't even know what all of those will be just yet. Not until you join us. In the EGC manifesto from the 1940s it was written the sexes are equal and complementary, the priestess must now function as well as the priest. Must now function. That time is now. And if you're read in the EGC Manifesto you would know that instruction came from the Secret Chiefs, not Baphomet. Equal and complementary ... Must now function ... As simple as it sounds, as much as we may, these days, take all of this for granted, that message is radical. This is the new radical Gnosticism. For the theory and practice of co-equality being asserted here - social, sexual, spiritual, sacramental - physical made one with the spiritual, is new. As much as we rest on tradition and inherited symbolism and practice, this experiment has not been done before in our context.

This is a Church of the new times. We are encountering new and evolving archetypes. Crowley said the formula of Horus was the spiritual made one with the natural. This is its - to borrow quantum physicist Wolfgang Pauli's term - psychophysical reality, the co-equality beyond us yet of us that we can reach through the co-equal practices and sacraments of the Aeon. Now, I am not saying all of this - how important your work is and will be for the Aeon - to make you all feel good and cajole your egos on the occasion of this historically significant conference. I've said it all before. This is my 27th year in the OTO and my 25th consecutive year as the Frater Superior's Representative. I want to share with you a story that dates to the very early 90s when I had first come to office. I was talking to a Sister who was giving me her perceptions of the masculine in OTO; in what initiations she'd done, in the Mass, and in our hierarchy. Back then, I didn't know how to handle the questions. I told her that I didn't have all the answers but what I needed, in the absence of us having any village elders here in Australia, was for her and other Sisters to stick around, work through the System, study it, understand it, and become the village elders - become the role models, mentors and guides we were lacking. In that particular case she didn't, like too many others. The inconvenient truth is she didn't get what she wanted, couldn't stay open minded, and didn't want to do the hard work, for the good of others. I can look into this group here and see a few who have. They've been solitary pioneers, trail blazers for women in this region. And I think the tide is now turning, with the demographics to gender balancing out and access to progressive initiation much more open and available. The Way is open to you.

I am a big fan of learning by doing. Earlier I said I think many of the Mysteries of Thelemic womanhood are still to be explored and how I feel the archetypes are brimming and awaiting our encounter. To try and evidence this, I'm going to quote from one of my talks - basically this is from a running commentary on the Mass that I was given by an anima figure named Nadia. I tend to prefix this by saying anima figures or any of the contrasexual archetypes for that matter, if you've ever encountered them, don't play by the rules or follow the textbooks. They do whatever it takes to balance you out so their message can be exaggerated. Keep that in mind. So, let's hear what Nadia, not Shiva, has to say - I should point out there was some liberal editing on my part to make it fit in with the lecture I'm quoting from:

> *The Priestess, part of the priest, is symbolically set upon the summit of the Earth, Binah, the City of Night, the Holy Mountain Zion, the City of the Pyramids - the Pyramid being the true shape of the Gnostic Mass Temple's dais, steps, shrine and high altar combined. The dimensions are also indicative of Binah, as too its crimson covering. The red three angled heart is set up in the shrine, the Priestess making a descending triangle with thumbs and forefingers over The Book of the Law. This sacred triangle, as declared in the sacred writings of Thelema, is symbolic of the life-blood of the aspirants to the Great Work for sacrifice in the Graal of BABALON. Here the Priestess sits with the sword*

and the balances - the balances being the co-equal A and L of Liber AL - as Adjustment, having just symbolically enacted the true adjustment, the fulfilling of the formula of Tetragrammaton associated with the Master of the Temple, as Adjustment or lamed.

Prior to the unveiling and disrobing for the Opus, she sits wearing the robe that no man weareth. Like the robe of the Master of the Temple, it is blue and symbolically or otherwise embroidered with gold stars. These stars of the Night of Pan are the Host of heaven, humanity, recalling the Virgin entering the Temple with the hosts that she placed on the altar before the Graal. The fleur de lys at the hem of the robe of the Magister now appear on the crimson altar-cloth, an ancient symbol of Motherhood, the purity of the Priestess reflecting that lily made from the breast milk of Hera, for she is also clothed in the white milk of the stars. The roses at the sleeves of the Magister's robe are now seen in our Temple on either side of the Graal on the super-altar. The ouroboros serpent on the hem of the robe of the Magister is now the uraeus serpent that Crowns the Priest - the temporal rather than sempiternal formula and task. The symbolism of the downward arrow on the robe of the Magister, whilst not seemingly apparent in our Mass, is now the Opus itself above, for the regeneration of humanity below.

> *It is not only possible but probable that the author of the Mass, a Magister Templi at the time, envisioned the Magister - another technical term for which is the Scarlet Woman - when not only picturing the Priestess, but encountering her formula in the New Aeon, in the sacrament of the Aeon & restoring her holy Office to the world. For this lofty formula of Initiation, the Great Work, finds its natural expression and symbology in the formula of the Mass of the Holy Ghost, of which the Gnostic Catholic Mass is its public expression and celebration, thus the Covenant of Resurrection on the Path in Eternity, is one with the new Covenant of the Open Way on the Path of the Great Return.*

Moral of the story is that while I definitely see a lot of my thinking and language in that passage, a significant component of it is stuff I'd never consciously entertained. I have a whole lecture which details a lot of other things just like that. Let me now give you two synchronicities. I met a Sister of the Order from overseas, a Priestess whom I didn't know prior, who told me of a dream where she was handed the robe of the Magister - she just didn't know it was the robe of the Magister until hearing my description and identification of what it was. The dream happened about the same time as my experience. And just recently in the US, a scholar heard the descriptions of lamed - from my talks one of which I just quoted - and shared with me strikingly similar identifications of its Arabic form in terms of sexual symbolism from mystic folk songs from Bangladesh he was translating and researching - where you have that curious mix of Islam/Sufism combined with the spiritual nomenclature and thinking of the Indian subcontinent. So you know, my point is there is a certain potency and potential waiting for us and our Work to encounter and experience it, rooted in our theory, practice, doctrine, Mass and Mystery. I would look to these and the sacred writings of Thelema as signposts on the way forward.

At this point I want to thank Annette in particular for having the vision and drive to make this event happen - something she first mentioned to me as an aspiration, a number of years ago now. We've both just been in Vancouver for the North American OTO centenary proceedings and I'm sure Netti can attest to the interest 'girt with the sword' has received overseas. I wouldn't underestimate the global impact you may be having without realising it; the karmic footprint you might be leaving here. If you share and disseminate whatever goes on here and engage your sisters and brothers from elsewhere, in your own way you're changing the world. And I'm a very passionate believer, as was Aleister Crowley, that the OTO can, and will, change the world. I'm going to let the cat out of the bag here and let you know that I've appointed Annette Grand Secretary General - she'll be taking that position up in times ahead & we'll formally announce that sooner or later. It should come as no real surprise. Annette has worked closely with me in Temple, here and overseas, in Governance, Publishing, Design, Talismanic construction and in many other ways. We've worked together across most of the limbs of OTO activity. We're very much 2 parts of the same Virgo! However, and this may be something that comes up over your next few days together, Annette's appointment should spell out the obvious: gender is no bar to appointment in OTO right up to our most senior levels, and it never has been. Crowley was organising the OTO with women in senior posts from our inception, they were instrumental to the Order's Californian operations in Agape lodge of the 1940s, and the transition, transmission and continuity through to Grady and up to the present day.

In fact, one thing few people know is that at the secret Tenth Degree meeting last year in Florence to vote in an OHO, one of the candidates was a Sister. And maybe on that note I may end off and just answer questions. I do apologise for the disjointedness of my composition. I was interstate last week so haven't had much time. I'd like to read a quote I've used many times before, from one of the world's leading feminist scholars, Elizabeth Grosz, now at Rutgers, who was my undergrad teacher in Philosophy many years ago - who really challenged me and anyone else who took her classes, to undo yourself: 'In refusing to seek answers, and in continuing to pose questions as aporias, as paradoxes ... is to face the task, not of revolution ... but, less Romantically or glamorously, of endless negotiation, the equation of one's life with struggle, a wearying ideal but one perhaps that can make us less invested in any one struggle and more capable of bearing up to continuous effort to go against the relentless forces of sameness, more inventive in the kinds of subversion we seek, and more joyous in the kinds of struggle we choose to be called into.'

So, enjoy your conference, and to give the Lord of the Aeon the closing word: 'Come with me, and I will give you all that is desirable upon the earth. Because I give you that of which Earth and its joys are but as shadows ... There is joy in the setting-out; there is joy in the journey; there is joy in the goal.'

Love is the law, love under will.

In the name of the Secret Master, hail and farewell.

OZ 37 ANNO VI - 23 SEPTEMBER 2015 E.V.

Our Church

The clarity of vocation

Tau Amrit

(Assistens Throno Primatio)

Greetings of the Spring Equinox. Winter is the natural period of dormancy where that which appears to be dead also conceals the hidden seed of new life. That new life waits silent and patient for the spring rains and warm sunshine, the necessary conditions for life to burst forth from the womb of its mother. I get to see this seasonal process quite explicitly at home where I am surrounded by nature and all its wonder. We have 10 new chicks in the chook pen, spring lambs and calves are appearing in the area, the wattle trees are flowering, the fruit trees are beginning to bud, the bees are out pollinating, the baby kookaburra is learning how to sing and the cockatoos bring their cacophony around most mornings and evenings.

One thing winter brings which I miss at other times of the year is the perfectly clear night skies. With the sun at its furthermost point from our hemisphere and the associated shortened daylight hours, the darkness has the opportunity to fully develop earlier in the evening which in turn gives us the opportunity to view the stars in the heaven with astonishing clarity. These obligatory nature analogies can tend to be almost cliché were it not for the synchronistic view of reality they impart. I reported in the winter solstice edition that the Temple of the Woman Clothed with the Sun in Adelaide had closed and in this edition I'm reporting that the fledgling Melbourne temple that we hoped would be operating soon will not be proceeding in the original context. What does that tell us? Staring up at the winter night sky alongside the Primate and Tau Cinxia recently I asked myself this question and the answer I received was 'Vocation'. When the nights are longer than the days, the work gets harder because it's cold and the life that once surrounded us seems to be fading we see - in the clearest darkest night - the difference between aspiration and vocation. Vocation is a 'calling', something that you must do no matter what circumstances come your way whereas aspiration is the motion towards something you'd like to do or be. The cold hard truth is that if decisions you make as a clergy member result in the closure of an existing Temple or the abandonment of plans for a developing one, you were never vocational. That is not to say that you wasted your or our time, just that experience is the best teacher and the great leveller.

The terms 'true vocation' and the 'clerical life' that I have used in these reports are not used merely for the purpose of churching up the identity of EGC. These informing principles are the building blocks of the Australian EGC of the future. Churches or public temples require dedicated clergy who put the well-being of their congregations and community before their own comfort. This pertains to much more than just performing *Liber XV*, which whilst a very important part of what our clergy are required to do, will probably amount to the smallest investment of time and resources in the job. For example, the meaningful celebration of the feasts of the times (as they are aligned in our cradle to grave model) will set our clergy fair and square in the midst of human development and emotion. Therefore our clergy will become the natural focal points for their congregations at the highest and lowest points in their lives. That is an honour, privilege and an ongoing responsibility that cannot be taken lightly, and the success of our Church will ride on this level of engagement. If you are an aspiring Priest, Priestess or Deacon working towards a public temple (or working within an existing public temple) I encourage you to consider this honestly. If it IS your Will to follow this path you will have all the assistance we can give you to realize it. If you THINK it is your Will you will receive the same level of assistance as long as you are working it out. Our only request is that you are honest about it. The proof is in the result. With spring having now arrived it will be interesting to see what new life lay dormant during the winter and what potential will be actuated.

OZ 41 ANNO VII - 23 SEPTEMBER 2016 E.V.

EGC Retreat Keynote Address

Grand Master Shiva X°

Can I start by saying that I am genuinely surprised by the turnout to this Retreat. I was expecting maybe half this size if I was lucky. That an event like this is filling a need and demand is something I'm going to have to go home and think about.

So, I'd first of all like to welcome you all on behalf of the OTO Gnostic Catholic Church, and I also want to specifically thank Brother Chris Selwood, Master of Alpha and Omega Lodge, and Bishops Tau Hanuman (Adam) and Tau Cinxia (Annette) for events and program management - once again the bar has been raised - plus everyone else who is helping or presenting. I also welcome our international brethren from China, Japan and New Zealand who are here - and again that shows the sort of cross fertilizing that is happening in this region and which I hope continues.

The events over the weekend I think will speak for themselves. I think they will take the EGC experience to a whole new level. But I don't want to talk about them now. I do want to talk about the Gnostic Catholic Church in Australia.

If you do the math, the EGC has been operative in Australia for 30 years. I started attending Mass a few years before joining the OTO, so about 4 years into things. I can tell you, things have changed a lot in that time. In pentagrammaton terms and with the wisdom of hindsight, I can analyse the Church's history in a fivefold elemental pattern of roughly 6 year periods. I'm not going to bore you with that, except to say that I think that as we approach an auspicious 31st year of operations, we commence a new era where the Spirit will be made one with the material, to shape our future. This event is its kick off.

Tonight though, I don't want to dwell on the past, or even the present for that matter. I want you to look through your mind's eye further afield and into our future. If you will, look through the Eye of Shiva for a moment.

Picture an OTO that is far more developed and mature than what we are today - all of the Triads are active, functioning and well resourced. Our members, from Minerval onwards, each according to individual rank and capacity, are firmly grounded and prepared in the rites, customs, fraternity, techniques, curricula and doctrine of the OTO. And this is our modus operandi. This is the norm.

Our experimental research in social and theurgical laboratories is producing creative, illuminist-based learning and results; our instructors, mentors and guides not only know their material but know how to properly teach it; our ceremonies are conducted with great skill and style in quality Temples; our sponsors are wise in judgment and ongoing in support; our membership retention and progression is high, our Aspirants truly attaining as Adepts of the Path in

Eternity; and our fraternal bonds grow from strength to strength with every generation.

Our operational apparatus - our leaders and government - are visionaries with intelligence, integrity, energy, motivation and initiated insight; our business strategies and organisational management are adroit and effective. We're not short on numbers in these roles and we're not light on cash either.

Our local groups are vibrant, well organised, and visible to those attracted to our Light. Our local people have taken real ownership and responsibility for semi-independently operating and promoting OTO regions and bodies. They can adapt and self-organise to environment, yet be no less accountable to inspection and the high standards and requirements of the central Executive, and its Electoral College and Councils.

I could go on and on, but I think you get the picture. In short, I am talking about a System where energised enthusiasm reigns supreme and holy in every aspect of OTO life. We know what we're doing, and there's a culture of joy and beauty in the doing of it.

Does all of that sound good to you?

Well, keep in mind that there's absolutely nothing of which I've just spoken, that on some level or other we're not already doing, that we don't already have, or that we haven't made progress - even if it's been very slow - and continuous improvement towards. Nothing I mentioned was wishful thinking - it is where we are heading, under the shadow of the wings.

Now, there's one portfolio that I did not mention. From the three internal OTO portfolios - that's what I was just speaking about, our initiate, governing, and administrative bodies - we seek a fourth external one - the Gnostic Catholic Church. Together, these are the four primary elements to our System, our four primary classes of membership. I say we seek a fourth, as we need the fourth, and this is an expression of an archetypal motif. Think of the 4 kerubim. As you know, 3 have animal faces indicative of the internal and unconscious, yet the fourth is human - the face of a man.

In a similar fashion, we have the 3 internal classes of membership - they are for OTO initiates only and for the most part only function within OTO. But we need a fourth to make a conscious impact outside of the OTO in the world, so we can bring the contents of our Mystery into the consciousness of our world, and enable a mystical participation in the Law of Thelema that belongs to all humanity.

This fourth element - the Church - is both private, in that the OTO trains its clergy, yet it is public, celebrating rites of public worship for the people. This paradoxia is resolved in a hidden or fifth element, secret and synthetic, a quintessence, a harmonizing centre to the Four, a quintessential One. That is our sacrament, our Secret, our Sanctuary of the Gnosis. For together, these five virtues create a sanctuary, or temenos, the 'sacred space' of the OTO. It is a guarded border - a temenos being a protected area - yet it shows the way to the Righteous. How? Through mystical participation in a central celebration, the Gnostic Catholic Mass. It administers the virtues to the brethren.

So, let's now look into a Church of the future.

First of all we will have members dedicated to following their vocation in the priesthood above all else. This is what they want to do. Of all the OTO options and pathways our System offers, this speaks to them intimately, this is what really interests them - it is their calling, perhaps primarily, or even exclusively.

As we further develop the OTO, we will have to have an organisation which recognises that call to service, and provide specialised pathways of progress in the Order, as well as training and support, for those who choose to take on the ecclesiastical Way of life. This is both our challenge and our commitment.

Our Mass is no longer a small, private local body event, but a public celebration put on by the Church in family friendly places of worship. Our congregations have diversified, open to all drawn to our celebration, not just initiates. Yes, some will be OTO members, past and present, as well as our friends, families and people interested in joining the Order - what happens now. But I see a time when most won't be OTO, with a Church that is our primary and most effective vehicle for community outreach and service.

We offer our congregations the Thelemic sacraments of baptism, confirmation, marriage, and last rites; we can have real kids doing the Child roles; the Clergy are immersed in the spiritual care and well-being of their congregations on a daily level - not just when they are celebrating Mass - getting to know the families and individuals, reaching out to hearts and minds, administering the sacrament to the sick, and providing spiritual instruction, guidance, and counselling.

These communities in turn support our Church and our clergy - we rely on their charity to support the livelihoods of our clergy, and sustain our places of worship; we have an OTO Executive that can resource the Church to ensure our clergy are professionally trained in counselling and as celebrants, and are equipped with whatever other skills are needed; we conduct all the necessary legal registrations at both state and national levels, to optimise the rights and entitlements open to the Church; further afield as communities grow, we then have the resources and the bench strength to establish Abbeys, homes and other facilities. I'm getting carried away I know, but quite seriously, the only limit to any of this is our imagination and the strength and smarts, of our resolve.

I often wonder - and I'll be painfully honest with you and say that in weaker moments this frustrates and depresses me - where we would be right now, for but one of many examples, if we had the organisational capacity I've been talking about, right now, and could reach out to the gay and lesbian community on the current same-sex marriage debate. How would we come across with our bisexual Prophet compared to the fossilized, homophobic doctrinal and moral positions that have been aired so far by the Christian churches. That is but one of many opportunities here in Australia right now for social change and social justice in the name of the freedom of man in whom is God, where the Church of the future, of the OTO, of Thelema - the EGC - could make its mark and have its place. If we start developing the Church now to be in that position, we can change the world. Or at least our little part of it.

What these future scryings offer is an insight into the opportunities, potential, but also the sheer magnitude of the work ahead. That in itself brings with it an element of risk. We should not be under any illusions that this will be easy and that it won't require the dedication and commitment of a lifetime. Likewise we should not forget - here I paraphrase one of Crowley's teachings - that if you're not finding joy and beauty in the work, you're doing it wrong. So no matter how hard it will get, let us always remember to proceed with joy and beauty. If you are, irrespective of your degree and level of experience, you will grow with our Mystery, our Mass and our Mission. And if you truly are, you would know that the joy and beauty I speak of is about what you give others rather than claim for yourself.

Nature favours the brave, and I think 30 years has taught us that the world isn't going to wait for us to get our shit together. I call upon the brave and the keen to take active steps to self-organise the Church in our communities. Don't wait for decrees from on high. I try to have as few of those as possible, and I think this has to be locally driven and adapted to local environments.

The focus questions I want to leave you with to think about, perhaps tonight before you go to sleep, are:

> What am I going to do about it?
> What am I really doing here at this Retreat?
> Who am I?

For in the Silence you may just hear the Call. In which case, come with me and let's make it happen.

Enjoy yourselves!

OZ 25 ANNO IVxx - 22 SEPTEMBER 2012 E.V.

SHADOW OF THE THELEMITES

The Abbot, the Abbey and the Nightmare

GRAND MASTER SHIVA X°

'England is at present hysterical with horror at my abominations. I am called "The King of Depravity", "A Wizard of Wickedness", and so on, and accused of theft, treason, sexual perversion, addiction to drugs, white slavery and murder! Columns and pages of weeklies are packed with this insensate drivel... All that we can say is that we are quiet, sensible people, very busy with our work and who wants to read that this place [the Abbey] is in reality a sort of stick in the mud Sunday School.' Aleister Crowley, 1923[1]

Aleister Crowley (1875-1947) considered the French Renaissance humanist and satirist Francois Rabelais (c. 1494-1553) a Master and Saint.[2] In 1898 at his Neophyte initiation into the Hermetic Order of the Golden Dawn, Crowley took the magical motto 'Perdurabo' - Latin for 'I shall endure unto the end.' Whilst clearly a reference to the biblical passages of Matthew and Mark,[3] Crowley would

---

[1] A. Crowley, letter to S.N. Robinovitz, 23 Mar. 1923. P.R. Stephensen Collection, Mitchell Library, State Library of New South Wales.
[2] See Section V of Liber XV, OTO Ecclesia Gnostica Catholica Canon Missa, 'The Saints.'
[3] "And ye shall be hated of all men for my name's sake: but he that endureth to the end shall be saved." Matt. 10:22 KJV; "But he that shall

most strongly identify it with the Prophetic Riddle of Rabelais' Gargantua and Pantagruel:

> To see the elect most joyously refreshed
> With every good thing and celestial manna,
> And as an honest recompense rewarded
> With riches; while the others at last,
> Will be stripped bare. So reason has it that,
> These labours once concluded, at this point
> Each man shall have what's due to him by fate.
> Such was the bargain. How praiseworthy he
> Who shall have persevered even to the end![4]

For Crowley, 'the great Magician of Touraine'[5] had centuries ahead of his time foretold the coming of 'Frater Perdurabo' and the Law of Thelema (Greek for 'Will') that he would bring to the world.

The history of Gargantua climaxes with the foundation of an *Abbey of Theleme* with its rule of 'Faictz ce que vouldras' -

---

endure unto the end, the same shall be saved." Matt. 24:13 KJV; "And ye shall be hated of all men for my name's sake: but he that shall endure unto the end, the same shall be saved." Mark 13:13 KJV.

[4] Quoted from the dedication in Crowley, A., Desti, M., Waddell, L., Magick: Liber ABA, Book Four Parts I-IV, 2nd rev. ed., ed. Hymenaeus Beta, Weiser, Maine, 1997 p.v. For a discussion and treatment of the original French see 'The Antecedents of Thelema', in Crowley, A., The Revival of Magick and Other Essays, Oriflamme 2, eds. Hymenaeus Beta & Richard Kaczynski, New Falcon and Ordo Templi Orientis International, Temple AZ, 1998 pp. 162–169.

[5] 'The Antecedents of Thelema'. p.167.

French for 'Do what thou wilt.' Crowley felt that throughout Gargantua his 1904 spiritual revelation *The Book of the Law* was implied. The book, unexpectedly dictated to him in Cairo by a praeterhuman intelligence, designated Crowley the prophet of a new Law and Aeon (or age) for mankind. Crowley was to be the Magus, The Master Therion (or To Mega Therion - the Great Beast) and Logos, sent by the sempiternal brotherhood known as A∴A∴ to promulgate and teach the Law of Thelema - the object of which was the complete emancipation of the human race.[6]

A few verses from the *The Book of the Law* are enough to show its striking resonances with the Gargantuan creed:

> 'Who calls us Thelemites will do no wrong, if he look but close into the word. For there are therein Three Grades, the Hermit, and the Lover, and the man of Earth. Do what thou wilt shall be the whole of the Law.' - AL 1:40

> '...So with thy all; thou hast no right but to do thy will. Do that, and no other shall say nay. For pure will, unassuaged of purpose, delivered from the lust of result, is every way perfect.' - AL I:42-44.

---

[6] See Crowley, A., The Book of the Thoth, Weiser, Maine, 1989, p. 113. For an account of the Law of Thelema and the reception of The Book of the Law see Magick, Pt. IV.

'There is no law beyond Do what thou wilt.' - AL III:60[7]

Crowley considered it his duty to realize the Abbey imagined by Rabelais.[8] Together with his consorts, in 1920 he established the 'Abbey of Thelema' in Cefalu, on the northern coast of Sicily. Not only would it be a retreat from the savaging he was receiving in the British yellow press for alleged wartime treachery,[9] but Crowley envisaged the Abbey as a spiritual retreat for the training of his disciples. In this regards he took his cue from the temporal religious Order of which he was Grand Master, the Ordo Templi Orientis (OTO). The OTO Manifesto called for 'a hidden Retreat (Collegium ad Spiritum Sanctum) where members may conceal themselves in order to pursue the Great Work without hindrance.'[10] These Abbeys, or 'profess-houses' as they are known in OTO parlance, 'are secret fortresses of Truth, Light, Power and Love... They are also temples of true worship, specially consecrated by Nature to bring out of a man all that is best in him.'[11] Like Rabelais' l'abbaye des

---

[7] Liber AL vel Legis, The Book of the Law, also referred to as Liber Legis or simply as (Liber) AL.
[8] See 'The Antecedents of Thelema'
[9] In fact the contrary is far more likely. See Spence, R.B., Secret Agent 666: Aleister Crowley, British Intelligence and the Occult, Feral House, Port Townsend, 2008.
[10] Liber LII, Manifesto of the OTO.
[11] ibid.

Thelemites, the Villa Santa Barbara (the Abbey's real name) would operate as an ideal of thelemic society. Crowley's diary entries from this time indicate that he had his copy of Gargantua on hand.

The history of the Abbey is best left to the historians.[12] However, life for the Thelemites there seems to have been far from the ideal Crowley portrayed in fictionalized accounts, nor as romantic and cool as the modern occult scene might imagine it. Whilst for a time it was a rustic paradise for the Thelemites - as for Crowley with his newfound family life of wives and children - for the most part they were impoverished and struggling for basic provisions; sanitary conditions meant illnesses were common and constant; tragedy overshadowed them - Crowley's baby daughter died, his favourite student died, and his unborn son was miscarried. He and the Thelemites were left shattered in a nightmare of grief and loss. The Beast was increasingly dependent on heroin and cocaine. He was not alone, and the fine line between the ecstatic use of sex and drugs in sacred orgia and the downward spiral of excess was fine indeed. Tension and jealousies between students - and lovers - got in the way of the Great Work. And as sensationalized accounts of the Abbey made it to England, the yellow press undertook what Crowley's future publisher P.R Stephensen rightfully described as 'a campaign of

---

[12] See for example Kaczynski, R., Perdurabo: the Life of Aleister Crowley, rev. ed., North Atlantic Books, Berkeley, 2010.

personal vilification unparalleled in literary history.'[13] Finally, in 1923 Italy's Ministry of Internal Affairs decided to act and expelled Crowley. A period of anxiety and exile for the Beast ensued, and the Abbey, the few residents left there struggling to make ends meet, was eventually shut down.

True to his motto, Crowley endured. Despite the sorrows and struggles of the Cefalu experiment, it is worth pointing out that nobody was there against their will and many went to great lengths just to turn up. Students came from as far afield as Australia, South Africa, and the United States. Some disciples genuinely attained under the guidance of their Master. And of those that didn't, many admitted they were still the better off for going. For the appeal of Cefalu was not the Abbey, but the Abbot - Crowley himself. William Breeze has aptly described his enigmatic personality and achievements:

'Crowley was many things and excelled at most: a record-setting mountaineer, a competition-level chess player, the best metrical poet of his generation in the estimation of some, a literary critic of international reputation, an innovative publisher, editor and book designer, a pioneer in the use of entheogens, and a lion of sexual liberation - he was above all a lover, of men, women, gods, goddesses and himself... the key to his appeal was (and is) that he was as

---

[13] Stephensen, P.R., The Legend of Aleister Crowley, ed. Stephen J. King, 3rd ed. rev. and enlarged, Helios (OTO), Sydney, 2007, p. 53.

fun as he was smart. In truth his only satanic feature was his pride, which was admittedly of Miltonian proportions.'[14]

He was also a lover of diaries - and his Cefalu ones record a staggering amount of magical activity and writing whilst there.

To get beyond the popular Cefalu narrative and offer a context for its goings on requires looking at two not unrelated creative disciplines: art and magick.

By the time of the Abbey, Crowley had embraced visual art with passion - paint and sketch in particular. He was demonstrably influenced by the French post-impressionist artist Eugene Henri Paul Gauguin (1848 - 1903). As he had done with Rabelais, Crowley added Gauguin to the list of saints in the OTO Gnostic Catholic Mass. At the age of forty-three Gauguin, a stockbroker, had abandoned Europe for art and Tahiti, establishing his 'House of Carnal Pleasure.' Crowley at the age of forty four had abandoned England for the Abbey (or the 'Whore's Cell,' or 'Hell,' as it was also called[15]) with his lovers and immersed himself in his

---

[14] 'Introduction' to Crowley, A., The Drug and Other Stories, ed. W. Breeze, Wordsworth, Hertfordshire, 2010, pp. ix-x.
[15] "And my house is going to be The Whore's Hell, a secret place of the quenchless fire of Lust and the eternal torment of Love, where every Idea is accepted as it is, without criticism, provided only that it presents itself with the power to occupy the "Void Place of the Spirit," that can never be filled, for its moment." Crowley, 1920 Diary fragment, undated, OTO Archives.

art. Crowley consecrated the Abbey to Gauguin, and as he set about painting it he wrote:

'I feel easier, but overexcited. Gauguin literally torments me; I feel as if by my own choice of exile rather than toleration of the bourgeois, I am invoking him, and this painting of my house seems a sort of religious-magical rite, like the Egyptian embalmers', but of necromancy. I would he might come forth "his pleasure on the earth to do among the living."... It is maddening to think that I might have known him in the flesh; he died in 1903, May 8, eleven months before the First day of the Writing of the Book of the Law. Just six months after I had met Rodin.'[16] For Crowley, art and magick were one:

'The Artist is a creative genius; that is, he is of the nature of Godhead which devised the Soul as a medium for self-realization. Also, as History assures us, the Artist is of the caste of the initiated rulers of Mankind; he understands the theory of the Universe, he is an Epopt of the Mysteries of Nature, and an Hierophant of the Inviolable Sanctuary.'[17]

---

[16] ibid.
[17] Crowley, A., 'Realism: A Note upon the Theory of Art,' quoted in Starr, M.P., 'Aleister Crowley: Virgin Painter or Old Master?', In An Old Master: The Art of Aleister Crowley ed. Hymenaeus Beta, catalogue for The October Gallery exhibition, April 7-18 1998, Ordo Templi Orientis International, London, p.3.

Crowley referred to himself as 'a subconscious impressionist... My art is really subconscious and automatic.'[18] He expressed his ideas in his Cefalu diary:

> 'There would be no fun (moreover) in creating dead things; the whole point of the game is that one's work lives and moves independently of one's conscious mind. It is not amusing to turn out objects according to a pattern, as any factory hand will tell you. My paintings are never what I wished to make them: they fight for themselves against my hand. I can't even correct what I see to be real errors, as often as not. The finished work always surprises me... Thus, each painting reveals an unknown part of me to myself; I gain real knowledge through my art. Is not that better fun than if it merely recorded my thought with mechanical precision? Art is a God's way of discovering his own mysteries, the most enthralling, most tireless of pleasures.'[19]

He also elaborated upon the method:

> '...one should absolutely discover the true subconscious Will (of the detail of Work for the time being) before starting: the Operation will then help to manifest in form.'[20]

---

[18] From the New York Evening World, February 1919, quoted in ibid. p. 6.
[19] Crowley, 1920 Diary fragment, undated, OTO Archives.
[20] Crowley, diary entry for 5 May 1920, OTO Archives.

Crowley's thelemic art theory was rooted in the magical theory of the universe, and in particular, in the central doctrine of Knowledge and Conversation of the Holy Guardian Angel, which he described as 'our Secret Self - our Subconscious Ego, whose magical Image is our individuality expressed in mental and bodily form - our Holy Guardian Angel.'[21] The artist must discover the Will of the Work in order to manifest form as the magician must converse with the Angel in order to discover his or her true will and accomplish it. Anything else was black magick. Anything else was bad art. Do what thou wilt. To 'manifest in form' - express the magical Image - was comparable to the subconscious expressions of the true Self. It was a matter of tuning in and letting true art or true instinct flow. The actual method becomes clearer if we consider that 'subconscious' is not a term used in psychoanalytic literature. It does not appear in theories of the Unconscious put forward by Freud or Jung - which Crowley was read in - Freud specifically rejecting it in favour of the Unconscious.[22] For Freud, the only mentation outside conscious awareness was das Unbewusste (the Unconscious) and das Vorbewusste (the Preconscious) - the former dynamic and the latter descriptive (i.e. unrepressed and able to be called forth through mentation).

---

[21] Crowley, A., The Equinox of the Gods, New Falcon, (1936 OTO) 1991, p. 100.
[22] See Freud's The Unconscious (1915) and The question of Lay Analysis (1926).

Crowley's use of 'subconscious' is an intentional repudiation of Freud's disdain for the term and he uses it in precisely the same way that Freud found frustratingly ambiguous - topographically (something below consciousness) and qualitatively (another consciousness). The 'Ego' of this subterranean consciousness was the true Self, revealed subconsciously through the hieroglyphs of instinct - the sexual in particular. The Great Work was a process of discovering the true Self and enabling its expression and fulfilment by understanding and overcoming the complexes and repressions that prevent or pervert it (in magical terms, the process of purifying the microcosm in order to unite with the macrocosm). The unveiling of this 'Subconscious Ego' went beyond the limits of personal abstraction - Blake's notion of imagination transforming to Divine vision and fruition comes to mind - and Crowley considered the Holy Guardian Angel a transpersonal and objective individual, 'something more than a man... and his peculiarly intimate relationship with his client is that of friendship, of community, of brotherhood, or Fatherhood.'[23] This

---

[23] Crowley, A., Magick Without Tears, ed. Stephen J. King, OTO, New York (in preparation). The historian James Laver discussed the matter with Crowley in June 1947, shortly before Crowley's death. According to Laver's memoir Crowley said "You realise that Magick is something we do to ourselves. But it is more convenient to assume objective existence of an Angel who gives us knowledge than to allege that our invocation has awakened a supernormal power in ourselves", quoted in Churton, T., Aleister Crowley the biography: spiritual revolutionary, romantic explorer, occult master - and spy, Watkins, London, 2011, p. 425. Crowley pondered the same at Cefalu. Writing about the

relationship is the source model for the thelemic bonds of Brotherhood behind his Orders, the OTO and A∴A∴ and achieving this Angelic knowledge and conversation was what Crowley considered the next step for humanity. The true artist as 'Epopt of the Mysteries of Nature' and 'Hierophant of the Inviolable Sanctuary' was already there.

The path to the Subconscious Ego is by no means an easy or even pleasant experience, initially at least, evoking deep-seated anxieties, fears, repressed memories, desires, fantasies - all expressions of the dark Unconscious archetype of the Shadow. Crowley made taking this descent into hell necessary training for the Thelemites at the Abbey. He called the main room La Chambre des Cauchemars - the Chamber of Nightmares - painting the walls with grotesque murals. 'The purpose of these pictures' wrote Crowley, 'is to

---

intelligence from the A∴A∴ named Aiwaz who communicated The Book of the Law to him (and who Crowley identified as his Holy Guardian Angel) he said "The Initiates' Logick is very necessary in all sorts of ways. Eg. Is Aiwaz a 'separate being.' I am bound to answer No, but I must explain that such No is to answer a question about any name soever. No difference between you, and Him, and a brick then? None. Not even in the sense that there is a difference between the Persons of the Trinity? Yes; in fact there is a perfectly real difference between the three things, and they are quite separate, though it is easier to think so of Aiwaz than of the brick. Any possible thought is both real and separate, and neither. Whatever the subject, one reaches the Fourth Formless State in a very short time." Crowley, diary entry for 2 June 1920, OTO Archives. The Fourth Formless State - the 'logick' of the Initiate - is the highest of the formless Buddhist jhanas (the 'peaceful formless liberations transcending material form' - santa vimokkha atikammarupe aruppa), described as 'neither-perception-nor-non-perception'.

enable people, by contemplation, to purify their minds.'[24] An indication of what the student encountered whilst in contemplation is given in the following description of some of the murals:

'Gross desires may be compelled to supply themselves with morose satisfaction, while their object is in the power of bestial lust. But equally "God helps those who help themselves", and services to others nourish oneself; while Beauty delights both by actively informing unenlightened Nature, and passively awakening ecstasy in merely animal instincts. The perfected Ideal of Human Beauty may be the prey of shameless degradation both as to the satisfaction of its active desire to creation, finding itself sterilized by the greed of society and of its passive aspiration to receive the Grace of God, in whose stead the Goat of Obscenity defiles it wantonly with agonizing abominations.'[25] Perhaps the chaos and crises of Cefalu were the externalised reactions, projections, symptoms, and coping mechanisms of the internal 'agonizing abominations' of the dark nights of its residents' souls as they worked through the Chamber:

> 'the predigestion of evil... which (the individual) carries out as part of the process of assimilating his shadow makes him, at the same time, an agent for

---
[24] Crowley, A., Unpublished essay on the Abbey, quoted in Perdurabo, p. 365.
[25] Crowley, A., Cefalu Part Two, Thelema Lodge Calendar, June 1995, OTO, Berkeley (title provided by editor).

the immunization of the collective. An individual's shadow is invariably bound up with the collective shadow of his group, and as he digests his own evil, a fragment of the collective evil is invariably co-digested at the same time.'[26]

From the initiated perspective then, everything seemingly wrong with Cefalu was right and part of the course - it was a place for the Great Work of initiation and transformation. Crowley never wavered from this work for his students. Perhaps at most, the Thelemites could have done a better job of sealing the magical circle at times and keeping the darker spirits contained within the triangle.

Crowley suggests the Thelemites were living with a different life orientation in a fictionalized account of the Abbey given in his 1922 novel The Diary of a Drug Fiend:

> 'It was a very curious detail of life at the Abbey, that one act merged into the next insensibly. There were no abrupt changes. Life had been assimilated to the principle of the turbine, as opposed to the reverberatory engine. Every act was equally a sacrament.'[27]

---

[26] Erich Neumann, Depth Psychology and a New Ethic, quoted in Shiva X°, 'Under the Shadow of the Wings' (lecture transcript), OTO, Sydney and Tokyo, 2011.

[27] Crowley, A., The Diary of a Drug Fiend, (1922) Weiser, York Beach, 1970.

Treated as a sacrament, the descent into hell in the Chamber of Nightmares was holy, and every byway of excess that resulted therefrom was but the path to redemption.[28]

Crowley was mindful - and taught - that you watch the faults in your house (of disciples) by correcting them in yourself: 'Therefore, watch heedfully the Fault of another, that thou mayst correct it in thyself. For if it were not in thee, thou couldst not perceive it or understand it.'[29] The descent into Hell at Cefalu suggests we need to look not only at the students but at the teacher.

In terms of the graded spiritual system of A∴A∴, Crowley had attained to the exalted grade of Magus - the second highest in a sequence corresponding to the qabalistic Tree of Life. He had uttered the Creative Magical Word of the Aeon - the hallmark of a Magus - with the reception of the *The Book of the Law* in 1904, something A∴A∴ doctrine held transforms the planet.[30] Crowley attained to the Grade

---

[28] Crowley's Australian student Frank Bennett provides fascinating insights into life at the Abbey in his Magical Record, which was edited and prepared in typescript (in all likelihood with Crowley's oversight). That it records discussions on the subconscious as well as chapter headings of his 'journey through hell' is telling. See Bennett, F., The Magical Record of Frater Progradior and other writings, ed. Keith Richmond, Neptune Press, London, 2004.
[29] Crowley, A. (The Master Therion), Liber Aleph vel CXI The Book of Wisdom or Folly in the form of an Epistle of 666 The Great Wild Beast to his Son 777, (1962), 93 Publishing, New York, 1991, Ch. 98 'On Watching for Faults in the House', p.98.
[30] These and other details of the Grades of the A∴A∴ are best studied in the paper 'One Star in Sight: a Glimpse of the Structure and System of

in full shortly before settling at Cefalu, sealing his initiation as To Mega Therion 666. As the Logos of the Aeon, he therefore joined the ranks of the historical Magi recognized by the A∴A∴ - Lao Tzu, Gautama (Buddha), Krishna, Dionysus, Tahuti (Thoth), Mosheh (Moses) and Mohammed. The Magus is the Master of Magick and of the Law of Change, whose work 'is to create a new Universe in accordance with His Will.'[31] For Therion, Cefalu was this new Universe's microcosm. By purifying this microcosm 666 could unite with its macrocosm - in this sense, to teach and preach his Law to mankind.

The highest grade of A∴A∴'. is that of Ipsissimus (lit. 'own very self'), 'the Master of all modes of Existence... free from internal or external necessity and Master of the Law of Unsubstantiality (anatta).'[32] The Ipsissimus was 'to keep silence during His human life as to the fact of his Attainment, even to other Members of the Order.'[33] Crowley's Cefalu diaries show him contemplating the Mystery of Selflessness as he was required to do as a Magus, a task that opens the Grade of Ipsissimus.[34] On the 31 May 1920 he recorded that after invoking Aiwaz 'I was instantly

---

the Great White Brotherhood A∴A∴., see The Equinox IV:1, Weiser, York Beach, 1996, pp. 5–22.

[31] Ibid. p. 13.

[32] Ibid. p. 12. Anatta (pali) or anatman (sanskrit) is generally translated as 'not-self'.

[33] Ibid.

[34] See Liber B vel Magi vs. 15–18.

rewarded by the Word of the Oath of an Ipsissimus.'[35] A few weeks later he wrote:

> 'I don't know whether to call myself Ipsissimus, nor does it matter. Only I feel that I have had enough 'personal attainment' for an infinitude of lives...'[36]

Nevertheless, he would formally take the Oath a year later on 23 May 1921, bringing on his final initiation. In a way this hermetically sealed the Cefalu experiment, Crowley's 'Selflessness in Self'[37] the complement to the 'Self of myself'[38] his students might discover. The initiation would last beyond his time at the Abbey, and true to his enlightened grade, he remained silent about it throughout his life.[39]

---

[35] Crowley, diary entry for 31 May 1920, OTO Archives.
[36] Crowley, diary entry for 18 June 1920, OTO Archives.
[37] Liber B vel Magi vs. 16.
[38] Liber Cordis Cincti Serpente III:64.
[39] Crowley did however note in Magick in Theory and Practice (1929) about his Angel; "Also He Made me a Magus...He wrought also in Me a Work of Wonder beyond this; but in this matter I am sworn to hold My peace." See Book Four p. 541. Kenneth Grant and John Symonds have also suggested that Crowley's pseudonymous name as author of Eight Lectures on Yoga (1939), Mahatma Guru Sri Paramahansa Shivaji - Paramahansa being an enlightened Master - was also a reference to the Grade of Ipsissimus, see Crowley, A., The Magical Record of the Beast 666: The diaries of Aleister Crowley 1914–1920, eds. John Symonds & Kenneth Grant, Duckworth, London, 1972, p. 124. (Mahatma - 'Great Soul' - is also applied to a person revered for wisdom and selflessness).

Crowley's Cefalu years and those following his expulsion are not always regarded as his brightest - his circumstances strained, his body drugged, his mind a maelstrom of wisdom and folly. I'd suggest he was in the thick of his greatest Initiation - in preparation, ordeal and attainment. He worked out the price he would have to pay at the Abbey - the Ipsissimus 'shews God Omnipresent, Dementia.'[40] He would later comment in 1924:

> 'I am by insight and initiation an Ipsissimus; I'll face the phantom of myself, and tell it so to its teeth. I will invoke Insanity itself, but having thought of the Truth, I will not flinch from fixing it in word and deed, whatever come of it.'[41]

And in word and deed he did. His initiation over, his final literary output on magick (*Magick in Theory and Practice*, 1929), life (*Spirit of Solitude [Confessions]*, 1929), the Law of Thelema (*The Equinox of the Gods*, 1936), moral philosophy (*Little Essays toward Truth*, 1938), initiation (*The Heart of the Master*, 1938), yoga (*Eight Lectures on Yoga*, 1939), tarot (*The Book of Thoth*, 1944) and a final book of letters on magick (*Magick Without Tears*, posthumously published in 1954) are the erudite and sublime last words of a Master. He only ever gave one indication of what really happened during the great Initiation which finally concluded in 1924:

---

[40] Crowley, diary entry for 31 May 1920, OTO Archives.
[41] Quoted in Perdurabo, p. 370.

'So in that Fire he was consumed wholly, and as pure Spirit alone did he return, little by little, during the months that followed, into the body and mind that had perished in that great ordeal of which he can say no more than this: I died.'[42]

The riddle of Rabelais for Crowley was that he who would endure would be praised rather than be, in the Matthew and Mark sense, saved. The Book of the Law likewise praised him - '...blessing & worship to the prophet of the lovely Star!' AL II:79[43] - and left the rest to us. We haven't saved his reputation yet, but Crowley has endured unto the end - and endures with us today. In these decades after his death there has been a gradual reappraisal of his life, and its spiritual, literary and artistic legacy. It's a slow road to salvation. May this exhibition take us a few steps forward. And may we endure unto the end.

OZ 26 ANNO IVxx - 21 DECEMBER 2012 E.V.

---

[42] 'The Master Therion: A Biographical Note', in Crowley, A., The Heart of the Master & Other Papers, ed. Hymenaeus Beta, OTO & New Falcon, Scottsdale, 1992, p.17.
[43] The Book of the Law.

IN THE FLESH

Manifesting Liber 194

FRATER O.I.P

Spotlight on the Electoral College: An interview with Frater O.I.P. (President, The Electoral College of the Knight Hermetic Philosophers) in regards to the instruction in *Liber 194*.

Liber 194 outlines the Electoral College should be comprised of 11 members; having operated with fewer members, do you think it is a hindrance having less than 11? Or would you say it is not essential to have 11 members within the Electoral College?

Firstly, I would like to thank you for the opportunity to respond to these questions. The Electoral College means a great deal to me, and as I approach the end of my 11 year term it has been helpful to be able to reflect on the College and give some potential new Electors some food for thought. There are certainly challenges involved in not having a larger membership sitting on the Electoral College (and this is true of other bodies within the Grand Lodge as well). The College really works by having 'boots on the ground'; working with local Senates.

Not having that more direct contact with the regions make governance more difficult and often issues are not identified early enough, meaning that at times we have had to be more reactive than proactive. It also makes some things much harder to get done without immediate and local interaction. This is especially true in such a large country with a significant geographical dispersion. You can see the strength of a functioning Senate and a local Elector in Sydney, where great and positive changes have occurred due to the level of engagement and regular meetings of the local leadership (Senate). Another factor is the original vision for the College, as I read it, is that Electors were meant to be full time in that role (although there is some ambiguity here in *Liber 194*). The reality is we are all part time volunteers, and have a multitude of other commitments that we have to balance like everyone else. I have tried to counter our lack of local representation as much as I can by hitting the road and touching base personally with the membership, and making it clear that I am always happy to get on the phone if any member wants to speak with me.

If you do think 11 members is important, what could be done/achieved differently should we reach the full criteria?

With 11 members (or at least an Elector located in each region) the College would be better connected to the members it governs and have its finger on the pulse more regarding the issues specific to the region and the Kingdom as a whole. Local people understand the subtleties of their specific culture and its strengths and weaknesses and how to work with them. It would also mean the College would be more visible to the membership, which I think would assist in its growth and health. Having more members with a broad range of skills would also assist the College to be able to achieve much more. Sometimes I feel we have stalled in some of our tasks due to lack of resourcing and direct engagement. Like most things the College works by harnessing human energy.

It is highlighted that any volunteer must possess 'First rate ability in a branch of athletics, first rate ability in some branch of learning, profound general knowledge of history, profound general knowledge of the art of government, and attention to philosophy.' Do you believe you met all of these criteria when you volunteered?

Quite frankly, no.

Do you believe you meet them now?

I have certainly worked since I was appointed to the College to meet these criteria as best I could (fully aware of my own limitations). I could have possibly ticked off 'attention to philosophy' at the start due to my University education, but athletics was probably low on the list when I first put my hand up. I addressed this by starting martial arts training (specifically Japanese) and since then have acquired Dan rankings in two separate schools; interpreting athletics as activities that require physical skill and some level of stamina. 'Some branch of learning' is suitably vague (as is first rate ability), but I also play classical guitar (if you can call it playing), which is extremely challenging and rewarding and creates an interesting nexus between the mental and the physical; both in the act of learning and playing a piece of music. There is also a large amount of theory to supplement your understanding. Every time I play in front of my teacher I also get a helpful check on my ego. I have also tried to read as widely as I can, and have involved myself in different associations to understand 'government' better. My current employment is as a Public Servant, which has given me some good experience with governance in a large organisational context, both good and bad, and taught me a lot about leadership (also both good and bad). With many of these historical documents (which I find with both OTO and A∴A∴ material) at times you need to look at the 'spirit' of what they are communicating. Some things are impractical, and sometimes impossible, to accomplish (or potentially illegal in a contemporary context). If we waited for everything to be perfect by the book very little would ever get done, and there needs to be a certain level of adaptability. Sometimes the fifth power needs to be the overarching principle, along with a level of pragmatism.

Could you elaborate on why each is considered so important to undertake the role?

Without going through these one by one, what I see Crowley was looking at here is a well-rounded and balanced individual. You can see in his writings a focus on both intellectual and physical accomplishment (I've dragged myself up 'La rocca di Cefalù'). He sought to develop a mental and physical robustness from his students, and I think appreciated the strong connection between all levels of our being - physical and mental - as modern science is more and more coming to appreciate. Being a somewhat sickly (but intelligent) child I think Crowley understood this well and sought to physically challenge himself as an adult.

Having undertaken the role, how important do you think each of these are?

> All these skills are important as they give a broad and historical understanding of governance, society and humanity; looking backwards to assist working in the present and planning for the future. They also ensure that Electors have a certain level of structure in their thinking that is vital in governance (not to underestimate the more intuitive side of this - governance is both an art and a science). Also, being in good physical health leads to better mental health that supports these other functions.

Are there any other criteria you think should be included in this list?

> I think this list is broad enough to cover most bases, but I also think knowledge of organisational communication and culture is important for anyone in a position of governance. I also think some understanding of psychology is a great tool when working in groups, and looking at what creates successes and failures. For instance I have recently become interested in the concept of 'cultural complexes', as opposed to just a focus on individual complexes, and how this could relate to our work.

It is highlighted that one must renounce personal progress within the order, what effect has this had for you? Do you think it was necessary to undertake the role?

The effect of renunciation is profound and I think the main thing that it has changed in me is a 'lust for result' in relation to progress in the OTO, and this seems common to all the Electors (although there must be an element of this from the start to volunteer in the first place - quite frankly I never thought I would make it this far). I have watched people progress to the higher degrees and important roles in the Australian Grand Lodge over the years, and I can remember watching them going through their Minerval initiation, or being an Officer through some of their Man of Earth degrees. I do not feel at all resentful about this, or feel like I am missing out, but happy that the Order is growing and developing in Australia, and members are benefiting from this (and hopefully I have played some small part). By the time I complete my 11 year term on the Electoral College next year it will have been over 20 years since I took my Minerval initiation, and with the perspective of this time I can see how far the Order has come, which may not be so apparent to our newer initiates. Over my term on the College my focus has not been on OTO degrees, but service to the Order - what I am actually doing. I have written previously that time in the OTO matters little, and I dislike it when people lord over other members just because of how long they have been hanging around. My question is, and I ask this constantly to myself, what have you actually done...what are you doing now? If I was never initiated into another OTO degree I would still be satisfied if I felt I was able to serve the Order in some capacity. Renouncing progress orientates your thinking towards service as an end in itself (or at least it has for me). I think renunciation is important for the role of Elector as it assures you are focused on that role, and also gives you an extended period of time in which to work. The Order works in different cycles (such as the rotation of local body Masters), and the 11 years helps you to think in a much larger cycle. This is important for more sustainable and long term strategic thinking. It makes me wonder how far down the road our Grand Master is thinking - and then the OHO! I also think the 11 year commitment ensures that people who are attracted to the College will be dedicated and service oriented. It is a long period and one I don't think any member would take lightly.

Also there's, 'must each live in solitude... for three months continually' How strictly is this enforced in reality?

I think this requirement is incredibly important for Electors, but due to our limited resources over the first 11 year term it is something we have not been able to actualise. This is something I want the next generation of Electors to be able to access in some form.

Do you think it is necessary and/or beneficial on a personal level? And for the role within the Electoral College?

Taking this time out enables individual Electors to spend time exploring the mysteries of the Order. Our governance must interact with our mysteries, and it is important that space and time is provided for this integration to occur. The interesting nuance here is over this period they are instructed that they are 'serving themselves' - a contrast with their main function as an Elector which is very much serving others. It enables Electors to shift from outward facing to inward facing for a period.

'The Electoral College of the senate is vowed to poverty.' How strictly is this enforced in reality? Can you continue to work a full time job? What about family and partners etc.?

Electors do not take a formal vow of poverty due to the obvious issues with this in a contemporary context, and the stage of development the OTO is in. I have a full time job, a partner, a small and often disgruntled dog, and a mortgage or two. The Grand Lodge is certainly not in a position to enable me to 'subsist on the charity of the Order, which is extended to [me] in accordance with [my] original rank in life', even if this were desirable. The way I try to tap into the spirit of this requirement is to make my purse, time and resources open to the OTO as much as possible.

Liber 194 was written in a 'different time' how does it translate in a modern world?

Liber 194 was written in a different time, and also with a particular, and quite grand, vision of what the OTO would be and I think it still translates well into the modern world, but also stands as a challenge to the modern world. In many ways *Liber 194* is like the manuscript of a piece of music (and Frater Shiva likes to remind us that the OHO is a musician). Played with robotic accuracy it is lifeless, but introduce human interpretation and improvisation and the music comes to life - you need to experiment and jam (unlock the spirit encoded in the notes). This spirit of exploration and experimentation allows us to ensure the OTO stays relevant, without compromising its core structure and principles - we're still playing the same tune.

Do the details need to be reviewed/revised?

> *Liber 194* is a foundational and historical document that I don't think should be revised, but it is expanded upon and made contemporary and workable through our bylaws and other operational and instructional documents. The Intimations and other foundational documents show the initial vision and spirit of the OTO as envisioned by its founders, but they are skeletal and we need to work with them to enable them to live today.

Do you have any advice for anyone considering volunteering to the Electoral College?

> Be realistic and be ready to be challenged about the image you might have about the Order (in my opinion the truth is far more satisfying). Governance is hard work at times and very challenging. You have to accept that people are not always going to agree with your decisions, and sometimes your decisions might be bad ones, and you need the humility to be honest about that and learn from it. At the end of the day you have to be ready to do what you think is right regardless of various contending forces (and emotions). However, the Electoral College really represents the democratic element of the OTO, so decisions will

be (or should be) made with the input and support of all the Electors, but there can be robust debate at times. Also make sure you are approaching the College for the right reasons - be clear about your motives. You need to be sure in yourself that this is what you want and that you are ready for it. Also make sure you understand your skill set and inclination - not everybody is wired for governance, but there are certainly skills that you can acquire through education and experience. If you think you have the raw material, the Electoral College want to hear from you.

Having almost completed your 11 years within the Electoral College, what would you say has been the most valuable experience during your service?

The most valuable experience (or experiences) has been working and developing relationships with some amazing people who make our Grand Lodge what it is today. This is one of the reasons I find it so rewarding hitting the road for the OTO - finding people who help me understand what this OTO gig is all about and reenergise me. We have inspired, energetic and insightful members who are helping to shape a new vision for Australia moving into the future. I have always been humbled when people have stepped up when we have needed them, and at times taken a Local Body from one about to close, to one that is now thriving - it is this drive and commitment that will help us take the Australian Grand Lodge to the next level.

The Electoral College is certainly not just about me, so I would also like to take this opportunity here to thank the two other Electors who stood at the threshold with me all those years ago with a beer in hand - Frater N.M.O.H.S. and Frater I.V.V.. It has been quite a trip, but the very considered and insightful council they have provided during difficult times and when difficult decisions have had to be made has always been greatly appreciated - mutual respect and honesty has been the hallmark of our work together. I have to also thank them for the times they have stopped me from doing something stupid.

OZ 41 ANNO VII - 23 SEPTEMBER 2016 E.V.

Freedom Requires Discipline

Brother Philip Tripp

It is often said that both individual and collective freedom is an important focus for those that practice Thelema. I can see that this is certainly true. For the past year I have reflected deeply on this idea of freedom and what exactly we mean when we say it.

Is the Thelemic concept of freedom different to the ordinary meaning of that word? Does a Thelemite have a different notion of freedom to that of the common man? My conclusion is that indeed he does. And I would formulate the distinction thusly. The common man thinks of freedom and he thinks that if he had freedom he could do what he likes, where he likes, when he likes, with whomever he likes and to whoever he likes. To the Thelemite freedom is a path that requires discipline, freedom indeed must be earned. Now many would say: What?! Have you gone mad?! How could this possibly be seen as freedom? What has discipline to do with freedom? Is not discipline entirely antithetical to freedom? Well the truth that Thelemites come to understand over time is that in fact: No!! That in fact those kind of responses are irrational and poorly thought through and demonstrate an untrained mind that is loose and given to meaningless drivel!

A brief tour through many of the ancient wisdom traditions of our world will show that there is a common base, a common ethic indeed, identified for those aspirants that wish to 'rise on the planes' as it were and achieve liberation in this very life. In the vedic wisdom of India the 'yamas' and 'niyamas' are prescribed as the first two limbs of yoga, setting out a moral code of ethical disciplines for the yogi to undertake before proceeding to the higher yogas of pranayama, asana, sense-withdrawal, concentration, contemplation and finally Samadhi. In the Buddhist tradition there is the notion of 'sila' or moral conduct which is prescribed as the foundational step that is required prior to entering into meditation practice. A universal principle that runs through all of this is that true freedom, true liberation is indeed earned by the aspirant by taking control of one's body and mind not by giving in to its every whim and desire in whimsical fashion.

Now let us not become confused here and assume we are speaking of self-denial! Many a lustful monk in a cave has fallen folly to this trip and suffered unduly for it! So be alert! For denial of one's earthly needs is no path to the freedom we are seeking. Self-acceptance is a virtue and to express oneself as one is, is no doubt part and parcel of truly being free, essential in fact! But yet the paradox still remains. That to truly be free, indeed to exert and express one's True Will, one must become free from his habitual patterns of behaviour, from the responses dictated by his conditioning, indeed from his own neuroses! And how is one to do this exactly? Well the ancient wisdom keepers, the sages and seers of the past, from whom the modern day Thelemite turns to for inspiration and guidance in these matters, have all invariably given the recommendation that freedom is EARNED through DISCIPLINE. Just as the kundalini Shakti is brought up from the base to the crown so too, the human experience must be elevated to the heights of real freedom through ardent practice to free oneself from the 'samskaras' the old traumas, the fears, the habituated ways of acting and seeing things the limited and conditioned responses of the human ego in order to express the True Will of the human personality that knows its own oneness with all that is and that, has been, and that could ever be. In this way we shine our own unique code out into the cosmos.

The Adam Kadmon, or the great cosmic man, is only fully formed when each human soul shines his light code in full freedom and radiance and thus completes the true collective cosmic ritual of the human race. By shining our own unique light as the stars that we each are we inspire others to become disciplined, to elevate themselves and to join in the celebration of human existence. Together then, will-directed creation is possible. Each in accordance with his own True Will. And here we must note that it is not a matter of one living his True Will at the behest of countless others being required to not live theirs. Ah! How could that be! We are such social creatures, we human beings. So in actual fact quite the contrary it is in practice, as we can only be free to the extent that those around us are free and hence the greatest act of service is to work for the emancipation and freedom of your fellow man. The march towards the True Will of freedom is as much a personal pursuit (read: to the Thelemite; an imperative!) as a collective one. And so, the practice of Thelema is not a solitary mission but a collective one. In undertaking this Great Work it is essential that a proper understanding is come to exactly what we mean by freedom and how it is earned. Of course it is a uniquely personal undertaking and it can take the aspirant to great lengths to make the progress required! But may none of us ever to the other say nay! To each may he hasten unto his work!

Through non-judgment, acceptance and community we can gather pace and proceed and exceed in this great and ancient endeavour. And the beauty of it is that it starts exactly where you are. One can proceed with a simple question. Does freedom mean sloppy clothing, a disordered home, chaotic personal relationships and finances and a generally haphazard and careless demeanour in one's life? Is that real freedom? Or is true freedom thoughtful and considered activity, spirited endeavour, orderly clothing and a disciplined approach to how to live one's life and work with others? What else does cultivated freedom look like to you in your life? I leave this stream of thought there for one to ponder.

OZ 45 ANNO VIII - 23 SEPTEMBER 2017 E.V.

ALAS! FOR THE KINGDOM WHEREIN ALL THESE ARE AT WAR

Battle of the Ants

BROTHER PHIL POPE

Spotlight on Brother Phil Pope, who after serving in the Navy for many years, joined the ranks of the Grand Master's Army and continues to do battle in the cause of Freedom.

Besides serving in the Electoral College for 11 years, Brother Phil has waged an ongoing campaign in his own community; fighting for the rights of returned service men and women in this country.

And if you think you have had a hard time getting temple equipment together.... worse things happen at sea.

Tell us about your early life and your first encounter with Thelema.

I grew up in Central Victoria. My parents had a cattle farm just outside of Bendigo. It was a great life as a kid, lots of freedom and time away from watchful adult eyes. Fishing, hunting, riding motorbikes and generally enjoying being a kid. My brother and I had discipline though. There were always chores on the farm and we spent a lot of time helping dad plough paddocks, run fences, get firewood; or helping mum skin rabbits, pluck chooks or tend the vege garden. In short, my brother and I were brought up to realise that you don't get a free ride. What you put into helping yourself in life determines what you will get out of it. I guess from a very early age, this upbringing gave me first-hand experience of the tenets of Thelema. My parents taught me that I could have great freedom, but if I screwed up, I would have to face the consequences and should do it without complaint. They also taught me that without the discipline to work and do things for yourself, you get nothing in life. Of course, it was not until I took the Minerval and started working through the OTO degree system that I heard these concepts explicitly expressed and given a name. I had, prior to joining the Order, read many of Crowley's works but Thelema did not really 'click' for me as an expression for my life and upbringing until my experience of the degrees.

You served for a long time in the navy, are the rumours true that you had a fully operational Golden Dawn Temple on board one of your ships?

I must admit, this question gave me a chuckle. Many happy memories that I am willing to share over a drink at OTO functions. Some of you at the 11th AUGL Anniversary will remember the story of the ill-advised attempts to make a Mars Incense in a closed air-conditioned environment and the subsequent panic as the hands were called to fire-fighting stations. Yes, some friends and I did have a functional temple on HMAS Melbourne (Aircraft Carrier). It was not an official G.D. Temple though. We were a collection of sailors that discovered in each other, a mutual interest in the esoteric and decided to start working rituals found in works by Aleister Crowley, Israel Regardie, Franz Bardon and a host of other authors. We were very eclectic and by necessity, resourceful. (I still have all my old elemental weapons made from whatever we could scrounge on a ship in the middle of the ocean. My ceremonial knife started life as a table knife nicked from the galley that I shaped over many nights with a whetstone, the handle made from a Telephone Exchange cotton cleaning tube and blackened with a mixture of parade gloss boot polish and yellow rubber glue.) Hiding ritual robes, weapons and books was a constant challenge also. We very quickly learnt the fine art of creating a temple in the mind and holding that image throughout a ritual. Up in the ships Radar Dome we would set up for a ritual, one of us would duck down to the bridge and check the ships heading on the compass, which would then give us our co-ordinates for the ritual. No matter the ship would change directions several times during the ritual. We had fixed the position of East, created our mental universe and did not give a thought or care for what the mundane world was doing around us for the duration of the rite. We were limited with temple furnishings as well, so we would discuss in detail, to build up a shared visualised image of things like the pillars Jachin and Boaz beforehand and then hold that mental image of them in place in the Dome until we finished. The ship acquired a reputation for being haunted amongst some crew members unlucky enough to be on deck in the middle of the night while we, under cover of darkness, in the catch nets below the flight deck were practising the fine art of vibrating divine names. When in harbour we spent time in temples, monasteries and sought out any occult bookstores or supply shops we could find. When in Sydney, we drove regularly out past Audley to the Royal National Park. We had a few secluded spots near creeks and rivers to conduct ritual work.

There's a great photo of you in the navy, reading an Alchemical text and giving the middle finger salute to the photographer, did the other blokes you served with think you were weird, or was it par for the course?

Definitely not par for the course. A lot of people avoided me as a weirdo, although my texta drawn image of the Goat of Mendes on my canvas tool bag probably did not help; I never had any tools stolen though. Having said that, I did have and still do, quite a few friends from the Navy who are not into the Occult but did not let my interests faze them. The finger photo was more a playful expression of the fact that I hate getting my photo taken, especially when in dress uniform, than annoyance at being busted reading an occult book. I had to edit out the non-occultist beside me in the picture though as I have lost contact with him, so cannot ask permission for it to be published with his image in it. For the record, the book was The Alchemists Handbook by Frater Albertus. My love of Alchemy started with school day obsessions with science and chemistry which nowadays has morphed into a fascination with art of alcohol distillation and ageing. A purely academic fascination of course.

How did you come to the OTO?

Some years after I had left the Navy, one of my friends who was part of the temple on HMAS Melbourne introduced me to an old mate of his from his recruit school days. David B, yes folks, the current Master of Templar Camp is also ex-Navy.

David and I formed a strong friendship which endures to this day. Some considerable number of years back he invited me to his 40th Birthday party (he will get me back for this comment. He is always quick to remind me I am several months older than him). At this party, I met our current Grand Master Shiva X° (then Frater Superiors Representative for Australia), and the multi-talented artist, Barry Hale. We instantly found a rapport with each other and I remember talking to them about my interest in trying to find musical note correspondences in the Enochian Alphabet with a view to playing the Calls of the Aeythers on an instrument. I am thoroughly ecstatic that Barry has taken that concept to heights way beyond my limited imaginings with his NOKO performances. I also remain humbled to consider both these men my firm friends. At that time, I was hosting a computer Bulletin Board System (BBS) called Alchemy that was a part of several FIDOnet Occult mail systems (an early precursor to the internet). I mainly hosted occult material for free download public access. GM Shiva put me in touch with the OTO Archivist in Australia and Bill Heidrick from the USA Grand Lodge. With the files those two people gave me, I started hosting a dedicated OTO and Thelemic Section on my BBS and maintained a close and valued friendship with Shiva and Barry.

In early 2000 David, Shiva and Barry approached me for advice on running a gathering in Canberra as they knew I had co-hosted the Australian Wicca Conference in 1994. This OTO gathering was duly held at a venue in the bush near the Cotter and Murrumbidgee Rivers. I was working at the Canberra Deep Space Communications Complex that weekend so I decided to drop by and catch up with my Order friends on the Saturday night. Unbeknownst to me, they were holding Minerval Initiations that night and I was invited to take the Minerval Degree. I took the plunge and have not regretted it since.

There are a fair share of ex-service and active military in the Order, is there a natural affinity do you think?

Oh definitely. The military trains you to respond to discipline while also taking responsibility for yourself and all those around you. There are consequences for failure, right up to and include death of you and your unit if you screw up, so it is a high stakes environment. You learn to be resourceful, fit and decisive. All of these qualities are embodied in the Order. It is run along quasi-military lines. Discipline is evident throughout the structure and taking responsibility for self, fellow brethren and local body or chapter are paramount for individual growth within the Order. The Order also encourages self-development while impressing that there are no shortcuts. This is totally resonant with military life for those that wish to progress.

You've been actively involved in working with returned veterans and servicemen. How well does this country treat those who've served in the armed forces? What sort of challenges do these men and women face when they return to civilian life?

Unfortunately this country does not do that well. The men and women that go into theatres of operations, do so at the behest of the government of the day to sort out problems that stem from failures of diplomacy by those same governments. The Political Leaders are always quick to jump in front of the camera to wave our troops off, or stand beside people with racks of medals on ANZAC Day to help bolster their election chances. It is very rare we see them lining up for a photo next to the coffins coming back draped in the Australian Flag or hanging out in the amputee or psych wards in the hospitals though. There is also a disconnect between the community at large and members of the Defence Force. Just to show how wide that is, how many reading this now can name a Base, Province or Valley in Afghanistan that we have been fighting in for the past 11 years? (Without resorting to google that is). Members of the public are more familiar with WW1 and WW2 than more recent conflicts. This does not make it easy for Vets to feel part of the community when they transition to Civvy Street. I have encountered many people that think the last war we were in was Vietnam and so they question young men and women as to their right to wear medals. This is particularly hurtful and frustrating for younger veterans.

Many Vets, if they have not already lost partner and family due to the distance and length of deployments, come home to a family that is used to doing everything at home for themselves, budgets, home and car maintenance etc. New friends and social groups that don't really know the deployed partner. The returning Vet has to try and fit back into a well-oiled machine that seems to have no need of assistance, or place for them. That coupled with the effects of deployment, both physical and mental can lead to marital breakdowns, homelessness and depressive illnesses. Jobs are hard to get and hold. The Military has a fairly rigid and unforgiving standard of work ethic and culture that everybody within is subject to so it seems the norm. This can lead to some pretty sharp things being said that often leads to a disciplinary visit to the manager's office. Apparently my critique of a really badly loomed set of cables in an electronics rack many years ago upset my co-worker to the point of a complaint being laid. How was I to know my constructive and helpful 'you really should lace up that bunch of cunts properly instead of the half-arsed way you did it' would be considered offensive and condescending.

The Military expends a lot of time and money training its members to fit in to a well-oiled machine that is purpose built to kill and deny the enemy. When someone leaves the Military, they expend exactly zero time and money training you to fit back into Civilian life. There are services and help available to ex-defence force members but they are not widely advertised and many remain unaware of what is available. The Department of Veterans Affairs does not have enough base level staff to quickly process claims by Vets, leading to long delays, frustration and in some cases death. It is unfortunate that DVA is colloquially known as DDD. (Delay, Deny, Die). Most of the work is being done by ESOs (Ex Service Organisations), like the RSL, Legacy, Soldier On, Wounded Warriors and Over-Reach. Last year alone veteran groups estimate we lost 84 to suicide. It is only recently that the government has commissioned studies into this issue. Veteran Suicides are not officially tracked as a separate statistic by the government. The rate for 2011 to 2015 was found to be twice that of the general population in Australia.

You've talked about the resilience of the human spirit in these cases, are you optimistic about the future of humankind?

I am optimistic for the future. Centuries ago life was hard and centred around existence. As a species we evolve, we find better ways to exist that give us more time for abstract thought.

Many use this time to dream up and implement ways we can become more caring and more involved in the world around us. Humans dare to dream and those dreams manifest into ways that enrich us all, in terms of medicine, ethical behaviours, science, education. We are on a journey, to where I do not know, maybe the journey is the end in itself. One thing I do know, the key teachings of Thelema have a very important role in that journey. The rights of the individual and freedom are paramount to the collective good of the species, and as a collective we are all on that journey together. I look around me and see good in people all the time, little random acts of kindness everywhere, I look to the stars and get a thrill as to where the evolution of humanity will take us.

If you wish to support our returning Veterans, please contact us via:

soldiersoffreedom@otoaustralia.org.au

OZ 47 ANNO V$_{IV}$ - 21ST MARCH, 2018 E.V.

APOKALYPSIS 418

The Temple of Christ, the Angelic priesthood and the Great Return of the Queen of Heaven

STEPHEN J. KING

'And there shall be no man in the tabernacle of the congregation when he goeth in to make an atonement in the holy place...' - Leviticus 16:17 (*KJV*)

'And they that walk upon their hands shall build the holy place.' - Liber CDXVIII, 16th Aethyr

'I understand that He - whoever, whatever He may be - is He for whom we all so long had waited.' - Khaled Khan,[1] *The Heart of the Master*

'And ye shall be hated of all men for my name's sake: but he that shall endure unto the end, the same shall be saved.' - Matthew 10:22 (*KJV*)

---

[1] [Aleister Crowley]

Do what thou wilt shall be the whole of the Law.

If Lutheran theologian and scholar Ernst Käsemann's dictum 'apocalyptic was the mother of all Christian theology'[2] holds, its corollary for the New Aeon of θέλημα might be '*The Vision and the Voice* is a primary scriptural source for the theogony of the Supernal Triad of the Crowned and Conquering Child, Chaos and Babalon.'[3] The latter remark is as understated as the former exaggerated. Yet it was just that theology which opened up this—*our*—theogony.

It was Aleister Crowley's Tunisian disciple Gerard Aumont, in all likelihood working under Crowley's direct supervision and oversight, who first described *The Vision and the Voice* as an Apocalypse:

> 'We are in possession of a certain mystical document which we may describe briefly, for convenience sake, as an Apocalypse of which we hold the keys, thanks to the intervention of the Master who has appeared at this grave conjuncture of Fate. This document consists of a series of visions, in which we hear the various Intelligences whose nature it would be hard to define, but who

---

[2] E. Käsemann, 'The Beginnings of Christian Theology,' *Journal for Theology and the Church* 6 (1969) p. 40.
[3] Frater V.V., 'Editor's Introduction,' *The Vision and the Voice with Commentary and Other Papers*, The Equinox IV:2 (1998) p. x.

are at the very least endowed with knowledge and power far beyond anything that we are accustomed to regard as proper to the human race.'[4]

When these words were penned in 1924 e.v., reference to *The Vision and the Voice* as an Apocalypse (*Gk.* apokalypsis, 'revelation') would have indeed been a 'convenience' given the (then) ambiguity of the term. This was long before the discoveries of the Dead Sea Scrolls (1945 e.v.) and the Nag Hammadi Library (1946–56 e.v.). Up until their discoveries and related research there was no scholarly consensus on what an apocalypse actually was: whether it referred to a genre of literature, millenarian belief, or simply revealed texts in general. A number of early works (including many of the Jewish apocalypses) do not bear the title—the first work to do so was the New Testament Book of Revelation—while others bear literary and narrative traits of more than one or composite genres.

It was not until 1979 that a now commonly accepted if broad definition of an apocalypse was applied in biblical criticism: 'a genre of revelatory literature with a narrative framework, in which a revelation is mediated by an

---

[4] 'The Three Schools of Magick (I),' in A. Crowley, *Magick Without Tears* eds. King and Warren, in preparation. Although identifying the unnamed 'mystical document' as *The Vision and the Voice* would be obvious to any serious student of Thelema, it was explicitly referenced as such in the first edition of *Magick Without Tears* by the editor, Karl Germer.

otherworldly being to a human recipient, disclosing a transcendent reality which is both temporal, in so far as it envisages eschatological salvation, and spatial insofar as it involves another, supernatural world.'[5] *The Vision and the Voice* meets this criteria in a manner uniquely set apart from the other sacred writings or holy books of θέλημα. It was therefore designated a publication of A∴A∴ in 'Class AB,' i.e. revealed *and* scholarly. In that the narrative framework of *The Vision and the Voice* is both temporal *and* spatial, the revealed transcendent reality speaks directly to the two teaching Orders of θέλημα, the temporal Ordo Templi Orientis and the spatial (or sempiternal) A∴A∴. The exquisite beauty of the *The Vision and the Voice* is that it shows the Unity of their respective natural and spiritual worlds in the new 'theogony of the Supernal Triad' and its Temple of Initiation.[6]

The Elizabethan enochian magic of Dr. John Dee and Edward Kelley that was employed by Aleister Crowley and Victor Neuburg for *The Vision and the Voice* is now widely known.[7] For our purposes, without in any way

---

[5] John J. Collins (ed.), *Semeia 14: Apocalypse: The Morphology of a Genre* (1979), quoted in John J. Collins, *The Apocalyptic Imagination: an Introduction to Jewish Apocalyptic Literature* 3rd ed. (2016) p. 5. See also *The Oxford Handbook of Apocalyptic Literature* ed. John J. Collins (2014).
[6] This Unity is discussed in the forthcoming book, Shiva X°, *Aspiring to the Holy Order, Book One: Hall of the Two Truths*, in preparation.
[7] For a brief and balanced assessment of Dee and Kelley's enochian system see Geoffrey James' Preface to *The Enochian Evocation of Dr John Dee* ed. G. James (1984), pp. xiii–xxvii.

underplaying its extraordinary canon and magical, theological (angelology), structural, linguistic and narrative depth, it is sufficient to say that in seeking the elusive *Book of Enoch* (also referred to as *1 Enoch* or the *Ethiopic Book of Enoch*), attributed to the biblical prophet Enoch[8] who 'walked with God: and he *was* not; for God took him' (Genesis 5:24 *KJV*), the angels instead revealed to Dee the revered Book of Life. This was the transcript and template of creation Enoch is said to have read from in heaven. This remarkable text, named by the angels to Dee as the *Holy Book of Loagaeth* ('speech from God'), would form the basis of the enochian system, of calling forth the angels and entering the gates of heaven.

The Hermetic Order of the Golden Dawn developed their own enochian system from the Dee and Kelley corpus largely concentrated in their 'The Book of the Concourse of the Forces.'[9] The major GD innovation was the rearrangement of the Watchtowers in line with Dee's Reformed Great Table of Raphael—for some a hotly debated and controversial revision—with the further addition of GD elemental attributions, correspondences and

---

[8] More likely a product of the Babylonian captivity circa 600 BCE. An English translation can be found in J.H. Charlesworth's two volume *The Old Testament Pseudepigrapha* (1983-85). The R.H. Charles 1893 annotated translation is widely available in print and online.

[9] Book Nine in the Israel Regardie edited *The Golden Dawn* (numerous editions and printings, 1971 onward) or Volume 10 of Regardie's *The Complete Golden Dawn System of Magic* (1984).

colour scales. The GD utilized the post-Dee *Book H* or *Clavicula Tabularum Enochi* which remains of uncertain authorship and provenance.[10] The GD also developed their own method of applying Dee's 48 Calls (from the *Book of Loagaeth* and originally intended for the 49 day Gebofal ritual) to the Watchtowers, and devised an enochian form of

---

[10] Also referred to as the *Booke of Invocations or Calls*, the *Tabula Bonorum Angelorum Invocationes* or *The Book of Supplications or Invocations*. For a discussion, see the Introduction to *Practical Angel Magic of John Dee's Enochian Tables: from four previously unpublished manuscripts on Angel Magic being a complete transcription of Tabula Bonorum Angelorum Invocationes in manuscripts BL Sloane 307 and 3821 and Bodleian D 1067 and D 1363 as used by Wynn Westcott, Alan Bennett, Reverend Ayton, Frederick Leigh Gardner, and other senior members of the Hermetic Order of the Golden Dawn*, ed. S. Skinner and D. Rankine (2004). See also 'The Hermetic Order of the Golden Dawn and The Book of the Concourse of the Forces' in A. Leitch, *The Essential Enochian Grimoire: An Introduction to Angel Magick from Dr. John Dee to the Golden Dawn*, pp. 57- 66. Leitch discusses the Reformed Table pp. 21-25. The Reformed Table as published by Leitch does not correspond exactly to that of Skinner and Rankine (their version includes a photograph of their mss. source). Nor do these correspond to those published in Regardie's *Golden Dawn* series or in Crowley's *The Equinox* I:VII, Plate III facing p. 234 (1912). As Joseph H. Peterson remarked, 'In [the GD] adapting Dee's system, various additions, omissions and mistakes were made. This departure was compounded by uncritical, although imaginative, treatments of the Golden Dawn and Crowley material by some authors. The net result is a maze of misinformation,' in *John Dee's Five Books of Mystery: Original Sourcebook of Enochian Magic from the collected works known as Mysteriorum Libri Quinique*, ed. J.H. Peterson, Introduction p. 3 (2003). This 'departure' has resulted in two broad schools of contemporary enochian practitioners, aptly described by Leitch as 'Dee-Purist' and 'Golden Dawn Neo-Enochiana.' The Thelemic practitioner schooled in the *The Vision and the Voice* apokalypsis represents their dialectical synthesis in what could be called

chess. Importantly, for the GD each of the 156 squares comprising the Enochian Tablets was a three-dimensional Pyramid, the whole referred to as the City of the Pyramids. In the transcendent reality of *The Vision and the Voice*, the City of the Pyramids was also the Supernal Binah, where the Masters of the Temple were entombed, with 156 the sacred number of BABALON, attributed to Binah. (For Crowley's comments upon the same, see below.)

Crowley codified some of the GD material into his Liber LXXXIV vel Chanokh ('The Book of Enoch').[11] He also intended to cover other Dee material such as the *Heptarchia Mystica* and *Loagaeth*, but these later studies never materialized. The GD system proper was the methodology employed for *The Vision and the Voice* as described by Crowley himself in his *Confessions*.[12]

The relationship of θέλημα to the enochian Watchtowers and Aethyrs is unique. In his Commentary to the 9th Aethyr of *The Vision and the Voice* Crowley wrote:

> BABALON = 156 = 12 x 13, which is the Formula of the Four Watchtowers of the Universe. These Watchtowers are composed of truncated Pyramids, each one concealing a Sphinx. They contain the

---

New Aeon Enochian.
[11] *The Equinox* I:VII and VIII (1912).
[12] Excerpted and adapted for the Introduction to *The Vision and the Voice* in *The Equinox* IV:II (1998).

Symbols of the Energies of the Four Elements. We may thus say that as each Watchtower contains 12 x 13 Pyramids, BABALON is indicated as Sakti. For the Elements are the manifested powers of the All-Father. Again, we may consider the Watchtowers as the 'City of the Pyramids' though in a sense less exalted than that usually implied in these Visions.[13]

The Vision and the Voice gives its own commentary about the Aethyrs and θέλημα:

But the knowledge of the Aethyrs is deeper than the knowledge of the Sephiroth, for that in the Aethyrs is the knowledge of the Aeons, and of θέλημα. And to each shall it be given according to his capacity.[14]

The enochian system as revealed to Dee is intimately connected to the New Testament Book of Revelation. Such a connection in these source texts helps to frame our reading of *The Vision and the Voice* given its apocalyptic, epistolary and prophetic nature, its enochian praxis and the relationship of θέλημα and its theogony to Revelation mysticism and criticism. While an analysis of the Dee enochian corpus to Revelation greatly exceeds the scope of this paper, it should be sufficient to note that Dee, an avid and devout millenarian, believed the true magical art the

---

[13] *The Equinox* IV:II p. 173 note 1.
[14] 12th Aethyr, Ibid. p. 153.

angels sought to teach would herald the coming of the Apocalypse. The *Book of Loagaeth,* said to be the Book of Life (mentioned seven times in Revelation)[15] and referred to as 'perfyted in the workmanship of him, which hath *sealed* it,'[16] has been identified with Revelation's 'book written within and on the backside, sealed with seven seals' (Rev: 5:1 *KJV*).[17] Out of *Loagaeth,* declared the Angel Uriel to Dee, 'shall be restored the holy books... And herein shall be deciphred perfect truth from imperfect falshode, True religion from fals and damnable errors...Which when it hath spred a While, THEN COMMETH THE ENDE.'[18] The 24 Seniors of the enochian Watchtowers are the 'four and twenty elders' that sit around the throne (Rev: 4:4 *KJV*), while *Liber Mysteriorum Secundus,* which is an exposition of the Sigillum Dei Aemeth, derived some of its practical formulae from the 7 trumpets and 7 Angels of Rev: 8:2. These few examples highlight not only the revelatory, but

---

[15] Revelation 3:5, 13:8, 17:8, 20:12, 20:15, 21:27 and 22:19.
[16] 'Quinti libri Mysteriorum Appendix.' *John Dee's Five Books of Mystery* p. 395. [Italics mine]
[17] See for example *The Essential Enochian Grimoire*, pp. 13–14.
[18] 'Quinti libri Mysteriorum Appendix.' *John Dee's Five Books of Mystery* p. 395. The angels explained to Dee how the *Book of Loagaeth* embodied the seven days of creation in Genesis and represented the entire span of history and knowledge from creation to destruction. The link to the Genesis creation story further links the enochian system with the symbolism of the Jerusalem Temple while the 'holy books' are the sacred writings of θέλημα. The 'ende' is that Abomination of Desolation, the New Aeon. See above.

the practical and doctrinal import of the Apocalypse of John to the enochian system.

Importantly, Dee's manifesto for a universal and magical science, the *Monas Hieroglyphica*,[19] references Rev:4 in theorem XXIV. This is the chapter of Revelation where an angel invites John the Divine to seership of the secrets of Heaven and is the point in the narrative just before the breaking of the seven seals and the appearance of the Four Horsemen of the Apocalypse. Deborah Harkness has suggested Dee's *Monas Hieroglyphica* 'was his attempt to take mankind to that point in cosmic history and that level of cosmic ontology through a universal, exegetical science so that a door would open in the heavens and further marvels could be revealed.'[20] It is tempting to conclude that Dee saw himself as a modern day John the Divine.

---

[19] See Dame Frances Yates' classic work *The Rosicrucian Enlightenment* (1972) for a discussion on the significance of the symbol and theorems of Dee's Hieroglyphic Monad. While the Yates study has aged in terms of contemporary rosicrucian scholarship, the thesis concerning the Monad is compelling. As an example of contemporary esoteric scholarship on the Hieroglyphic Monad and its relationship to core Golden Dawn doctrine, see for example T. Burns and J.A. Moore, 'The Hieroglyphic Monad of John Dee
Theorems I-XVII: A Guide to the Outer Mysteries' in the *Journal of the Western Mystery Tradition*
No. 13, Vol. 2. Vernal Equinox 2007
(http://jwmt.org/v2n13/sign.html).
[20] D.E. Harkness, *John Dee's Conversations with Angels: Cabala, Alchemy and the End of Nature* (1999) p.90.

From the perspective of Scientific Illuminism, Dee was successful. The opening of the *secret door* of the heavens and those 'further marvels' are the revelations of θέλημα and *The Vision and the Voice*.[21] For while the enochian angels certainly foretold the end times they also foresaw the new: 'But I begynne new worldes, new people, new kings, & new knowledge of a new Gouernment;'[22] 'New worlds, shall

---

[21] In the cosmic historical cycles of the A∴A∴ of 600 and 300 year currents and sub-currents respectively, Crowley attributed Dee and Kelley to the 300 year sub-current prior to Aiwass and To Mega Therion. See the Commentary to Liber LXV:IV:22, *The Equinox* IV:1 (1996) p.143. In Chapter 187 of *Liber Aleph*, Crowley commented 'This nevertheless is sure (or the learned Casaubon, publishing the Record of that Word with the Magician Dee, sayeth falsely) that an Angel did declare unto Kelly the Very Axiomata of our Law of Thelema, in good Measure, and plainly; but Dee, afflicted by the Fixity of his Tenets that were of the Slave-Gods, was wroth, and by his Authority prevailed upon the other, who was indeed not wholly perfected as an Instrument, or the World ready for that Sowing.' See *Liber Aleph* (1991) p. 187. For the 'door that would open in the heavens' or the secret door, see AL:III:38. On the currents and sub-currents of A∴A∴, see the forthcoming title by Shiva X°, *Aspiring to the Holy Order, Book Two: The Flight of the Bennu Bird*, in preparation.

[22] King Bynepor (Thursday, Jupiter) from the Heptarchia Mystica, 20 November 1582.

spring of these. New manners: strange men;'²³ 'The old ways cease, the new begin.'²⁴

The Angels of Dee and Kelley in some measure foresaw the New Aeon as had the seers and prophets of the Old. It is not surprising that key among these prophecies is as we have seen, Revelation in the New Testament canon, while in the Old Testament, the Book of Daniel stands out. *The Vision*

---

²³ The Angel Medicina Dei (i.e. Raphael, 'Healing of God' referred by Dee in his journals as Medicina Dei 'Medicine of God'), 24 March 1583. While what follows must be classed as highly speculative (the generous reader may afford it intuitive status!), in the change in Angelic discourse from 'new' to 'strange' may be prophecy of the remarkable and highly influential current brought into the world by the great Jewish mystic Sabbatai Tsevi, 'the Messiah of 1666,' at the height of revived millenarian fervour. Sabbatai Tsevi advocated and practiced the doctrine of *ma'asim zarim* (mystical 'strange acts') incorporating antinomian sexual practices and other strange and seemingly heretical behaviours. The movement flourished in Jewish circles even after Tsevi's conversion to Islam (with a few hundred of his followers). Sabbatianism in turn influenced the Frankist school which had significant bearing on the famed Asiatic Brethren, an Order generally held to have had a seminal influence on western esoteric currents such as the Hermetic Brotherhood of Luxor, the Golden Dawn and Ordo Templi Orientis. With the latter embracing θέλημα, the new and universal Law, religious current and related movement the angels prophesied was made manifest. I am indebted to my Brother in strangeness, Barry William Hale the Apocalyptic, for introducing me to the teachings of the remarkable Sabbatai Tsevi - verily, a strange man of kindred transgression. The doctrine of *ma'asim zarim* should be kept in mind when 'strange' is referred to in the Holy Books of θέλημα.

²⁴ The Angel Michael (i.e. 'Who is like God' Fortitudo Dei), 23 May 1583. (The selected quotes in footnotes 15–17 should be studied in relation to the function of these Angels in the enochian hierarchy and revelations.)

and the Voice brings to bear Daniel's 'the abomination that maketh desolate' (Daniel 12:11, *KJV*), something pointedly referenced at various times in the scriptural narrative of *The Vision and the Voice*.²⁵ While a standard exegesis of Daniel points to that 'abomination' as the desecration of the (Jerusalem) Temple by 'the wicked King' Antiochus Ephipanes (I Maccabees I:10-28), as J. Daniel Gunther remarked:

> The biblical prophets of the 'old time' proclaimed that they beheld the 'end of days,' and in this they were partially correct. They had the vision of the end of *their own* time - when the sacrifice would indeed be removed from the Temple, when sacrifice would be declared abrogate and the oblation cease.²⁶

Gunther's description is telling. The *new time* is θέλημα and it is revealed in *The Vision and the Voice* which *is steeped*

---

²⁵ Compare with Daniel 9:27 and 11.31. See also the Olivet Discourse, Matthew 24, Mark 13:14, AL:III:19, and the 26th, 21st and 16th Aethyrs. As J. Daniel Gunther comments, 'There is a far deeper meaning of the Abomination of Desolation that is understood by Initiates. Aspirants should carefully study Liber VII and Liber CDXVIII' [i.e. *The Vision and the Voice*], J. D. Gunther, *Initiation in the Aeon of the Child*, p. 31 (2009).

²⁶ *Initiation in the Aeon of the Child*, p. 30. See Daniel 9:27 'And he shall make a firm covenant with many for one week: and in the midst of the week he shall cause the sacrifice and the oblation to cease; and upon the wing of abominations shall come one that maketh desolate; and even unto the full end, and that determined, shall wrath be poured out upon the desolate.' See also Daniel 11:31 and 12:11.

in Temple symbolism, a Key to its reading. As Aaron Leitch matter of factly put it, 'you might say that if the *Book of the Law* were Thelema's Torah, then *The Vision and the Voice* would be Thelema's Talmud.'[27] In that '*talmūd*' תַּלְמוּד means 'instruction, learning' - he has a point. 'This book of the law shall not depart out of thy mouth; but thou shalt meditate therein day and night, that thou mayest observe to do according to all that is written therein: for then thou shalt make thy way prosperous, and then thou shalt have good success' Joshua 1:8 *KJV*. The Key to that meditation is *The Vision and the Voice*.

If *The Vision and the Voice* is steeped in Temple symbolism (that is, the Jerusalem Temple and specifically, the cult of the First Temple), moreso is Revelation, which as we have already seen has strong associations with both θέλημα and Dee's enochian. Much of this can be explained by the ubiquity of Temple imagery in western magic, alchemy and qabalah. This is so deep and intrinsic a symbolic or archetypal template that it can get overlooked or remain unrealized (unconscious) as the source *Imago* in the western esoteric tradition.[28] Likewise, the Temple can be forgotten,

---

[27] *The Essential Enochian Grimoire*, p. 67.
[28] While digressionary to this paper, it is no coincidence that Crowley's spiritual biography detailing his progress through the grades of A∴A∴ (mystically encountered in *The Vision and the Voice*) was called 'The Temple of Solomon the King' or that he reconstituted the Order of Knights Templar - with its historical Temple links and later Freemasonic Temple and Templar lore - in the form of Ordo Templi Orientis (OTO). In enochian magic, the archangel Michael revealed the magical

trivialised or taken for granted amidst the tradition's evolutionary and syncretic blending with classical paganism, hermeticism, and other more modern and universal currents. Yet the Temple remains a structural semiotic Key. The implications of a Temple setting have consequences for how we read Dee, and for that matter, *The Vision and the Voice* and the *new* Temple. As theologian Margaret Barker astutely put it:

> ...the original gospel message was about the temple, not the corrupted temple of Jesus' own time, but the original temple which had been destroyed some 600 years[29] earlier...The restoration of the first temple was the hope of the first Christians, and to set them, their writings and presentation of Jesus anywhere else than in the temple setting distorts what they were preaching and misrepresents the original gospel. *The Book of Revelation is the key to understanding early Christianity. Because it is steeped in temple imagery*, most people find it an opaque and impossible text, but people who thought in this 'temple' manner also wrote and read the rest of the New Testament. If we read it in any other way, we are reading our own meaning into the texts and are

---

ring he had given Solomon, commanding Dee to use the same, 'Without this, thou shalt do nothing...' (14 March, 1582), See John Dee's *Five Books of Mystery*, pp. 78–79.

[29] See note 21.

not connecting to the original teachings of the Church.'³⁰

The early Christians regarded *The Book of Enoch* (*1 Enoch*) - recalling that the intent of Dee's enochian work was to obtain this text - as scripture. Importantly, in *The Vision and the Voice* 4th Aethyr it is written 'And in the Book of Enoch was first given the wisdom of the New Aeon.' The Dead Sea Scrolls indicate *The Book of Enoch* was one of the most widely used books in Jesus' times. In one passage it recounts how after the judgement of fallen angels the Lord of the sheep would carry away the Temple and set up something greater in its place (1 Enoch 90.28-29). It would have been a common expectation in and around Palestine at the time of Jesus that the Messiah to come (the Good Shepherd) would destroy and rebuild the Temple. In John 2.19 Jesus claims that prophecy of Enoch for himself when he said 'Destroy this temple, and in three days I will raise it up' *KJV*. This would become one of the two charges laid against Jesus (Mark 14:58 KJV). The other likewise relates to his claiming of the prophecy of Enoch - that of being the Messiah (Matthew 26:63).³¹ Critically, this gives us two of the most important but probably more overlooked attributes

---

³⁰ Margaret Barker, *Temple Theology: an introduction* (2004) p.1. [Italics mine]

³¹ In responding to the charge Mark 14:62 differs from Matthew 26:64 with the addition of two important words: 'I am.'

and expectations of the Messiah - to destroy and rebuild the Temple.

We may recall that it was on the *third day* of the writing of *The Book of the Law* the prophet was adjured to 'Get the stele of revealing itself; set it in thy secret temple' (AL:III:10) and told 'That stele they shall call the Abomination of Desolation' (AL:III:19).[32] In *The Vision and the Voice* 26th Aethyr comes the vision of that Stele of Revealing signifying the death of the past Aeon. 'So when you see the abomination of desolation spoken of by the prophet Daniel, standing in the holy place (let the reader understand), then let those who are in Judea flee to the mountains' Matthew 24:15-16. Verily and Amen.

The 'holy place' is a direct reference to the Temple. The holy place was separated from the 'most holy' or 'most holy place' - the holy of holies - by the Temple veil. The Temple replicated the Tabernacle of Moses, the tent that housed the Ark of the Covenant: 'And thou shalt hang up the vail under the taches, that thou mayest bring in thither within the vail the ark of the testimony: and the vail shall divide unto you between the holy *place* and the most holy' Exodus 26:33 *KJV*. The veil therefore concealed the ark and the chariot throne. Both the Temple and Tabernacle were microcosms of creation - but whereas the holy place was a *passive* holy,

---

[32] See note 25 and related text.

the most holy actively *imparted* holiness.[33] Only the High Priest entered the holy of holies, the second or *secret Temple* once a year on the Day of Atonement, 'But into the second *went* the high priest alone once every year, not without blood, which he offered for himself, and *for* the errors of the people' Hebrews 9:7 *KJV*.

Of the veil of the Temple, the Romano-Jewish historian Josephus (born to a priestly family) wrote: 'it was a Babylonian curtain, embroidered with blue, and fine linen, and scarlet, and purple: and of a contexture that was truly wonderful. Nor was this mixture of colours without its mystical interpretation: but was a kind of image of the universe' Of the War, Book V:5:4. Josephus went on to interpret the colours as signifying the elements, as did the Hellenistic Jewish philosopher Philo of Alexandria. In other words, the veil of the Temple represented matter and was the *boundary between heaven and earth*. To enter the holy of holies therefore, *was to enter heaven*. The vestments of the High Priest represented the veil ('For in the long garment was the whole veil' Wisdom 18:24 *KJV*) which he divested upon entering the holy of holies. Thus Jesus, described as the High Priest in Hebrews - 'But Christ being come an high priest of good things to come, by a greater and more perfect tabernacle, not made with hands, that is to say, not of this building' Heb. 9:11 *KJV* - is likened to the veil of the

---

[33] See for example Haggai 2 and Ezra 2.63 for discussion and distinction on 'holy' and 'most holy.'

Temple, 'By a new and living way, which he hath consecrated for us, through the veil, that is to say, his flesh' Heb 10:20 *KJV*. Beyond the veil the High Priest was in *heaven* and *divine*; a shining one robed in the garments of glory of the resurrection body. 'No man' but divine - 'And there shall be *no man* in the tabernacle of the congregation when he goeth in to make an atonement in the holy place...' Leviticus 16:17 *KJV*[34]

This followed a long tradition ranging from the shining Moses at Sinai (Exodus 34 29-30), to the veiling of the divine brilliance. Theodotus 38 says:

> A river goes from under the throne of Space and flows into the void of the creation, which is Gehenna, and it is never filled, though the fire flows from the beginning of creation. And Space itself is fiery. Therefore, he says, it has a veil in order that the things may not be destroyed by the sight of it. And only the archangel enters it, and to typify this the high priest every year enters the holy of holies.

In the early Hekhalot literature this originated with the veiling of the Father YHVH:

> The glorious king [i.e. YHVH] covers his face, otherwise the heaven or Arabot would burst open in

---

[34] [Italics mine]

the middle, because of the glorious brilliance, beautiful brightness, lovely splendour, and radiant praises of the appearance of the Holy One, Blessed by He. (3.En.22B.6)

And: 'R. Ishmael said: Metatron said to me: Come and I will show you the curtain (*pargod*) of the Omnipresent One, which is spread before the Holy One, blessed be he... (3.En.45.1.64).'

While *The Vision and the Voice* heralds a New Aeon where 'the Name יְהֹוָה is broken in a thousand pieces (against the Cubic Stone)' (30th Aethyr) and Jehovah himself bewails 'Woe, woe unto me! These are they that hear not prayer...Accursed am I unto the aeons' (26th Aethyr),[35] the brilliance of the Father - as distinct from that of Jehovah the jealous and ignorant demiurge - with its association to the Temple veil is a recurring theme:

> Verily, I say unto thee, many are the adepts that have looked upon the back parts of my father, and cried, 'our eyes fail before the glory of thy countenance.'
>
> And with that he gives the sign of the rending of the veil...

---

[35] See also the 16th Aethyr.

- 18th Aethyr[36]

For *the Temple veil has now become the Veil of the Abyss.* That the seers and priests and prophets like Ezekiel, Enoch and the authors of Revelation had extraordinary visions of the holy of holies - in some cases long after its furnishings had disappeared from the Temple - suggests in priestly practice and otherworldly visitation and vision the most holy could indeed traverse a threshold between heaven and earth, the human and the divine. That experience undergoes a systemic and aeonic transformation in θέλημα as revealed in *The Vision and the Voice* and other sacred writings.

Within the context of the Temple, reading θέλημα and *The Vision and the Voice* in particular take on extraordinary new dimensions. To revisit Daniel Gunther's comments quoted earlier:

> The biblical prophets of the 'old time' proclaimed that they beheld the 'end of days,' and in this they were partially correct. They had the vision of the end of *their own* time - when the sacrifice would indeed be removed from the Temple, when sacrifice would be declared abrogate and the oblation cease.[37]

While further reference to the Temple symbolism in θέλημα will be made, a full appreciation and study of

---

[36] See also Exodus 33:22–23.
[37] See note 26.

'Temple theology' in θέλημα greatly exceeds this paper's scope.[38] To speak plainly if perhaps over-simplistically, we may see in *The Vision and the Voice* the establishment of the new Temple and the worship of the true theogony, no longer the exclusive purview of the High Priest, but open to all aspirants to the Mysteries who genuinely pursue its Great Work.[39]

What is consistent in the old accounts of the prophets (for example 2 and 3 Enoch) is that beyond the veil of the Temple there would be an anointing, a vesting in garments of glory (the resurrection body) and the seer-prophet-priest would *become an Angel.* In Blessings 1QSb IV from the Dead Sea Scrolls is the tender and beautiful surviving fragment of an old hymn:

> May you be as an Angel of the Presence in the abode of holiness To the glory of the God of [Hosts]. May you attend upon the service in the temple of the Kingdom. And decree destiny in company with the Angels of the Presence.

This is a radical mysticism. If the priests of the Temple were angels, the High Priest would be their chief, the Mighty Angel, and if we treat the angels (the priests) as the host of

---

[38] This is however the special research interest of the Saint Augustine Theological Circle in the Australian section of Ecclesia Gnostica Catholica.
[39] See Liber X Porta Lucis 17–18.

heaven - the angelic hosts צבאות (sabaoth) - the High Priest must be the Lord of Hosts (hence Jesus was referred to *both* as Lord and High Priest).⁴⁰

The key is in the same hebrew word being used for 'angel' and 'messenger,' מלאך שליח (malak or malak yhvh - messenger of god). This allows us to reread scripture in terms of a tradition of angelic priests (for example, Malachai 2.7 'a priest... is the angel of the Lord of Hosts' KJV).⁴¹ 'The high priest was the chief of the angels, the Mighty Angel, the Great Angel. He was the key figure in the Book of Revelation, emerging from heaven, that is, from the holy of holies.'⁴² The high priest, resurrected and 'no man' beyond the veil, was an angel figure, the Son of God: 'Neither can they die any more: for they are equal unto the angels; and are the children of God, being the children of the resurrection' Luke 20:36 *KJV*.

In the Tarot of θέλημα, this has some bearing on the tarot card, Atu XX The Aeon. The Master Therion notes that in the Old Aeon this card was called The Angel or The Last

---

⁴⁰ This tradition continues in the worship of θέλημα where the OTO Priest of Ecclesia Gnostica Catholica is referred to in Liber XV, the OTO Gnostic Mass, as 'Priest *and* King' [Italics mine]. Likewise, the initiate of θέλημα must unite - achieve Knowledge and Conversation and Consummation - with the Angel, ultimately constituted a Master of *the Temple*. [Italics mine.]
⁴¹ I have substituted 'angel' for 'messenger.'
⁴² M. Barker, *The Revelation of Jesus Christ which God gave to him to show to his servants what must soon take place (Revelation 1.1)* (2000) p. 35. See for example Rev 10 1–11.

Judgment, and represented the destruction of the world by fire (ie. The New Aeon). The new card represents the Stele of Revealing (i.e. the Message of the Angel) for the 'children of the resurrection,' referred to in θέλημα as 'the children of the light.'[43] This repeats the theme mentioned above, that the new Temple and Angelic consummation are open to all aspirants to the Mysteries who genuinely pursue its Great Work.

The texts of the prophet Enoch are graphic. 'And the Lord said to Michael, "Go, and take Enoch from his earthly clothing and anoint him with my delightful oil and put on him the clothes of my Glory."... And I looked at myself and I had become one of his glorious ones' (2 Enoch 22).[44]

The anointing transforms the High Priest into a Messiah, a Christ (the anointed) - one who has been raised or resurrected:

> And as he prayed, the fashion of his countenance was altered, and his raiment was white and glistering. And, behold, there talked with him two men, which were Moses and Elias: Who appeared in glory, and spake of his decease which he should

---

[43] See *The Vision and the Voice* 19th, 9th and 8th Aethyrs. See also Liber XC Tzaddi 3, 27; AL I:5,12,15, Liber CCCLXX A'Ash 30. Compare to the lopsided 'children of light' of 1 Thessalonians 5:5. See also Ephesians 5:8.
[44] Compare with the doctrine of the chosen ones in θέλημα, see AL:I:15,17,31,51 and AL:II:19,25,53,65.

accomplish at Jerusalem. But Peter and they that were with him were heavy with sleep: and when they were awake, they saw his glory, and the two men that stood with him (Luke 9:29–32).

In the New Aeon, with the sacrifice abrogate and the oblation ceased, the new High Priest of the Temple is the Master of the Temple (Magister Templi), NEMO (no man):

> And he saith: No man hath beheld the face of my Father. Therefore he that hath beheld it is called NEMO... but there is one among them, which one I know not, that shall be a man - child, whose name shall be NEMO, when he hath beheld the face of the Father, and become blind.
>
> - *The Vision and the Voice*, 13th Aethyr[45]

The Angel of the Presence mentioned earlier, in hebrew *Mal'ak ha-Panim* or *Mal'akh ha-Panim*, מלאך הפ or the The Angel of *his* Presence (see for example Isaiah 63:9) is literally The Angel of the *Face* i.e. *those that have beheld the face (or presence) of the Father*.

The Vision and the Voice details the preparation (initiation) of the High Priest - who perfects the consummation with the praeterhuman Angel through the ordeal of the Abyss in

---

[45] This doctrine is referenced throughout this Aethyr. See also the 12th Aethyr.

this new Angelic priesthood. What distinguishes the new Temple from the old is that *all of us* may take up the inward journey to this exalted office. The sacrifice has been removed from the Temple and salvation is no longer through the blood of another but by your own in the Graal of BABALON. This is both the consecrated life of aspiration as well as the new worship and Sacrament of the Aeon:

> And this is the comedy of Pan, that is played at night in the thick forest. And this is the mystery of Dionysus Zagreus, that is celebrated upon the holy mountain of Kithairon. And this is the secret of the brothers of the Rosy Cross; and this is the heart of the ritual that is accomplished in the Vault of the Adepts that is hidden in the Mountain of the Caverns, even the Holy Mountain Abiegnus.
>
> - 12th Aethyr[46]

The Vision and the Voice shows the way, the truth and the life - 'for no man cometh unto the Father, but by me.'[47]

The Temple tradition continues in the fourfold method the Master employs tending to his disciples. Certain disciples

---

[46] Crowley commented 'All these Mysteries are taught in the O∴T∴O∴', *The Equinox* IV:2 p. 151.
[47] John 14:6. It is telling that the evangelist reflected on the Cleansing of the Temple (John 2:13-22) with the words 'But he spake of the temple of his body' (John 2:2).

are especially anointed to follow the Way of their Master, and to work and walk with that Messiah who anointed the Magister.[48] 'The Holy Oil is emblematic of Grace and the Chrism of the Holy One, a gift which originates from above... It was used only on those set apart for Holy Service. Those who have received this sacred anointing may come to perceive that this is the least merciful of all the Hierophantic methods of the Magister, for it unfailingly affirms that the one so anointed treads upon the Path that is both beautiful and terrible, the Path of sacred Service to Mankind that leads ultimately to the lonely frontier of the Abyss.'[49]

The original Temple veil, as matter, made visible what passed through it from beyond the veil.[50] This is now reflected in the Work of the Masters *below* the veil for 'every man that is called NEMO hath a garden that he tendeth' 13th Aethyr. Those who have followed the averse Path of θέλημα will indeed establish the 'abomination of desolation spoken of by the prophet Daniel, standing in the holy place' Matthew 24:15–16. This averse path is referred to as walking upon your hands - 'And they that walk upon their hands shall build the holy place' 16th Aethyr.[51] That is to

---

[48] On this difficult topic and doctrine, see *Initiation in the Aeon the Child*, Ch. 5 and *The Angel and the Abyss* Ch 8. See also the 25th Aethyr.
[49] *The Angel & the Abyss*, pp. 197–198. See also the 13th Aethyr.
[50] In θέλημα, this is graphically depicted in the OTO Gnostic Mass where the Priestess appears before the veil of the Temple with the words 'Greeting of Earth and Heaven!'
[51] There is an associated technical Mystery: 'Blessed are they who have turned the Eye of Hoor unto the zenith, for they shall be filled with the

say, 'Thy kingdom come. Thy will be done in earth, as *it is* in heaven.' Matthew 6:10 *KJV*. 'Blessing unto the name of the Beast... And the throne of his spirit is a mighty throne of madness and desolation, so that they that look upon it shall cry: Behold the abomination' 16th Aethyr.

In the Temple we learn from Enoch (1 Enoch 14 and *Similitudes*) the throne was surrounded by the hosts of heaven, typically treated as the angelic hosts צבאות (sabaoth) as mentioned earlier. However, we also learn from the apostates of Deuteronomy 4:19 and Kings 23:4 that hosts of heaven could refer to the sun, moon and stars, and most specifically the stars (Psalms 33:6 and Isaiah 34:4). In the New Aeon this has returned as the *Knowledge and Conversation of the Angel, in the angelic priesthood, open to all* with 'The unveiling of the company of heaven' for 'Every man and every woman is a star' AL:I:2-3, the Star Goddess Nuit herself imploring 'Help me, o warrior lord of Thebes, in my unveiling before the Children of men!' AL:I:5. 'Now

---

vigour of the Goat' (16th Aethyr), Crowley commenting 'The Eye of Hoor turned to the Zenith refers to a Mystery of Magick, practical and puissant, which the student must be left to solve for himself,' *The Equinox* IV:2 p. 126. See however both the New and Old Comments to AL:I:57, *The Law is for All* (1996) pp. 77-78. It should be remarked of the fortress or Tower, Atu XVI in the Tarot, that 'Tower' was a common designation of the holy of holies, the House of God, for eg. The Assumption of Moses 2.4 reads 'The court of his tabernacle and the tower of his sanctuary', while in Christian adoption, Hermas *Parables* 9.7.1 'The Son of God is Lord of the tower.' The Tarot is as much a history and ontology as it is an alchemy and mystical anatomy of the New Aeon, collective and individual.

ye shall know that the chosen priest & apostle of infinite space is the prince-priest the Beast; and in his woman called the Scarlet Woman is all power given. They shall gather my children into their fold: they shall bring the glory of the stars into the hearts of men. For he is ever a sun, and she a moon. But to him is the winged secret flame, and to her the stooping starlight.' AL:1:15-16.[52]

There is one final and what might seem like a pretty 'out there' point to make, on the Angelic priesthood of the Temple. In Crowley's notes for a New Commentary on *The Book of the Law* he wrote that Aiwaz, the praeterhuman messenger of *The Book of the Law*, 'is the true most ancient name of the God of the Yezidis, and thus returns to the highest Antiquity. Our work is therefore historically authentic, the rediscovery of the Sumerian tradition.'[53] In the published 'New Commentary' (*The Law is for All*), these remarks make more sense of his comment to Chapter One verse One, where on Nuit and Hadit, Crowley notes his colleague Samuel Bar Aiwaz 'identifies them with ANU and ADAD the supreme Mother and Father deities of the Sumerians. Taken in connection with the AIWAZ identification, this is very striking indeed.'[54]

---

[52] Note that the stars on the robe of the Magister Templi represent the stars of the Night of Pan or humanity, the Host of heaven.
[53] Warburg File K.I., quoted in Tobias Churton, 'Aleister Crowley and the Yezidis', in *Aleister Crowley and Western Esotericism*, eds. Henrik Bogdan and Martin P. Starr.

Samuel Bar Aiwaz was wrong about Anu and Adad being the supreme Mother and Father deities of the Sumerians. And Crowley was wrong to identify the Yezidi with the Sumerians. Crowley's identification was based on the scholarship of British archaeologist, Leonard Woolley, who mistook Ur in southern Mesopotamia (modern day Iraq), which he excavated, with Ur Kaśdim, 'Ur of the Chaldees,' referred to in the Bible as the birthplace of the Patriarch Abraham (Genesis 11;28, 11:31, 15:7, Nehemiah 9:7). The Ur of the Chaldees was Urartu, the biblical 'Ararat' (Genesis 8:4, 2 Kings 19:37, Isaiah 37:38, Jeremiah 51:27), the Kurdish mountains of South Armenia and Turkey. Abraham is said to have been the son of an Armenian Mithani ('One House') King. The historian Eusebius, writing in the early fourth century, quoted fragments of Eupolemus, a now-lost Jewish historian of the second century B.C.E., as saying that 'around the time of Abraham, the Armenians invaded the Syrians.' This is held to correspond to the arrival of the Mithani.[55] The Crowley

---

[54] Aleister Crowley, *The Law is for All*, eds. Louis Wilkinson and Hymenaeus Beta, p. 25.

[55] See http://www.newworldencyclopedia.org/entry/Mitanni. While not germane to this discussion, but certainly connected to it, the radically innovative Pharaoh, Akhenaten, who sought to revolutionize Egyptian religion through the worship of one sole God, the solar disc or Aten, had close relations with the Mithani royal house. His family for generations had more and more empowered and favored the Heliopolitan priesthood over the Theban, while intermarriage with the Mithani had led to a rich cross fertilization of ideas and reputation as free thinkers. This possibly or more likely probably, extended to new religious ideas. Importantly,

biographer and Yezidi scholar, Tobias Churton, believes 'there is a relationship between their [Yezidi] ancestors and the Mithani of Urartu and the Paddan Aram... On this basis, the Jews and Yezidi Kurds have common ancestry,' which makes sense given the traditional Yezidi locales.[56]

This lengthy digression was necessary as Crowley's quite unusual identification of Aiwaz to the 'God of the Yezidis,' could be a reference to Melek ('Lord or King') Tawus (Aiwass?), the Yezidi 'Peacock Angel'. In Hebrew, Melek would be מלאך שליח (malak or malak yhvh - 'messenger of god'), but noting from before that the same word signifies an angel (i.e. The Angel of the Presence, in hebrew *Mal'ak ha-Panim* or *Mal'akh ha-Panim*, מלאך הפ or the The Angel of *his* Presence). As I said, this allows us to reread scripture and Temple lore in terms of a tradition of angelic priests, which in the New Aeon is represented by those 'Lords or Kings' who have consummated the Knowledge and Conversation with the Great Angel. 'For I am not only

---

Akhenaten's forebears (Amenhotep II, Tuthmose IV, Amenhotep III) increasingly saw in the Aten, forms of Ra-Horakhti (Ra Hoor Khuit), such as 'Ra-Horakhti-Khepra-Atum of Heliopolis.' This ultimated in Akhenaten's monotheism for Ra-Horakhti. Likewise, Abraham's belief in a single deity may also be of Mithani influence. These connections behind the Mithani, the bloodline of Akhenaten, their radical religion of Ra Hoor Khuit, and the Abrahamic religions - the People of the Book - may well explain the revelation of the theogony of *The Book of the Law* in this New Aeon. This theme is taken up in Shiva X°, *Aeonic Psychology*, in preparation. See also above.
[56] Tobias Churton to Stephen J. King, private communication, Jan 19, 2017.

appointed to guard thee, but we are of the blood royal, the guardians of the Treasure-house of Wisdom. Therefore am I called the Minister of Ra Hoor Khuit: and yet he is but the Viceroy of the unknown King.' (8th Aethyr). 'And there cometh a peacock into the stone, filling the whole Aire. It is like the vision called the Universal Peacock, or, rather, like a representation of that vision. And now there are countless clouds of white angels filling the Aire as the peacock dissolves.' (20th Aethyr) 'And now the peacock's head is again changed into a woman's head sparkling and coruscating with its own light of gems. But I look upwards, seeing that she is called the footstool of the Holy One, even as Binah is called His throne.' (7th Aethyr)

Recalling again the initial reference to the 26th Aethyr that led to the elaborations of past paragraphs, it is only after the vision of the Abomination of Desolation that the new Temple, its theogony and officers, are revealed. After a manner, these too are straight out of Revelation which is straight out of First Temple lore. By this measure *the officers in the new Temple for the preparation of the High Priest in The Vision and the Voice are the Temple kerubim.* In their aeonic and theogonic sense they are of course, much more than just the Four Beasts who now keep watch and ward at the Abyss in the ceremony of the Magister. However the *Imago Dei* of their archetypal substrates are the Lion, Eagle, Man and Bull (Ezekiel 1:10). While now thought of and worshipped by men as Chaos and BABALON,[57] the Fire Kerub (the Lion God of Horus, the Beast) appears in the 25th Aethyr; the Water-Kerub, the Scarlet Woman appears in the 24th Aethyr. The assisting Earth and Air Kerubs appear in the 23rd Aethyr.

In Temple lore, two representations of these creatures were placed in the holy of holies (1 Kings 6:23–28; 2 Chronicles 3:10–14) and two on the mercy seat above the ark (Exodus 25:18-20). In Revelation they summon the four riders (Rev. 6:1–7) and one hands over the seven golden bowls of wrath to the angels leaving the Temple (Rev. 15:7). While with a mythological presence throughout Near Eastern religious impulses, the kerubim are best viewed as heavenly guardians of the holy of holies.

The composite Beast of θέλημα, like the similarly composite Beast of Rev:17, carries 'the woman drunken with the blood of the saints, and with the blood of the martyrs of Jesus' Rev 17:6, 'BABYLON THE GREAT, THE MOTHER OF HARLOTS AND ABOMINATIONS OF THE EARTH' Rev 17:5.[58] The conjunction of BABALON and the Beast in the kerubic sense indicates a new set of relations, a juxtaposition,

---

[57] See the Comment to the 24 Aethyr in the 'Synopsis to *The Vision and the Voice*,' *The Equinox* IV:2 p. 32. See also the Creed in the OTO Gnostic Catholic Mass, Liber XV.
[58] The corrected spelling BABALON was revealed in *The Vision and the Voice*. It was spelt Babylon until after the 10th Aethyr, i.e. after the passing of the Abyss.

a functional opposition or *coincidentia oppositorum*[59] that is enunciated in *The Vision and the Voice*. We may call this the *kerubic shift*.[60]

With the Great Return of the Mother of Abominations, redemption in the New Aeon is no longer represented by the coronation of the elements through the name of Jesus (יהשוה) - one of the 'gods of men' (AL:III:49) cursed in *The Book of the Law*.[61] As mentioned above, redemption now follows the averse path, described as a transfiguration from Virgin to Mother and her coronation in the City of Night, referred to as the Holy Mountain Zion, the City of the Pyramids.[62] The transfiguration from Virgin (daughter) to

---

[59] A term coined by the great German theologian and philosopher Nicholas of Cusa. Interestingly, Morimichi Watanabe, citing a German paper by Fritz Nagel, notes that Dee was indebted to Cusa's *De coniecturis* for Dee's term 'experimental science,' which included his conception of magic. M. Watanabe, 'An Appreciation' in *Introducing Nicholas of Cusa: a guide to a Renaissance Man* eds. Bellitto, Izbicki & Christianson (2004) note 5 pg. 401.

[60] In Jewish mythopoeia, we may treat this as the return of the kerubim to the Temple in the time of the Messiah, foretold in *Numbers Rabbah* XV.10. That time is now!

[61] See AL:III 49–54. In other words their formula or worship has been superseded. See *The Vision and the Voice* 3rd Aethyr: 'And Satan is worshipped by men under the name of Jesus; and Lucifer is worshipped by men under the name of Brahma; and Leviathan is worshipped by men under the name of Allah; and Belial is worshipped by men under the name of Buddha. (This is the meaning of the passage in Liber Legis, Chap. III.).'

[62] See for example the 14th, 12th, 8th and 6th Aethyrs. For a thorough examination consult the works of J. Daniel Gunther referenced in this paper.

Bride (mother) signifies in Temple lore the return of the Queen of Heaven,[63] historically the ancient goddess of Jerusalem *banished by Temple reformers in the seventh century BCE.*

The Queen of Heaven (מלכת השמים, *Malkath haShamayim*) was an archetypal Goddess figure worshipped throughout the Near East. In Jeremiah 44:16–18 we read:

> As for the word that thou hast spoken unto us in the name of the LORD, we will not hearken unto thee.
>
> But we will certainly do whatsoever thing goeth forth out of our own mouth, to burn incense unto the queen of heaven, and to pour out drink offerings unto her, as we have done, we, and our fathers, our kings, and our princes, in the cities of Judah, and in the streets of Jerusalem: for then had we plenty of victuals, and were well, and saw no evil.
>
> But since we left off to burn incense to the queen of heaven, and to pour out drink offerings unto her, we have wanted all things, and have been consumed by the sword and by the famine. *- KJV*

---

[63] See AL:I:27, 33.

She appears in the vision of Isaiah (7:15), 'Behold, the virgin shall conceive and bear a son, and shall call his name Immanuel' (i.e. 'God with us') and is transformed in the visions of the prophets to symbolize the plights of the exilic people. She appears as Wisdom in the Wisdom literature of the *Ben Sira* and 1 Enoch, while the Jewish refugees in Egypt following the destruction of Jerusalem in 586 BCE (the papyrus of Yeb) worshipped her as the goddess Anat-Yahu.

Both Jesus and John the Baptist reference the Wisdom literature (Luke 7 and 11). While in Revelation the Goddess is a key and antagonistic figure in the form of the Woman clothed with the Sun and the Harlot, the formula is corrected and resolved in θέλημα in the forms of Nuit and BABALON, of Virgin (ה heh final) becoming the Bride (ה heh prima), that is הה, the daughter is the mother. However, as mentioned earlier before this digression into the goddess archetype θέλημα draws from and fulfils, the new theogony laid forth in *The Vision and the Voice* - '... our Lady the Scarlet Woman, Babalon the Mother of Abominations, the bride of Chaos, that rideth upon our Lord the Beast' (Liber Cheth 1) - requires a shift in kerubic arrangements, given the woman now rides the Beast and the new averse path of redemption.

As evidenced in The Hierophant and the Universe cards of the Thoth Tarot, the Eagle kerub is now in the upper left position and the Man kerub in the upper right, a reversal of the traditional arrangement. While too complex to get into in this place,[64] the Eagle is also named the Dragon or Eagle-Dragon and the Man is now represented as a Woman. When aligned diagonally to the pentagrammaton, the (Scarlet) Woman is now functionally opposed to the Bull (Beast) and the Lion to the Eagle-Dragon (i.e. Lion-Serpent), thus giving the Signs of N.O.X. and in another sense, the Kerubic Officers in the ceremony of the Master of the Temple. 'Therefore is the Eagle made one with the Man, and the gallows of infamy dance with the fruit of the just' Liber LXV III:59.

It is no surprise that concomitant to this unveiling of the new Temple, *The Vision and the Voice* conceals and reveals the doctrine of the Messiah in the New Aeon. This is one of the most sacred and secret doctrines of θέλημα, beloved of its adepti. The reader is encouraged to consult the works of J. Daniel Gunther on this recondite subject, which can serve as a study guide through *The Vision and the Voice*.[65] The recourse to scripture in this paper is sufficient to indicate a continuous Temple apocalyptic and the rest can be left to one's own Vision and Voice!

What can be mentioned here is that in the mystical rapture of the 7th Aethyr, where the averse qabalistic New Aeon formula of the Virgin (ה heh final) becoming the Bride (ה

---

[64] See *The Angel & The Abyss*, Ch. 5 The Fruit of the Just.
[65] See *Initiation in the Aeon of the Child* Ch. 5 and *The Angel & The Abyss* Ch. 8.

heh prima) is experienced,[66] the Master of the Temple encounters the path of ד (daleth). It is significant to note that here the Woman of the Apocalypse is experienced and the Edenic serpent Nechesh נָחָשׁ is described as the Messiah מָשִׁיחַ,[67] the Child of Adam and Eve. This parallels Revelation where the Woman of the Apocalypse[68] gives birth to the child Messiah (Rev. 11.19–12.6) who is then 'caught up unto God, and to his throne.' The vision of John in Rev 11:19 is replete with pure Temple symbolism. As the Aethyr is also a commentary on the doctrine 'The word of Sin is restriction' (AL:I:41), the Temple related apocalyptic of the text - and indeed, the High Priestly origin of the Apocalypses[69] - is further illustrated by the quoting of the prophet Ezekiel (18:23) and the Proverbs of Solomon (1:26) in the Aethyr.

---

[66] This can be compared for historico-spiritual context with the gates of righteousness in the *Haqdamat Sefer ha-Zohar* 1:8a. Daniel Matt's commentary explaining 'Shekinah is called Righteousness. Through her one enters the realm of sefirot and can eventually ascend to Wisdom.' The *Zohar* states in the same passage 'Whoever attains one attains the other' as the higher Wisdom is reflected in the lower Wisdom (Shekinah), *The Zohar* Vol. 1 Prizker Edition, translated and commentary by Daniel C. Matt (2004) p. 50

[67] This further relates to the doctrine of the Great Name that has a practical application in both OTO and A∴A∴.. See *Initiation in the Aeon of the Child*, p. 135. The Serpent is the Redeemer.

[68] Rev 12:1 should be compared to Liber LXV:I:28.

[69] See for example, M. Barker, 'Beyond the Veil of the Temple. The High Priestly Origin of the Apocalypses', http://www.margaretbarker.com/Papers/BeyondtheVeil.pdf.

The connecting of the serpent, the Messiah, the Great Name, Eden and the Temple to AL:1:41 and the exhortation of Ezekiel reflect the key principle and formula of θέλημα, that of the spiritual being made one with the material, i.e. the formula of Horus, the child, the future. 'Thy kingdom come. Thy will be done in earth, as *it is* in heaven.' Matthew 6:10 *KJV*. If we recall that the original Temple was designed to replicate the days of creation in Genesis,[70] what we now see in the 7th as well as other Aethyrs with Edenic and creation themes, is a new sense of how this is to be applied in the New Aeon, in the new Temple with the transition from High Priest to Magister. It is explained in the 27th Aethyr where Crowley comments 'This is the use to which BABALON puts the Blood of the Masters of the Temple...to vivify the Rose of Universal *Creation*, i.e. the Attainment of the Master of the Temple fills the World with Life and Beauty.'[71]

This is the creation of the new world, communicated to Dee by the Angels. Governed by a new spiritual law with a Tradition that emanates from Temple law and its ancient antecedents, and no less from the radical and reforming Jesus:

'Do what thou wilt shall be the whole of the Law...
It is the Law that Jesus Christ, or rather that

---

[70] The works of Barker noted above should be studied in this regards.
[71] *The Equinox* IV:2, note 5 p. 54. [Italics mine]

Gnostic tradition of which the Christ-legend is a degradation, attempted to teach; but nearly every word he said was Misinterpreted and garbled by his enemies, particularly by those who Called themselves his disciples. In any case the Aeon was not ready For a Law of Freedom. Of all his followers only St. Augustine appears to have got even a glimmer of what he meant.'[72] - *The Equinox of the Gods*

'Love, and do what thou wilt.' - Saint Augustine, *Tractatus* VII 8

'Love is the law, love under will.' - AL:1:57.

'Open the Mysteries of your Creation, and make us partakers of the undefiled knowledge.'[73]

And on that note, I think it is time to stop. For the *Vision and the Voice* must be experienced in your own vision and voice, not mine. If I have at least partially succeeded in intimating some its vast scope and depth, and in particular how the Law of θέλημα connects through it to the great Angelic, Temple and Mother of Heaven traditions - the

---

[72] Crowley, *The Equinox of the Gods* (New Falcon: Scottsdale, 1991 pp. 135–136.

[73] Translation of the Call or Key of the Thirty Aethyrs, *The Equinox* IV:2 pp. 28–29. See also the rendition given in the 2nd Aethyr of *The Vision and the Voice*, pp. 226–229.

spiritual inheritance of humankind - I am happy. I will elaborate on such themes in future papers.

And may you partake of the undefiled knowledge.

> On my head is the crown, 419 rays far-darting. And my body is the body of the Snake, and my soul is the soul of the Crowned Child. Though an Angel in white robes leadeth me, who shall ride upon me but the Woman of Abominations? Who is the Beast? Am not I one more than he? In his hand is a sword that is a book. In his hand is a spear that is a cup of fornication. Upon his mouth is set the great and terrible seal. And he hath the secret of V. His ten horns spring from five points, and his eight heads are as the charioteer of the West. Thus doth the fire of the sun temper the spear of Mars, and thus shall he be worshipped, as the warrior lord of the sun. Yet in him is the woman that devoureth with her water all the fire of God.
>
> - *The Vision and the Voice*, 25th Aethyr

'He fell on his face and saw him uprooting mountains, kindling lights in the palace of King Messiah. He said to him, Rabbi, in that world you will be neighbours, empowered masters in the presence of the blessed Holy One.'

Haqdamat Sefer ha-Zohar 1:7b

Love is the law, love under will.

In Nomine BABALON.

Amen.

Restriction unto Choronzon.

OZ 48 ANNO Vɪᴠ - 21 Jᴜɴᴇ 2018 ᴇ.ᴠ.

TEMPLE MOUNT

The Oriental Templar crusade for Verità

STEPHEN J. KING

'...there is an Ascona within each of us... It is easy to link it with Berkeley, the Paris May, the Berlin Communes, the peace movement, women's emancipation, the gay movement, and the greens... Half a century later, Ascona is everywhere.'

Nicolaus Sombart[1]

Early in 2016 the Italian Grand Master of Ordo Templi Orientis (OTO), Frater Phanes, informed me of a letter dated September 1, 1935, from Olga Fröbe-Kapteyn to Swiss psychologist Carl Jung. In this she mentioned the existence of a Templar Order in Ascona, Switzerland.[2] Fröbe was the founder of the Eranos Foundation at Ascona. Beginning in 1933, the Foundation held seminars on comparative religion, philosophy, history, art and science,

---

[1] Nicolaus Sombart, 'Nachrichten au Ascona,' W. Prigge, ed., *Städtische Intellektuelle* (Frankfurt: Fischer, 1992), 113–115. Quoted in Gottfried M. Heur, *Freud's 'Outstanding' Colleague/ Jung's 'Twin Brother': The suppressed psychoanalytic and political significance of Otto Gross* (Oxon and New York: Routledge, 2017), 123.
[2] Frater Phanes, personal communications April 30, 2016.

with a penchant for mystical symbolism.³ Originally centred around Carl Jung, some of the twentieth century's leading thinkers met at Eranos, including Mircea Eliade, Erich Neumann, Gershom Scholem, Karl Kerènyi, D.T. Suzuki, Paul Tillich, Erwin Schrödinger, Joseph Campbell and others.⁴ Neumann called Eranos 'a navel of the world, a small link in the Golden Chain' while for Jung, it was 'the only place in Europe where scholars and interested lay participants could come together… unrestricted by academic boundaries.'⁵ Kerènyi described Eranos as 'one of the most creative cultural experiences in the modern Western world.'⁶ Why would its two key actors even show any interest in some type of quasi-Masonic group operating in the Swiss Alps?

For now, it is a question that cannot be conclusively answered. My application to the Eranos Foundation for a copy of the letter did not get a response. As a result, the specific content and context of the letter (and whether or not Jung responded) is not known. If unanswered however, it needn't be unexplored. The presence of the Oriental

---

³ The Eranos Foundation continues to operate, http://www.eranosfoundation.org/index.htm.
⁴ For the definitive study of Eranos, see Hans Thomas Hakl, *Eranos: an alternative intellectual history of the twentieth century* (Montreal & Kingston: McGill-Queen's University Press, 2013).
⁵ Ibid., 7.
⁶ Ibid.

Templar Order (OTO)[7] in Ascona, at the Monte Verità bohemian colony in the early 20th century, seemed too big a coincidence and legitimate grounds for enquiry. The immediate problem however was the date of Fröbe's letter to Jung. The popularly held view in the English-speaking world has been that the official OTO organizational presence in Switzerland - in the early 20th century at least - ended with the Outer Head of the Order (OHO) Theodor Reuss' departure from his cultural project at Monte Verità. We can locate that to be at some point between about the end of World War One and Reuss' death in the early 1920s. Fröbe's letter is from 1935. What happened in between? It suggested that to explore this problematic would require setting aside some generally held assumptions about formal OTO history, and looking into research and disciplines not in the typical domains of OTO studies.

According to the Monte Verità chronicler Robert Landmann, Reuss was at Monte Verità for more than a year.[8] Hans Thomas Hakl tells us he came in 1916 at the invitation of the colony's co-founder, pianist Ida Hoffman.[9] Given that Reuss' OTO Anational Congress took place at

---

[7] Ie. Ordo Templi Orientis, the Order of Oriental Templars, or Order of the Temple of the East.

[8] Martin Green, *Mountain of Truth: The Counterculture Begins, Ascona, 1900–1920* (Hanover and London: University Press of New England, 1986), 148. Green is citing Robert Landmann, *Ascona, Monte Verità: Auf der Suche nach dem Paradies* (Zurich: Benziger, 1973).

[9] Hakl, *Eranos*, 37.

Monte Verità in August 1917, at the earliest he must have departed the colony later that year. We know Reuss attended the Congress of the International Masonic Federation in Zurich in July 1920,[10] and died in Munich in 1923. Monte Verità itself was sold in 1920, and what remained of the community was managed by a triumvirate leadership of artists.

Ida Hoffman's husband and co-founder of Monte Verità, Henri Oedenkoven, helped Reuss set up OTO in Ascona.[11] An English woman named Isabelle Adderly, who would later be Oedenkoven's second wife,[12] served as Reuss' OTO secretary.[13] The fact the OHO was invited to Monte Verità by its founders, who then joined and helped establish OTO at the colony, is little known but highly significant. It locates OTO as participant to and influential within, for a short while at least, the then burgeoning European counterculture that has informed the intellectual history of the 20th century.

Mindful of this, to use a methodology put forward by the scholar of religion and ideas, Ioan Couliano, I've treated OTO as an *ideal object* existing in its own logical

---

[10] Ellic Howe, 'Theodor Reuss: Irregular Freemasonry in Germany 1900-1923,' February 16, 1978, http://freemasonry.bcy.ca/aqc/reuss/reuss.html
[11] Green, *Mountain of Truth*, 148.
[12] https://de.wikipedia.org/wiki/Henri_Oedenkoven
[13] Sabazius X° and AMT IX°, 'History,' http://oto-usa.org/oto/history/

dimension.[14] What Ascona demonstrates is how that system of consciousness interacts with other objects, such as the Monte Verità ideal and the currents that emerged from it, to form history. Looking at how these objects interact becomes what Couliano termed *morphodynamics* - the study of events in space-time. This can uncover an object's lateral but not necessarily lineal inheritances and transmissions: a history of ideas. The centrality of OTO to the Monte Verità collective and ideal is a good example.

Fröbe's 1935 Templar reference can be linked to OTO if we look into references with an Asconan focus. Hakl tells us that a former collaborator of Anthroposophy founder Rudolf Steiner, Alice Sprengel, had aligned herself with Reuss around 1914. Reuss had authorized her to establish OTO Lodges.[15] This is supported by Martin Green, who says that Sprengel was Reuss' Secretary and was head of the Locarno branch of OTO, nearby to Ascona, as late as 1937.[16] We also know Sprengel attended the 1935 Eranos Conference, which ran from August 12–22.[17] Jung attended as well.[18] Fröbe's letter to Jung was written the following month in September. And we know Fröbe was quite aware of

---

[14] Ioan Couliano, *The Tree of Gnosis: Gnostic Mythology from Early Christianity to Modern Nihilism* (San Francisco: HarperSanFrancisco,1992).
[15] Hakl, *Eranos*, 99–100.
[16] Green, *Mountain of Truth*, 177.
[17] Bibliographic citation for the 1935 Eranos Yearbook, http://www.eranosfoundation.org/publications_b.htm#an03.
[18] Hakl, *Eranos*, 97.

Sprengel. Until she received letters of protest from supporters, Fröbe originally intended to refuse Sprengel admission to the conference.[19] Sprengel was a Jewish emigrant, and while Jewish emigration was still the official German policy in 1935, the National Socialists were against Jewish attendance and participation at the Eranos Conferences.[20] It is highly unlikely Fröbe and her circle would not have known of Sprengel's OTO involvement. She had by now been organizing OTO in and around Ascona for about 20 years. We also know Fröbe was writing to Jung at this time about the increasing pressure on Eranos from the National Socialists. It is reasonable to conclude that Sprengel and OTO were a topic of discussion.

That Sprengel, a Jew, was even running a Reuss-era styled OTO group in Locarno into the mid-late 1930s is extraordinary. In 1939 for example, a report submitted by the German Consulate in Locarno to the National Socialist regime said the Eranos Foundation 'did not serve the interests of Jews, Freemasons and foreign interests.'[21] The Foundation was nevertheless under scrutiny and other reports were nowhere near as dismissive. An anonymous report from 1936 stated that to the contrary, Eranos wished 'to infiltrate our 'Western' Christendom with Oriental

---

[19] Ibid., 99–100.
[20] Ibid., 97–103.
[21] Ibid., 98.

occult elements'[22] while a 1937 report from the Security Service of the SS described Eranos as a 'Freemasonry-like endeavour.'[23] If Eranos was on tenuous ground, a Jewish woman who was actually running a 'Freemasonry-like endeavour' infiltrating 'Western' Christendom with Oriental occult elements' - an Oriental Templar Order[24] - was a radical and potentially dangerous proposition. But topical for Fröbe and Jung it could have been. Importantly, what we see from the morphodynamic perspective is lateral, logical continuity between OTO, Monte Verità and the later Eranos Foundation ideals (with its nexus in Jungian analytical psychology). Sprengel warrants acknowledgment in OTO history as an exemplar of the Monte Verità OTO ideal object.[25]

---

[22] Ibid. Hakl cites a memorandum in the archives of the Reich Ministry for Science, Teaching and People's Education.

[23] Ibid.

[24] Reuss referred to OTO as the 'Gnostic Neo-Christians.'

[25] Most biographical information about Sprengel relates to her childhood and involvement with Rudolf Steiner. For a survey, see Virginia Sease, *Rudolf Steiner's Endowment: Centenary Reflections on his attempt for a Theosophical Art and Way of Life, 15 December 1911* (Forest Row: Temple Lodge, 2012), 45–55. Most authors cite her death as 1949 (although I have also seen 1941 and 1947 given). In materials on Peter-Robert Koenig's 'The Ordo Templi Orientis Phenomenon: a research project' website (http://www.parareligion.ch/), Sprengel is said to have initiated Hermann Metzger into OTO. Upon Sprengel's death, Metzger established a Swiss branch of OTO, citing permission from Felix Pinkus, a surviving member of the Reuss era Swiss OTO. (Metzger's branch was eventually regularized in OTO by Aleister Crowley's successor as OHO, Karl Germer, 'but Germer and Metzger fell into disagreement toward the end of Germer's life,' Sabazius X° and AMT IX°, 'History'). While

A comment on the constitutionality of the Asconan activities is warranted. Reuss appears to have quite liberally authorized people with Lodges or affiliations to the umbrella of Rites at his disposal, including his Oriental Templar Order. His OTO successor Aleister Crowley certainly thought he authorized too many people, complaining in a 1943 letter to Wilfred Smith that Reuss 'hastily issued honorary diplomas of the Seventh Degree to various people, some of whom had no right to anything at all and some of whom were only cheap crooks.'[26] Certainly Reuss' revised OTO Constitution, issued in January 1917 'on Monte Verità, in the Republic of Ticino (Switzerland),'[27] made clear the OHO had 'paramount authority regarding all matters which concern the welfare and administration of the OTO.'[28] This authority was then vested in Crowley as the succeeding OHO, who had reconstituted OTO away from Reuss-styled Freemasonry and in accord with his revealed scriptural tradition of Thelema, the new Temple of Initiation it called for, and his new system of 'Magick.' That groups such as Sprengel's Locarno branch were not aligned

---

Koenig has done considerable research into the Swiss history, his bias against the modern OTO and selective quoting of primary sources (often without citing provenance), should be treated cautiously.

[26] Aleister Crowley, letter to Wilfred Smith, March 1943, cited in Sabazius X° and AMT IX°, 'History.'

[27] Merlin Peregrinus X° 'I.N.R.I. Constitution of the Ancient Order of Oriental Templars, Ordo Templi Orientis, With an Introduction and a Synopsis of the Degrees of the O.T.O.', *The Equinox* III(10) (New York: 93 Publishing, 1990), 191.

[28] Ibid., 187.

to OTO Headquarters under Crowley technically invalidates them as 'official' bodies of the organization.[29] However for the purposes of this paper, it is clear Sprengel believed she was faithfully and legitimately carrying on the work of OTO from Reuss.

Some supporting evidence for a surviving OTO at Ascona into the 1930s, comes from the British historian Elizabeth M. Butler. In OTO studies, Butler is better known for the disparaging account in her 1959 biography *Paper Boats* of meeting Aleister Crowley in the 1940s.[30] Less known is that she also mentions visiting Ascona in 1937, at the invitation of the wealthy banker, art collector and philanthropist, Baron Eduard von der Heyt. The Baron had purchased Monte Verità in 1926, building a hotel on the site as a venue for artists. Butler noted in *Paper Boats* that the 'Order of the Temple of the East, purporting to be a London Lodge of Freemasonry, initiated orgiastic rites in what was by then a flourishing hotel.'[31] This is a clear reference to OTO. It may indicate that Sprengel's Locarno lodge continued to use Monte Verità for its work, or that she continued to use her authorization from Reuss to establish OTO lodges. It seems less likely that after Reuss' departure as well as the closure of

---

[29] For the succession from Reuss to Crowley, see Sabazius X° and AMT IX°, 'History.'
[30] Elizabeth M. Butler, *Paper Boats: an autobiography* (London: Collins, 1959), 166–177. See also Hakl, *Eranos*, 304–305, n. 46.
[31] Butler, *Paper Boats,* 137. See also Hakl, *Eranos*, 38.

the colony in 1920, vestiges of the original Reuss OTO group may have carried on at Monte Verità into the 1930s.

Returning to the early years of Monte Verità and Reuss, with OTO organizers such as Ida Hoffman, Isabelle Adderly and Alice Sprengel, it is clear Reuss' pro-women approach to OTO blended with Hoffman's anarcho-feminist Asconan ideals. This was one of the many bohemian currents promulgated at Monte Verità, a hotbed of the counterculture, which Reuss was seeking to position in tactical alliance with OTO. Hoffman recalled that OTO included 'several significant women.'[32] The feminism born of Ascona, which Reuss and OTO were participant to and collaborative in (remembering that it was Hoffman who invited Reuss and OTO to Ascona in the first place), was connected to Hoffman's alternative healing practices - a mix of herbal and mineral treatments, nude sunbathing, vegetarianism, and physical exercise. It was a rejection of patriarchal industrialism, government, armed forces, institutionalized medicine, orthodox religion, sedentary urban habits and diets, and other perceived authoritarian, capitalist structures. Among those who embraced the Asconan and OTO anarcho-feminist discourse were Hugo Ball and the Zurich Dadaists, who frequently visited Ascona.[33] While neglected in art history, Reuss and OTO

---

[32] Hakl, *Eranos*, 177.
[33] Theresa Papanikolas, *Anarchism and the Advent of the Paris Dada: 1914–1924* (Oxfordshire and New York: Routledge, 2016), 92.

have their place in influencing this seminal artistic movement and expression.

Further to this, Reuss would also initiate other 'significant women' and their male leader at Monte Verità, who would then go on to make a lasting contribution to modern culture. Reuss initiated the dancer, choreographer and movement theoretician, Rudolf von Laban and his female troupe of dancers, into Monte Verità's Anational Swiss Grand Lodge of OTO, Verità Mystica. Laban had an interest in Freemasonry and also ran his own Lodge, the 'Lodge of Women,' for his dancers. The Laban all-women troupe performed a cycle of solar dances at the 1917 OTO Conference, often cited in modern dance literature, and were active participants in Reuss' OTO work. It suggests the 'Lodge of Women' was either OTO or at the very least, heavily OTO influenced. Their signature style of dance 'employed improvisation and encouraged intense and often violent personal expressiveness in performances that consistently reflected broader anti-patriarchal attitudes.'[34] The Zurich Dadaists mentioned above collaborated with the Laban troupe in numerous performances at a time when the OTO influence at Ascona and Reuss' influence on Laban were at a peak (1917). In June 1917 the Laban School incorporated a Dadaist program and with the opening of the

---

[34] Ibid.

Galerie Dada in 1917, a Laban dancer led '400 people in a celebratory dance.'[35]

Laban had come to Ascona to establish a summer school for the arts. He had an unconventional relationship with his wife Maya Lederer and his mistress, the Dalcroze-trained dance teacher Suzanne Perrottet. Other than his free-love lifestyle, he embraced the exploration of Love-Work-Play, the threefold foundation of the Monte Verità philosophy and the currents it generated. Here Laban developed his own application of the Asconan doctrine in Tanz-Ton-Wort (Dance, Sound, Word). Karen K. Bradley aptly summarised Laban's Monte Verità period, saying 'the confluence of various art forms with the ideas of free love, feminism, organic gardening and freemasonry led to new forms of creating and sharing dance.'[36] The Freemasonry Bradley refers to is OTO.

Just after the OTO Anational Congress, in October 1917, Reuss chartered Laban to co-run Libertas und Fraternitas, a 'Johannis lodge of ancient Freemasons of the Scottish-and-Memphis-and-Misraim Rites in the Valley of Zurich.' Reuss, ever the tactician, could be ambiguous in his authorizations about where the constituting masonic pedigrees ended and OTO proper began, but this was

---

[35] Valerie Preston-Dunlop, *Rudolf Laban: an extraordinary life* (London: Dance, 1998), 43–46.
[36] Karen K. Bradley, *Rudolf Laban* (Oxon and New York: Routledge, 2009), 7.

basically an OTO charter. Then in early November, Laban took over Reuss' position at Ascona as Swiss OTO Grand Master of the Anational Grand Lodge, Verità Mystica. Later in the month Laban closed Verità Mystica and focussed on his Zürich OTO Lodge.[37] In time the Zürich Lodge would drop its OTO affiliation and regularized under the Swiss Grand Lodge of Freemasonry.

Green says that Reuss provided serious stimulus for Laban's theories on dance, religion and culture. The commonality was liberation and expression: personal, social, political, artistic, spiritual, cultural and sexual. A rejection of the dominant paradigm. A rejection of what Freud termed the *Unbehagen* or 'discontent' afflicting industrialized Germany and German-speaking Europe, in favor of *Lebensreform*, 'reform of life.' In 1920 Laban would write 'If the result, namely the extinction of a great number of habitually accepted ideas, feelings and actions is achieved, then there shall be space for knowledge and function which meanwhile has been developing. Only then shall we be able to speak of the coming transference of the pure reason expressed in the dance to human life.'[38] Commenting on this, Bradley observed, 'He [Laban] saw himself as both an artist and a researcher (what we might now think of as a social scientist). Science, religion, philosophy and art were spokes on a wheel, ways of understanding the nature of humanity. Dance

---

[37] Sabazius X° and AMT IX°, 'History.'
[38] Bradley, *Rudolf Laban*, 12.

reflected all of it and was a part of advancing that understanding.'[39]

Laban saw OTO as useful to arouse curiosity and hypnotic suggestion - of that 'pure reason' - and thought that Reuss' 'personal aims and ideas are sometimes very valuable, even related to eurhythmics.'[40] In that simple acknowledgement we can see Theodor Reuss and his OTO doctrine as having an influence on Laban, the father of modern dance; on the eurhythmy of Rudolph Steiner (who had an early OTO affiliation from Reuss) which found practical application in the arts, education and anthroposophic medicine and therapies; and via Laban and Steiner, on somatic bodyworks generally, in particular the work of Joseph Pilates.[41] From the perspective of morphodynamics, OTO appears again as a 'seed' idea and community permeating cultural expression and evolution. In this particular instance, Reuss' approach to religion, culture and in particular, yoga and Mystic Anatomy as practiced in OTO, must be singled out as influencing modern movement theory and the performing arts.[42]

---

[39] Ibid. For the depth of Laban's contribution to the social sciences, see also Ciane Fernandes, The *Moving Researcher: Laban/Bartenieff Movement Analysis in Performing Arts Education and Creative Arts Therapies* (London and Philadelphia: Jessica Kingsley Publishers, 2015).
[40] Green, *Mountain of Truth,* 106. Citing the Suzanne Perottet archives.
[41] See for example Leena Rouhiainen, 'The Evolvement of the Pilates Method and its relation to the Somatic Field,' *Nordic Journal of Dance*, vol 2 (2010): 57–68.

More broadly, Reuss as an activist in matters of sex, gender, religion, culture and political economy, is telling of OTO's symbiotic relationship with the Monte Verità collective. If OTO was Reuss' Templar crusade and doctrine, Monte Verità was the Temple Mount. He sought for a time to infuse the colony with OTO ideals. History it would seem has remembered the ideals of Monte Verità, but forgotten the Templars who taught a large part of them. It has remembered some of the more well-known initiates, but overlooked their Initiation. Why is that? Martin Green has noted that the Eranos Foundation, which we have already discussed, 'was certainly a continuation of old Asconan interests, in theosophy and the occult.' That is a reference to Monte Verità, the 'seed' idea behind the currents of

---

[42] This was taken up by Keith Cantù in his paper delivered at the Ascona conference, 'The 'Mystic Anatomy' of Theodor Reuss'. Reuss adopted the term from Hargrave Jennings' *Phallicism, Celestial and Terrestial, Heathen and Christian: Its connexion with the Rosicrucians and the Gnostics and its foundation in Buddhism, with an essay on Mystic Anatomy* (London: George Redway, 1884). I am indebted to Keith for pointing out to me that Reuss copied passages from the Jennings essay on Mystic Anatomy almost verbatim into his own paper. Keith noted, "the fact that Reuss was lifting material directly from Jennings implies that there is a logical connection between Reuss' idea of 'Mystic Anatomy' and Jennings, but I'm not sure how much it extends to technical aspects. My hunch is that Reuss expanded this to include material from Indic Hathayogic and tantric sources, specifically the *Siva Samhita*, but that originally 'Mystic Anatomy' had more of a hermetic / mystic / qabalistic valence linked to the Genesis account." Keith Cantù, pers comm., September 11, 2017. For the Reuss paper, see Theodor Reuss, 'Mystic Anatomy,' *The Magical Link* 8, nos 1–2 (Spring–Summer 1994):8-9. See also the discussion on Otto Gross above.

'theosophy and the occult' being OTO. Green noted however that with Eranos, these currents were now 'on a transcendental and respectable level.'[43] Maybe that is it - respectability? Yet, while not on the same 'respectable' scale and scope as Eranos, which Hakl rightly framed as the *alternative* intellectual history of the 20th century, OTO influence at Ascona contributed to what I call an *underground* intellectual history of the 20th century.

The founding Eranos ideal and archetype was of a *meeting place* of East and West. Reuss decades earlier encountered the same, but sought not only a meeting but their *mystical marriage* in the practical work of OTO. David L. Miller has suggested the Eranos Foundation 'encouraged thinking and living at the radical edge.'[44] I would suggest the Monte Verità community of bohemians, artists, anarchists, feminists, pacifists, vegetarians and Oriental Templars - the latter including all of the former - needed no encouragement and were *already* at that radical edge. When supporters protested to Fröbe that Alice Sprengel should be allowed to attend the 1935 Eranos Conference, they said it was Sprengel who taught them the Eranos ideal.[45] How? Sprengel was OTO. She was already practicing what Eranos was preaching.

---

[43] Green, *Mountain of Truth*, 154.
[44] Hakl, *Eranos*, back cover review.
[45] Ibid., 100.

In an undated letter to Crowley, which Crowley annotated as 1917, Reuss gives some indication of his work and activity. He said his 'Anational Grandlodge for Switzerland' had 42 candidates of various nationalities; that a New Temple on Monte Verità had been consecrated; and that Crowley's 'The Message of Master Therion'[46] had been read to a 'gathering of Vegetarians' who had 'foregathered on Monte Verità for establishing a cooperative settlement.'[47] Reuss said the cooperative 'in part, was united with OTO, for tactical purposes styled the "Hermetic Brotherhood of Light" - as foreshadowed in the OTO Constitution.'[48] Reuss goes on to mention his activities to get influential Freemasons and Theosophists initiated.

The 'tactical purposes' why Reuss referred to OTO as the Hermetic Brotherhood of Light are open to speculation. The revised OTO Constitution from Ascona states in Article 1 that OTO, 'formerly known as: "The Hermetic Brotherhood of Light," has been reorganized and reconstituted.'[49] The historical justification for this is far from clear and several theories have been put forward.[50]

---

[46] Liber II, 'The Message of Master Therion,' *The Equinox* III:10, 23–26.
[47] "Crowley and Reuss: Some Correspondence," II - Reuss to Crowley, *The Magical Link*, vol. 7 no. 3, (Fall 1993): 3.
[48] Ibid.
[49] Merlin Peregrinus X° 'I.N.R.I. Constitution of the Ancient Order of Oriental Templars, Ordo Templi Orientis, With an Introduction and a Synopsis of the Degrees of the O.T.O.', 186.
[50] See for example, Richard Kaczynski, *Forgotten Templars: The Untold Origins of Ordo Templi Orientis* (privately printed, 2012), 249–250.

What seems apparent however, is that Reuss was claiming a continuity pre-dating OTO's formative patents to the 'HBL' brand, be that the 1895 Hermetic Brotherhood of Light and/or the earlier Hermetic Brotherhood of Luxor.[51] The implication and impression would have been that OTO, unlike the 'Esoteric Buddhism' of the Theosophical Society (TS) that enjoyed massive popularity in German-speaking countries, was like the HBL: an Order of practical occultism. Esoteric Phallicism.

For the connotation may also well have been that the practical occultism of OTO continued the sexual teachings of the Hermetic Brotherhood of Luxor, adopted from the African American sex magician, Pascal Beverly Randolph.[52] This would have served a twofold purpose. First, it would give the legitimacy of lineage to the sexual teachings and mysticism Reuss had introduced into OTO, drawn from the 'Spiritual Father' of OTO, Carl Kellner.[53] Second, given the

---

[51] See Jocelyn Godwin, Christian Chanel and John P. Deveney, *The Hermetic Brotherhood of Luxor: Initiatic and Historical Documents of an Order of Practical Occultism* (York Beach: Weiser, 1995).

[52] See John Patrick Deveney, *Paschal Beverly Randolph: A Nineteenth-Century Black American Spiritualist, Rosicrucian, and Sex Magician* (Albany: State University of New York Press, 1997).

[53] Patrizia Ebner explored this theme in her paper delivered at the Ascona conference, 'The Man, the Mystery, and his Legacy: Carl Kellner.' For a recent study, see Karl Baier, 'Yoga within Viennese Occultism: Carl Kellner and Co.' in Karl Baier, Philipp A. Maas, Karin Preisendanz (eds.),
Yoga in Transformation: Historical and Contemporary Perspectives (Göttingen: Vienna University Press, 2018).

nature of these OTO teachings, it would demonstrate a blending of western Freemasonry and neo-Gnostic and Rosicrucian sexual occultism with Hatha yoga and tantra, positioning OTO as the foremost Oriental (or Theosophical) Masonic Order. It is worth considering that in the then volkish awakening in German-speaking lands, there was tremendous interest in Theosophical, Buddhist and Indo-Aryan currents.[54] Reuss was laying claim to all of it. The Asconan OTO Constitution even had a specific class of membership (Probationers) just for 'embracing Theosophists, etc.'[55]

Reuss' organizational machinations aside, you cannot live at the 'radical edge' without courting controversy. Robert Landmann recorded that Reuss' lodge taught 'ecstatic release' as part of its 'paths to enlightenment.'[56] According to the Laban biographer Evelyn Dörr, Reuss used these rites to seduce women, including the wife of Henri Oedenkoven (who initially set up OTO with Reuss). Dörr doesn't specifically name her, but it had to be Ida Hoffman, which might in turn explain Oedenkoven's second marriage to Reuss' OTO secretary, Isabelle Adderly. Adderly had the

---

[54] See Douglas T. McGetchin, *Indology, Indomania and Orientalism: Ancient India's Rebirth in Modern Germany* (Madison and Teaneck: Fairleigh Dickinson University Press, 2009).
[55] Merlin Peregrinus X° 'I.N.R.I. Constitution of the Ancient Order of Oriental Templars, Ordo Templi Orientis, With an Introduction and a Synopsis of the Degrees of the O.T.O., 189.
[56] *Ascona*, quoted in Evelyn Dörr, *Rudolf Laban: the Dancer of the Crystal* (Lanham: Scarecrow Press, 2008), 68.

first of their three children in 1920. Dörr writes, 'insulted as a charlatan, imposter and devourer of women, Reuss left the colony.'[57] This would explain Laban's appointment as Grand Master, his closing of the Verità Mystica Lodge at Ascona, the focus he then put on his own OTO Lodge in Zurich, and the subsequent dropping of its OTO credentials and regularizing under Freemasonry.

There is some supporting evidence for this view. On November 3, 1917, the day Laban was elevated to OTO Swiss Anational Grand Master, he wrote to his mother saying 'the summer in Monte was in this respect fruitful, as I decided to transform my up to now external activities in various secret societies into internal ones and to take on the president of a supreme council.'[58] However, only 11 days later he wrote to his mother again, this time saying 'The lodge at Monte has been closed down, the unsuitable members there - Henri, Ida, etc. - have been excluded, and I've transferred the headquarters from there to here [Zurich].'[59] Laban's wording suggests that as far as he was concerned, the Anational Swiss Grand Lodge 'headquarters' had transferred from Verità Mystica to the Libertas und Fraternitas OTO body.

---

[57] Ibid.
[58] Laban, November 3, 1917, Ibid. Laban is referring to the Supreme Grand Council of a Grand Lodge of OTO.
[59] Quoted in http://www.parareligion.ch/consider.htm.

Referring to Reuss, Laban later noted in his manuscript 'The Character of a Secret Society,' that he saw his ideals of freemasonry 'abused by the leader of the sect.'[60] On his part, Laban passionately busied himself in Lodge work. Writing to his sister Renée, he said 'to the physical-spiritual-intellectual development of young people belongs without doubt information, knowledge of traditional forms of training for humanity that only secret societies have... some things must be a part of life, become an attitude towards life, such as virtues and good manners, character and will, and only those who are wise know how to produce this and pass it on, and only in the customary form of a mixed cult between science and religion that has existed since primitive times.'[61] While this 'mixed cult' is the Reuss approach to Theosophical Freemasonry, for Laban, Reuss failed to measure up. Laban would express the very best of his OTO and Asconan experience on the Mountain of Truth, of community and self-empowerment through the creative spirit, in his dance *Die Tänzer vom Berg* ('The Dancer from the Mountain').

This wasn't the only time Reuss' morals were called into question. Richard Kaczynski gives this measured and considered treatment in *Forgotten Templars*. Importantly, Kaczynski notes that 'Reuss is known to have been a sexual reformer, supporting suffrage and women's rights. There is

---

[60] Dörr, *Rudolf Laban: the Dancer of the Crystal*, 68.
[61] Ibid., 68–69.

also evidence that, outside of lodge, he practiced the liberal views on sexuality that he espoused'[62] and that 'he made no secret of his unconventional lifestyle.'[63] We are left to question whether Reuss' 'unconventional lifestyle' was too countercultural for the counterculturalists of Monte Verità?

As already mentioned, in 1920 Monte Verità was sold. Hoffman and Oedenkoven, who still worked together, went on to Brazil to set up a new colony. Laban's main dancer, Mary Wigman, also an OTO initiate, broke from him, ironically because, as Nina Macciachini noted, 'things were already going so wrong for Laban, on account of his many women, the so-called Lodge, she was rebelling against him.'[64]

It would be misreading this as Laban throwing stones at Reuss from a glass house. Whatever Reuss and Laban did - or did wrong - was in genuine pursuit of the spiritual impulse behind the Asconan feminist doctrine: 'the divinity of woman is one of the ideas the Asconans propagated.'[65] Reuss was one of its prime advocates.[66] To explore this

---

[62] Kaczynski, *Forgotten Templars*, 250.
[63] Ibid.
[64] Quoted in Green, *Mountain of Truth*, 152.
[65] Ibid., 5.
[66] Hymenaeus Beta has noted, for example, that 'Reuss declared mothers to be saints' in his introduction to Crowley's 1915 paper, 'The Whole Duty of Woman,' *The Magical Link*, vol. 3 no. 9, (Fall 1995): 3. OTO under the direction of Reuss also took the revolutionary step of restoring the clerical office of Priestess to the western liturgy. See 'Liber XV, OTO Ecclesia Gnostica Catholica Canon Missa,' in Aleister Crowley, with Mary Desti and Leila Waddell, *Magick: Liber ABA, book 4, parts I-*

Asconan ideal we must now introduce 'the most brilliant of the Asconans,'[67] Otto Gross.

Gross was a well-known resident of Monte Verità, a psychoanalyst, one time assistant to Freud, and anarchist. In fact he combined these currents together in a type of anarcho-psychology that rejected Freud's premise of the necessity for psychological repression. Probably as a result, Jung credits him with identifying the extravert as a psychological type. Gross was a drug user and advocate of free love - forcibly interned at times in mental institutions - and died in poverty, his fascinating and revolutionary contribution to psychology and politics for the most part suppressed until only recently.[68] Author Werner von der Schulenberg indicates just how influential and pervasive Gross psychoanalysis was at Monte Verità:

> 'In this strange world of astrology and occultism, psychoanalysis had its heyday. There was nothing new about it, though. Dr Gross, the thoroughly exploited source of Jung, inventor of the world-soul

---

IV, ed. Hymenaeus Beta 2nd rev ed. (York Beach: Weiser, 1994), 584–597.

[67] Green, *Mountain of Truth*, 6.

[68] See Gottfried M. Heur, *Freud's 'Outstanding' Colleague/ Jung's 'Twin Brother': The suppressed psychoanalytic and political significance of Otto Gross* and Otto Gross, *Selected Works 1901–1920*, trans. Lois L Madison (New York: Mindpiece, 2012).

and Swiss psychoanalytic pope, had introduced it to Ascona.'⁶⁹

Schulenberg's remarks cry out to the serious researcher to lift the suppression of Gross and give his stunning intellectual contribution a long overdue reappraisal. Such is beyond the scope of this paper. It must suffice to say that this force of nature indelibly impacted Monte Verità, his ideas extending to its residents and many visitors, including Jung (who treated Gross and who Schulenberg says exploited his ideas), D.H. Lawrence, Franz Kafka, Franz Jung and the Dada movement. Gross' 'Nietzschean matriarchalism'⁷⁰ was adopted en masse at Ascona. It influenced the feminist politics and spirituality of Monte Verità, Laban's dance dramas and quite probably the OTO doctrine and practices of Reuss. Gross was at Ascona in 1917 when the OTO presence there was in full bloom. If we need find a source or inspiration for the OTO 'ecstatic release' as part of its 'paths to enlightenment,' as practiced by Reuss and recounted by Landmann above, we probably need look no further than Dr Gross and his therapeutically prescribed *orgia*.⁷¹ In fact,

---

⁶⁹ Werner von der Schulenberg, "Ascona," Westermanns Monatshefte, no. 75 (February 1931): 568–71. Quoted in Heur, *Freud's 'Outstanding' Colleague/ Jung's 'Twin Brother': The suppressed psychoanalytic and political significance of Otto Gross*, 123.

⁷⁰ A term applied to Gross in Paul Bishop, *Carl Jung* (London: Reaktion Books, 2014), 17.

⁷¹ Heur, *Freud's 'Outstanding' Colleague/ Jung's 'Twin Brother': The suppressed psychoanalytic and political significance of Otto Gross*, 124.

E.M. Butler's account of OTO 'orgiastic rites' at Monte Verità reported they were 'said to vie with those instituted by a scandalous *habitué*, the "uninhibited" psychoanalyst, well-named Dr. Gross.'[72]

There is some theoretical justification for such a position. Earlier, commenting on the 'Mystic Anatomy' of Reuss, I footnoted religious scholar Keith Cantù's observation that Reuss copied some of his writings from the esoteric phallicist Hargrave Jennings' essay on Mystic Anatomy. Cantù noted that Reuss expanded upon yogic lines Jennings' approach which was 'more of a hermetic / mystic / qabalistic valence linked to the Genesis account.'[73]

The psycho-sexual therapies and politics of Gross were centred around a modern day restoration of the cult of Astarte and rooted in his understanding of 'the Genesis account.' He wrote, the 'thinker of Genesis must have been motivated by the struggle between the authoritarian-theocratic monotheism of the prophets and the Astarte cult.... All that at that time remained intact of feminine freedom and dignity must have been concentrated in the Astarte cult. The orgy as cult act was a defense by the free matriarchal society itself of the positive value judgment of the sexual aspect, and in the priestly authority of women the past spirit of womanhood was still alive... the poet of Genesis recognized the last flicker of a dying human ordeal,

---

[72] Butler, *Paper Boats*, 137.
[73] See note 42.

the end of the great struggle for the old matriarchal ideal.'[74] From here devolved patriarchy and authority. Gross' remedy reads like a Monte Verità manifesto: 'The true liberation of woman, the dissolving of the existing patriarchal family through the socialization of maternal care, re-establishes every individual's vital interest in the society, which forthwith guarantees him the potential of highest freedom, of boundless freedom... the groundwork for such a revolution must effect the liberation of each individual from the principle of authority that he carries inside...liberation from original sin itself, from the will to power.'[75]

Reuss was working along similar lines, not only socially through the OTO cultural project at Monte Verità, but mystically, that is, by yogic and sexual means yet no less responding to 'the Genesis account' and predicated on 'the positive value judgment of the sexual aspect' : 'the Ancient Masters of Hermetic Science... were enabled in a spiritual way, to penetrate the truth of the real meaning of the Original Fall of the Angels, of the Original Fall of Adam and Eve.... The Masters of Hermetic Science hold that it is possible, by the right application of the meaning of "Original Sin" and "Fall of Angels," to arrest in magic art, i.e. Sex Magic, the Supernatural S.E.E.D.S. operating in every and through every being, for purposes of

---

[74] Gross, 'The Basic Concept of Communism in Paradisal Symbolism,' *Selected Works*, 280, n. 5.
[75] Ibid., 279.

understanding "GOD ITSELF" and "UNITING WITH GODHEAD." This is called the great act of Transmutation of the Reproductive Energy. This Great Mystery is also embodied in the Eucharist of Churches. It is a Hermetic Mystery.'[76] Therefore, it may well be that Gross, whether directly or indirectly through his widespread influence on the Asconans, provided or helped to frame a political and

---

[76] Theodor Reuss, 'Mystic Anatomy,'. Reuss, quoting a yoga paper he attributes to Carl Kellner, describes 'The Transmutation of the Reproductive Energy' exercise in his essay 'Our Order,' which was republished alongside of 'Mystic Anatomy' in the OTO newsletter *The Magical Link*. They originally appeared in Reuss' *Oriflamme* OTO journal. He writes 'This exercise of the transmutation of the reproductive energy is not done for sexual excesses…The reproductive energy is a process of creation. It is a Godly act!…the performer of the exercise must concentrate all his thoughts on withdrawing and lifting the reproductive energy from the organ into the solar plexus, where he "wills" that it be stored for transmutation purposes. This is connected with precisely controlled breathing. The act of transmutation of energy is connected with this, and finally the great "merging" or reunion occurs and the performer becomes the seer while remaining fully conscious and experiences what he sees. This is white sexual magic!'. Taoist scholar Tony Edwards remarked on this passage, 'what I find particularly interesting from my perspective is that the Reuss/Kellner techniques mirrors exactly the Taoist one using almost identical language. The very first stage in Taoist alchemy is "Gathering" which consists of drawing generative energy at precisely a time known as "Living Midnight" or the "Growth of Yang"…Then the generative energy is lead by the will into the lower *dantian* where it is "Sealed" and stored for "Transmutation."' Tony Edwards, pers comm. October 11, 2017. Since delivering this paper, I have subsequently (2018) found out from the Baier paper cited in note 53 that 'The Transmutation of the Reproductive Energy' was written by William Walker Atkinson, who wrote under the pseudonym Yogi Ramacharaka, in *The Hindu Yogi Science of Breath* (1904).

psychological rationale to the Reuss methodology for personal transformation and unity with Godhead via OTO sexual magic.

The intuitive researcher by definition must adopt a trans-historical methodology, something Gottfried M. Heuer considered 'a trans-temporal, trans-generational and transpersonal approach to the past as an intersubjective web of ideas and concepts...'.[77] This 'arcs backwards to the past with the intention to contribute to healing present and future. This orientation equalizes meaning and fact and contains a redemptive and numinous dimension - numinous in the sense in which intimate interrelating, conditional for healing, invokes the presence of the holy.'[78] This paper, as an introduction, has sought to present an 'intersubjective web of ideas' and the holy Order with which they were intimately interrelated.

Too easily dismissed in both positive and negative narratives as scandalous bohemians, degenerate artists, dissidents, drug addicts, black magicians, mentally unstable, political revolutionaries, misfits, sexual deviants, and 'proto-hippies,' Monte Verità may well have been all of that but was also a serious countercultural proposition of radically Gnostic proportions. The Asconans were firmly located in the German intellectual inheritance, not just in its Theosophical

---

[77] Heur, *Freud's 'Outstanding' Colleague/ Jung's 'Twin Brother': The suppressed psychoanalytic and political significance of Otto Gross*, 3.
[78] Ibid.

Freemasonic fringe of esoteric philosophy, or psychoanalysis and the other countercultural currents mentioned above, but in the *eschaton* of Jacob Taubes, in the Western tradition's 'permanent revolution.'[79] Although 'Marx destroys the capitalist-bourgeois world, Kierkegaard the Christian-bourgeois world,'[80] the countercultural currents of Monte Verità were *creating* a new world - a revolution of creativity.

While superficially the Monte Verità project may appear as an expression in the Romantic and Mytho-Poetic Hegelian sense of German Idealism, 'in the service of a new, sensuous, practical rationality and a motivating political praxis,'[81] the Hegelian reform fails to overcome externality. It acts 'according to the insights of something or someone external.'[82] Ascona acted according to itself. Internally. It was an inner experience, an alternate social reality, and decidedly anarchic. The Asconans took their cue from Otto Gross: 'It is the inner fate and determination of the revolutionary, alone, if it must be so, knowing his own insular orientation, among enemies and allies alike, to the proclamation of his message from the future, to carry the revolutionary secret of redemption and to take on himself, if

---

[79] See Jacob Taubes, *Occidental Eschatology*, trans. David Ratmoko (Stanford: Stanford University Press, 2009). See also, Couliano, *The Tree of Gnosis*, 255–259.
[80] Taubes, *Occidental Eschatology*, quoted Ibid., 258.
[81] Philip Quadrio, 'Morality, Politics and Mytho-Poetic Discourse in the Oldest System-Programme for German Idealism,' *SOPHIA*, no 50 (2011) 625-640, https://doi.org/10.1007/s11841-010-0223-3.
[82] Ibid., 639.

it may be so, responsibility for the overthrow of all that now exists and for the struggle and force released, perhaps against the will of an entire world.'[83] It was this individual and interior impulse in the first instance. In social dynamics, the counterculture aims for critical mass not open warfare.

From this perspective Reuss departed Ascona a heroic failure. Not for his indiscretions, but for politicizing and propagandizing the Anational Congress at Monte Verità - for taking it into the realm of the Mytho-Poetic in the service of an external 'motivating political praxis.'[84] This was not the praxis of Ascona. What Ioan Couliano said of Christian theology and Gnosticism applies equally to Monte Verità and OTO: they 'were "ideal objects" or systems in a logical dimension, having nothing intrinsically to do with the games of power that were played in their name, which belonged to other dimensions of reality.'[85]

His departure was swift. And so began a new era in OTO history.

Epilogue: the Horus Principle

I began by suggesting a meeting point between OTO and analytical psychology. It was an underlying theme in the

---

[83] Gross, *Selected Works*, 280.
[84] William Breeze explored this in his paper at the Ascona conference, 'Conflict, Disinformation and Intolerance on All Points of the Triangle: the OTO at War in World War One.'
[85] Couliano, *The Tree of Gnosis*, 267.

'intersubjective web of ideas' this paper sought to introduce and uncover. We see them contrasted in the Monte Verità colony and the Eranos Foundation, and reconciled to some extent in the enigmatic character of Otto Gross, who in Heuer's intellectual estimation was Jung's 'twin brother.' Others as we saw like Schulenberg, were far less generous about Jung! But long before Olga Fröbe-Kapteyn's 1935 letter to Jung about a Templar Order, by six degrees of separation or synchronicity they already had an Asconan connection.

In 1912, about the time Aleister Crowley and Theodor Reuss started actively collaborating on an OTO movement, Jung published his revolutionary *Wandlungen und Symbole der Libido* (later published in English as *Psychology of the Unconscious*).[86] *Wandlungen* is not an easy read. Jung gets over excited and hasty in composition, too eager to share his revelations before their maturation and expression in a coherent doctrine. Jung's promulgation of the 'numinous' (borrowing the term from Rudolf Otto) was treated by some Freudian critics of *Wandlungen* as a neurosis, what Freud would have called a misdirected father complex.[87]

---

[86] Carl Jung, *Psychology of the Unconscious: a study of the transformations and symbolisms of the libido, a contribution to the history of the evolution of thought,* trans. Beatrice M. Hinkle (London: Kegan Paul Trench Trubner, 1916).

[87] For a discussion, see Mark Greene, *Adventure in Archetype: Depth Psychology and the Humanities* (Hong Kong: Mercury Pier, 2011), Ch 2 'Jung and Freud on Religion: The Numinous versus Neurosis', Kindle edition.

At risk of oversimplifying the *Wandlungen* methodology, it applied the German construct of *Wisseschaften* (multi-disciplinary systematic research) to comparative philology, comparative mythology, evolutionary biology and psychology. Jung blended Freud's genital stages of psychosexual development with Johann Jakob Bachofen's stages of cultural evolution, while unifying biology and evolution through Ernst Haeckel's 'ontogeny recapitulates phylogeny' thesis. In doing so Jung was boldly elevating his new psychology simultaneously into the *Geisteswissenschaften* ('sciences of spirit') *and* the *Naturwissenschaften* ('natural sciences') of the German Academy. In other words, Spirit *and* Matter combined in the scientific syncreticism of a new analytical psychology.

In the white heat of *Wandlungen* ecstasy, Jung underwent an intellectual and some would assert, a spiritual, transformation. He had already openly declared in 1910 that he sought a spiritual dimension to the psyche. He wanted psychoanalysis 'to transform Christ back into the soothsaying God of the vine... and in this way absorb those instinctual forces of Christianity for the one purpose of making the cult... a drunken feast of joy where man regained the ethos and holiness of an animal.'[88]

According to Richard Noll, a clinical psychologist and historian of science, with *Wandlungen* Jung's transformation

---

[88] Program statement, 11 February 1910, quoted in Paul Bishop, *Carl Jung*, 107.

along these lines was complete. He was no longer a Freudian, a Christian in the ordinary sense, or a monotheist. Jung embraced the volkish currents of the times, and advocated solar worship and Aryan paganism. Noll considers this 'the beginning of an Aryan psychoanalysis in Zurich. It was the beginning of Jung's return to his *Volk*, and to the inner fatherland.'[89] Noll even suggested Jung underwent a Mithraic deification - a mystic union with God - and now saw himself as the Aryan Christ, with analytical psychology his new religion.

Noll's controversial books, *The Jung Cult*[90] and *The Aryan Christ*, have not surprisingly been met with mixed reactions. The Jung biographer, Paul Bishop, gives more balanced consideration in his 2014 study when he wrote although 'some of its assumptions and conclusions [have been] questioned, his [Noll's] historical contextualization of Jung's work in relation to Ernst Haeckel and evolutionary biology, to the Nietzschean matriarchalism of J.J. Bachofen and Otto Gross, and to the project of cultural renewal embodied in the Stefan George circle, underscores how deeply and profoundly Jung belongs to a broader stream of thought in German culture.'[91]

---

[89] Richard Noll, *The Aryan Christ: the secret life of Carl Jung* (New York: Random House:1997), 49.
[90] Richard Noll, T*he Jung Cult: origins of a charismatic movement* (Princeton: Princeton University Press, 1994).
[91] Bishop, *Carl Jung*, 17.

Noll's approach, however, is supported in part in Carrie B. Dohe's 2016 critical study, *Jung's Wandering Archetype: Race and religion in analytical psychology*.[92] Commenting upon the posthumous editorial handling of Jung's works, she said 'they point to an attempt to suppress the evidence of Jung's particular interest in and hope for a hypothesized collective German psyche. Nor can his utilization of colonialist and anti-Semitic discourse be shrugged off... Jung was deeply, personally invested in these discourses of hierarchy and inequality, due to his belief in the superiority of a presumed Germanic-Christian psyche.'[93]

Wandlungen had a direct connection with OTO's establishment at Ascona. Gross, who as we saw in all likelihood bore some influence on Reuss and OTO, was treated by Jung. But more directly, Rudolf Laban underwent analysis with Jung or one of his assistants, in Zurich. According to Richard Noll, 'Laban had read *Wandlungen* and shared it with his Dionysian dancers in Ascona, including Mary Wigman...'.[94] Those 'Dionysian dancers' are the OTO. Noll goes on to say that after 1916 (the year Reuss arrived at Ascona), 'Asconans flooded the consulting rooms of Jung's colleagues... they revealed their dreams and their drawings, their poems and their dances.'[95]

---

[92] Carrie B. Dohe, *Jung's Wandering Archetype: Race and religion in analytical psychology* (Oxon and New York: Routledge, 2016).
[93] Carrie B. Dohe, *Jung's Wandering Archetype*, 246.
[94] Ibid., 118–119.
[95] Ibid.,119.

That sounds like the Asconan OTO underwent therapy. While something in need of specialized research, it is fair to assume Reuss would have known about this, and through the analytical process Jung would have known about Reuss and OTO.

It is not only possible but probable, that the solar exuberance of the second part of *Wandlungen* had an influence on the development of Reuss' 'Gnostic neo-Christian,' solar-sexual OTO doctrine. It is fair to also assume it influenced the solar dances by Laban, Wigman and the Lodge of Women, at the OTO Ascona Congress. In terms of the morphodynamic we have been tracing, *Wandlungen* must be included as one of the Asconan currents that influenced and impacted upon OTO. From the psychological perspective, Reuss' politicizing and propagandizing the Anational Congress was consistent with a belief, perhaps an unconscious one, in the 'superiority of a presumed Germanic-Christian psyche' as promulgated in *Wandlungen*.

Crowley read the 1916 English translation of *Wandlungen* and immediately wrote a review in *Vanity Fair*, 'An Improvement upon Psychoanalysis.'[96] Crowley felt Jung had at best, *unconsciously* 'paved the way for the revival of the old magical idea of the will as the dynamic aspect of the self,'[97]

---

[96] Reprinted in Aleister Crowley, *The Revival of Magick and Other Essays*, eds. Hymenaeus Beta and Richard Kaczynski, 76–81.
[97] Ibid. p. 78.

but rightly questioned the logic and strength of many of Jung's assertions and arguments. I think Crowley's realization and revelation of a universal Thelema went beyond the inner Fatherland of Jung, and possibly for that matter, of Reuss. It looked to the new universal-Thelemic psyche or emergent *Imago Dei* of humankind, the God-Image of the New Aeon, not the hypothesized superiority of a Jungian Germanic-christian one. While sharing in solar-libidinous celebration, psychologically this is the point of departure between Crowley and Jung, and probably Crowley and Reuss as well.

Ioan Couliano suggested 'systems that have been sufficiently run in time would tend to overlap not only in shape but in substance. With complex data at hand... portions of the map of the Buddhist system would overlap with portions of the Christian system with portions of German idealism with portions of modern scientific thought, because all systems are infinite and tend to explore all possibilities given to them. Accordingly, when sufficiently extended their maps of reality would certainly coincide.'[98] That complex data from the Thelemic perspective is the procession of the Aeons. It leaves open for an overlap between the anatomy of the psyche proposed by Jung and that of Thelema.

We approximate just such an overlap in Jung's 'Horus principle' from his African period in the mid-1920s, post the

---

[98] Couliano, *The Tree of Gnosis*, 268.

Reuss-Ascona time. Here, from observing tribal customs and exploring tribal beliefs, Jung had profound inner realizations about the Sun God Horus. In seeing baboons, like himself, waiting patiently for sunrise and then greeting the sun, 'Jung felt that he was participating in a process older than human consciousness itself.'[99] These experiences were cemented when he saw the Temple of Abu Simbel as he travelled down the Nile on a steamboat. The Temple, built by Rameses II in Lower Nubia, was dedicated to in Thelemic parlance, Ra Hoor Khuit. Framing the colossi of Rameses with Horus in the centre was a row of baboons, looking east, greeting the sunrise. 'On Elgon, Jung had witnessed both human and animal reverence for the rising sun. When Jung saw the same gestures carved in stone at the Egyptian doorway to sub-Saharan Africa, the connection was confirmed.'[100]

At the time, Jung felt he had made a significant discovery locating an African source for Egyptian religion. However, he was by no means the first. E.A. Wallis Budge did the same in his 1911 study, *Osiris: The Egyptian Religion of Resurrection*, which Jung had read.[101] Jung was also read in the 'solar worship' thesis of comparative religious scholar, Frederick Max Müller. However, Jung nevertheless announced that he had made a 'discovery' regarding the

---

[99] Blake W. Burleson, *Jung in Africa* (New York and London: Continuum, 2005), 168.
[100] Ibid.
[101] Ibid., 169–170.

source of the Nile. As Blake W. Burleson commented, 'Jung's claim should have been that he provided evidence that the source of Egyptian religion was further south than what Budge had argued; Jung believed that Osiris, Horus and Set were originally Nilotic Gods.'[102]

For our purposes, however, in Africa Jung encountered the *universal* Imago Dei in the form of Horus, what he termed a 'preconscious archetype'[103] in that it was 'older than human consciousness itself.' And older than 'a hypothesized collective German psyche.' This encounter with archetype then constellated in the vision of Ra Hoor Khuit at Abu Simbel. From a Thelemic perspective, we could view this 'Jungian synchronicity' as a sublimated apprehension of the new archetypal dominants - transformed for a new age in Thelema, if articulated by Jung in terms of the old. However, it suggests from this 'discovery,' largely overlooked in the current literature, more overlaps between analytical and aeonic psychology will occur.

Something that first commenced on the Mountain of Truth.

OZ 50 ANNO VIV - 21 DECEMBER 2018 E.V.

---

[102] Ibid., 170.
[103] Jung, *Collected Works* (8 411), quoted Ibid., 168.

Living in the Sunlight

The Mutations of the Tao working

Grand Master Shiva X°

At the recent Mutations of the Tao retreat I talked about a little known practice called 'Living in the Sunlight.' Crowley mentions it in a 1915 letter to Charles Stansfeld Jones. Crowley was writing formally to Jones as 'Baphomet X°' and the letter is a specific instruction about the VII° practices of OTO. Living in the Sunlight is mentioned to illustrate points about VII° practice and effect by way of analogy - a different practice that works with the same underlying principle, whose practical results could benefit and validate VII° work.

In the letter, Baphomet remarks:

> I must tell you more, too, about 'living in the sunlight,' which is our beloved Sister Hilarion's[1] way of saying 'the way of the Tao.' I had hoped she would speak of it the other night, but she was shy. She taught it me, and from that hour my whole life has been transfigured. In material matters, even, all has suddenly gone well. I will ask her to write you about it. The main point seems to be the

---

[1] Jeanne Foster

conception of yourself as a King - Vide Liber CCXX Cap 2. It's damnably hard to explain, but it's merely a trick, like all great skill, perfectly easy once you find the way. The elements of struggle, worry, desire, must be eliminated.

He adds the following PS to the letter:

About this 'living in the sunlight,' I ought to add that it involves making everybody in your sphere reflect your radiance. This is the measure of your success. If you have anybody about you miserable, it shows that your light is failing to penetrate. This primarily applies to the private life, and to the Lodge, but also to casual strangers. And remember, if you can do this, you can get away with robbery and murder! They won't care how strict you are; they'll all obey cheerfully without knowing they are doing it. It will all be part of a glorious romp through life. I've not been a very striking success in the past, but in the last few months I've had a great teacher - not only precept, but example.

I was given a copy of this letter 21 years ago. While I can make no great claim to either striking success let alone a romp through life, after searching for what the *actual* practice was for years with no luck, I eventually devised my own based upon what I thought it might be and got to work. I believe a more refined or advanced application of the Living in the Sunlight method is given in Liber Aleph, with the underlying principle - which I will call the Radiation of the Light - referred to throughout the book and applied in different contexts.[2]

It wasn't until relatively recently when I was in Poland lecturing that Brother Krzysztof Azarewicz, Frater Superior's Representative for Poland, told me Charles Stansfeld Jones had a lecture called 'Living in the Sunlight.' The title of the lecture had to be more than just coincidence. The lecture was published in the Swedish journal *Fenris Wolf*, which has never really been on my radar - those interested should try to get their hands on this. To my knowledge this is the only published version of the lecture. In it, Jones describes the actual Living in the Sunlight practice Crowley was taught. I'm not aware of any other written description of it.

That in Crowley's estimation Living in the Sunlight 'primarily applies' to 'Lodge' management, as noted in the PS above, gave me the idea that adapted for the 21st century, Living in the Sunlight could be a useful practice for

---

[2] In the particular approach to Living in the Sunlight I suggested at the Retreat, see for example Liber Aleph Cap. 18 'On the Sleep of Light.' Sovereign Sanctuary members might also want to revisit Liber 451. As we see with Crowley's use of Living in the Sunlight to demonstrate VII° principles, its benefits and effects resonate with and resemble more heightened results generated from high degree practices of OTO, which Crowley had revised and codified. This might explain why Crowley never developed the practice as taught to him by Soror Hilarion, as a standalone technique.

OTO members of all degrees. Crowley's recourse to it to explain VII° work further suggested it could be a nice foundational practice that develops with the practitioner over time. In that sense it could be preparatory for the higher aspirations of our membership - a bit like the 3 stages of Liber Resh that Crowley details in his *Confessions*, from beginner through to advanced.[3] While Baphomet mentions applying Living in the Sunlight to Lodge governance with an almost Machiavellian cheekiness, by the time Liber Aleph was written the Radiation of the Light could be read as sound mystical cultivation and magical hygiene for all, entirely in accord with our solar doctrine, worship, subtle energetics and bonds of the Order.

The lecture was delivered by Jones on May 7, 1922. Like a few of Jones' other lectures from this period, it clearly bears strong traces of Crowley's influence - the teachings he received from him during the WW1/US period, adapted for the North American public with a typically Jones flavour.[4]

---

[3] Living in the Sunlight and Liber Resh are mutually complementary. Both build together with regularity. For a workable OTO application of Resh see the notes in *Book Four*, where Crowley instructs Grady McMurtry 'Use at start signs of grades, 0°–III° OTO, and Sign of Enterer, followed by Sign of Silence, at the "Hail"-Damn it, you saw me do it!' (Letter, March 30, 1944).

[4] I recommend students develop an appreciation for the uniquely North American alt-spiritual milieu at the time Jones was lecturing, with its associated lecture circuits, town hall meetings and other media. It is typified by a lack of Old World 'occult' and esoteric elitism. For general introduction, check out the books by American historian Mitch Horowitz (Mitch has an interview-podcast on the Tasmanian OTO

Its publication in *Fenris Wolf* seems to be along the lines of a 'From the Archives' type of history piece, with no substantive editorial treatment contextualizing its relationship to OTO magical and taoist practice, its historical location at a particular time in Crowley's spiritual development, the organisational development of OTO, etc. While I haven't looked at the source typescript used for publication ('an original typescript preserved at the OTO archives'), it doesn't strike me as 'probably a transcription written by someone in the audience' - it seems way too detailed for that. But I haven't examined the source tss. I could be wrong.

As I mentioned at the Retreat, in considering Living in the Sunlight as a practice, keep in mind the solar, biblical, OTO, AL, pranic and kundalini references I mentioned from the Jones lecture. These are important. That said, here is how Soror Hilarion's method of Living in the Sunlight is given in the Jones lecture, as published in *Fenris Wolf*:

> When we were in Vancouver, some years ago, a certain sister of the Order whom we called [Soror Hilarion] came to visit us with the Master Therion. She it was who first used this expression 'living in the sun light' and who has most shown it forth in her own life... the remembrance of her is always, as

---

body's Hieros Gamos Radio show that is worth listening to). This can help put Jones' efforts and style into cultural perspective (irrespective of his content and later history).

it were, a ray of sunlight. She is one of the most wonderfully bright, cheerful, soothing individuals and yet at the same time so full of passion that is[sic] arises within one all the latent forces that I have ever known... she had a method all her own which everyone of us may adopt. It consisted in this: she said whatever may have been the cares and trials and troubles of the day, no matter how many people may have gone against us and appeared to be unkind to us and so on - no matter what state of mind we may have been in - there was one great secret... This world, itself, is more or less of an illusion and we create to a large extent our own illusions... we are looking at it from an illusionary point of view. Now, the idea was that every morning - every night, when she laid down to sleep, she put aside the cares of the day - all little annoyances and sorrow and shadow, with a firm determination, before sleeping, to wake up to the sun and wake up to a new day - to a clean sheet, to look at the world afresh every morning and to live that day in the sunlight and with the sun

This is not the place to recount my talk at the Retreat - you had to be there. But the salient point is 'every night.' Do it and sleep on it.⁵ By way of example, I made reference to the dream and nocturnal yogas of Tibetan Buddhism, and pointed out how Liber Aleph opens with chapters on the interpretation and nature of dreams. Keep in mind that the US period was also when Crowley developed his psychoanalytic theories, especially after reading Jung for the first time in 1916. This was running parallel to his exploration of the Tao and the development of OTO. (We see the Order, psychoanalysis, Thelema and the Tao all come together in the Simon Iff detective stories he wrote in this period.) That sleep naturally affects the immune system, hormonal functioning, emotional and psychiatric well-being, learning and memory, and clearance of toxins from the brain, underscores the references Jones made to the mystical benefits and subtle body processes. If you can get hold of the lecture, look at his references to the manipura carefully and align that with where this chakra sits in the OTO chakra kshetram series of the Man of Earth, a sequence which can serve as our own Oriental Templar 'microcosmic orbit.' Reading footnote 76 in my Ascona paper elsewhere this issue⁶ may give you some ideas to work with.

We'll revisit and develop all of this at future Retreats - with more from Chris Wong, Tony, Barry as well as Dan if we can get him down here again. Look out for Tony's paper in

---

⁵ This is not to say that is the only time you can use this method. Oceania Lodge in Sydney, for example, have adapted it into a group guided meditation with favourable results.
⁶ This can be found on page 283 of this publication (ed).

the forthcoming new edition and series of *The Waratah*, which Chris Carr & the Australian Grand Lodge Publishing Guild are currently preparing. Tony coined the term we're using to describe our work with Thelema and the Tao - Amalantrine Alchemy - after the Wizard Amalantrah (see Liber 729). Which reminds me of another thing I said at the Retreat: balance meditation with mentation (ie. rigour, research, reflection). All the texts I mentioned on the timeline I used should be studied. Trace the 'most daring thesis' Crowley mentions in *The Book of Lies* from the early (pre-OTO) studies I referenced right through to Liber 157 Tao Te Ching, the Amalantrah Working, Liber Aleph etc. We will call this reading list the 'Baphomet program' and we'll revisit that too. 'COMPASSION is really a certain Chinese figure whose names are numerous. One of them is BAPHOMET.' (Liber 71 Part III:94, Commentary) Try as best you can to get to the body of the garment beneath these texts. As you get more familiar with the corpus, you can extend your studies to Crowley's pre-1904 works, to consider his ontological evolution from Buddhist to the Tao (eg. the morphing of the skandhas into the ba gua in *Soul of the Desert*), and his later magical writings right through to *Magick Without Tears*. There's more texts and practical techniques to add to the program next time. My cheat sheet would be to get the $0=2$ equation under your belt.

While Living in the Sunlight as recounted by Jones might superficially appear to be a light, feel good, affirmation or mindfulness type of exercise (and it could certainly be used like that profitably), 'once you find the way' as Crowley put it, it is more closely connected with Shen Gong work and when developed, Nei Dan, while cultivating the art and energetics of Wu Wei. There are reasons Crowley called Soror Hilarion's method - quite possibly the only practice developed by a Sister of the Order adopted by Crowley - 'the way of the Tao.' Its beauty is in its subtlety and simplicity, its healing and rejuvenating nature, its transfigurative radiance. For all.

I am delighted to see awareness of Living in the Sunlight reintroduced into OTO some 100+ years since Soror Hilarion introduced it to Baphomet. May it enliven your travels with the Sun. The experiments must continue.

> 'That which I have said of ye operation of ye Sun is accomplished & ended.' (*Emerald Tablet*, Isaac Newton translation)

OZ 50 ANNO VIV - 21 DECEMBER 2018 E.V.

For publication in 2020 e.v.

THE LEGEND OF ALEISTER CROWLEY
A STUDY OF THE FACTS

by

P.R. Stephensen

A new Australian edition*

The Legend of Aleister Crowley is a literary biography and defence of the much maligned British poet and mystic. Published in 1930 in the pamphleteering style and spirit, it was written by Crowley's publisher at the Mandrake Press in London, the Australian P.R. 'Inky' Stephensen. Inky described the book as "a study of the documentary evidence relating to a campaign of personal vilification unparalleled in literary history." It calls out the smear campaigns and literary bias that hounded Crowley's literary and mystic career – the 'fake news' of the times.

The Legend of Aleister Crowley is a useful primary source document that curates, contextualizes and comments upon numerous press critiques of Crowley. These would otherwise be unavailable to the general reader. The study complements the many contemporary biographical studies of Crowley and is a useful case study for students of 20th century journalism and the British press. While the work might appear quaint in the modern age, it remains relevant at a time when journalistic integrity, and the power of new media, are being questioned and challenged.

This new edition incorporates digital scans from the first edition and includes for the first time the unpublished *suppressed* Introduction to the book by P.R. Stephensen. There is a new foreword by Stephen J. King together with a new critical essay, 'The Legend of P.R. Stephensen'.

Illustrated.

* *This is not a reprint of our 2007 scholarly edition, but a new general edition. The Australian OTO is the legal copyright owner of this work, in agreement with the estate of P.R. Stephensen. We have no connection with American editions where authorship or co-authorship is falsely credited to Mr. Israel Regardie.*

If you want
FREEDOM
You must fight for it

If you want
TO FIGHT
You must organise

If you want
TO ORGANISE
Join us

ORDO TEMPLI ORIENTIS
Grand Lodge of Australia

• Sydney • Melbourne • Brisbane • Canberra •
• Hobart • Perth • Adelaide • Ballarat •

www.otoaustralia.org.au

The OTO does not include the A∴A∴ with which body it is, however, in close alliance. While the curricula of A∴A∴ and OTO interpenetrate at points, this is more by nature than design, and the exception, not the rule. The respective systems and their methods are distinct. One follows the Path in Eternity. The other, the Path of the Great Return. The Grand Lodge of Australia openly supports the work of the Great Order by providing resources to its Outer College, hosting lecture tours to Australia by its senior instructors, and collaborating on joint projects and learning events.

Those of you whose will is to communicate with the A∴A∴ should apply by letter to the Cancellarius of the A∴A∴.

www.outercol.org

secretary@outercol.org

www.ingramcontent.com/pod-product-compliance
Lightning Source LLC
Chambersburg PA
CBHW050304010526
44107CB00055B/2105